Praise for Canterbury ...

Kim Letson has created a curative elixir with *Canterbury and Other Tales*, a sumptuous blend of adventure-memoir, escape, loss and healing shared in concise, engaging vignettes. Letson's prose shuttles us into each trek, as though granting exclusive peeks into the author's personal travel diary. A series of stories you won't want to end.
Bill Arnott, poet and bestselling author of the *Gone Viking* travelogue series and *A Season on Vancouver Island*.

This book vividly brings back the joys of walking and riding many of the same pathways and facing some of the same challenges which Letson presents with unvarnished candour. While the journeys do not all carry the title of pilgrimage, they all share the pilgrim sense of an inner search – a need to fill the void of the tragic loss of her husband and mother with both a rationale for her own existence and her relationship with the world.

Weary with toil, I haste me to my bed,
The dear repose for limbs with travel tired;
But then begins a journey in my head,
To work my mind, when body's work's expired:
William Shakespeare, "Sonnet 27," 1609
Paul Chinn, author of the Lightfoot Guidebooks.

Kim Letson has done it again. In this latest collection of journeys, she shares intimate moments, challenges of the terrain, encounters with both fellow travellers and those who host pilgrims such as her. Walking alongside shadows of the past, she describes intriguing details and the broad sweep of historical context for her travels and

surroundings. Her insights are often humorous and sometimes wry, but it is her accomplishments and tenacity which leave us in awe and just a little envious.
Christine Dickinson, historian and co-author of *Atlin: The Story of British Columbia's Last Gold Rush, Watershed Moments: A Pictorial History of Courtenay and District, Step into Wilderness: A Pictorial History of Outdoor Explorations in and around the Comox Valley,* **and** *The Ladies and the Lake Trout: Atlin Remembered.*

Like their namesake, these tales are much more than a guided tromp across some of Europe's best treks and pilgrimages. They are also reflections on love, friendship, loss and what it means to be human. Letson shares lyrical glimpses of the landscapes and history she encounters: the uphill grinds, the wet boots, the soaring cathedrals and sweeping views. In her deft hands we are changed.
Jeanette Taylor, historian and author of *River City: A History of Campbell River and the Discovery Islands, Tidal Passages: A History of the Discovery Islands, The Quadra Story: A History of Quadra Island,* **and** *Sheltering in the Backrush: A History of Twin Islands.*

Canterbury And Other Tales

Canterbury And Other Tales

Treading Ancient Trails

*For Marie
Happy Wandering*

Kim Letson

Kim Letson

Copyright © 2023 Kim Letson

All rights reserved. No part of this publication may be reproduced, stored in a retrieval system or transmitted in any form or by any means – digital, electronic, mechanical, photocopying, and recording or otherwise – without the prior written permission of the author, except for brief passages quoted by a reviewer in a newspaper, magazine or social media forum. To perform any of the above is an infringement of copyright law.

Edited by Trevor McMonagle,
The Right Words Editing.

Cover images by Kim Letson.

Book design by Greg Salisbury,
Red Tuque Books.

ISBN: 978-1-83952-716-6

Published by:

and under licence by Brown Dog Books, 10b Greenway Farm, Bath Rd, Wick, nr. Bath BS30 5RL

Photo Credits Kim Letson, Pat Gould and others with author's camera.

Printed and bound in the UK by CPI Group (UK) Ltd, Croydon CR0 4YY

> *... And heavy is the tread*
> *Of the living; but the dead*
> *Returning lightly dance:*
>
> *Whatever the roads bring*
> *To me or take from me,*
> *They keep me company*
> *With their pattering, ...*

Edward Thomas, "Roads," 1914

To all the wanderers, ramblers, hikers, trekkers, walkers and pilgrims who don a pack and set off to discover themselves and to seek an understanding of the wider world – saunter on dear friends, saunter on.

Canterbury and Other Tales: Treading Ancient Trails

Chapter 1　From Coast to Coast 1

Chapter 2　Becoming a Pilgrim on a Portuguese Camino 27

Chapter 3　In the Company of Chaucer on The Pilgrims' Way 59

Chapter 4　Upping and Downing on the Cornish Coastal Path 99

Chapter 5　Revisiting the Ridgeway 143

Chapter 6　Walking the Via Francigena 157

Chapter One

From Coast to Coast

The fleeting hour of life of those who love the hills is quickly spent, but the hills are eternal. Always there will be the lonely ridge, the dancing beck, the silent forest; always there will be the exhilaration of the summits. These are for the seeking, and those who seek and find while there is still time will be blessed both in mind and body.

Alfred Wainwright, Book Seven, The Western Fells, 1966

So many styles of stiles. Mum rests on a ladder stile with Mary, Joan, Barb, Sandy, Kay and Sandra behind. Gaps in the dry-stone walls are just wide enough for a rambler, but too narrow for sheep or cattle.

2 September 2006. In Victoria, BC, Canada.
I sit by my husband's bed, holding his hand, blinking back tears. "Who are you?" he manages, his whisper slurred.

Having been airlifted from our remote kayak camp on the west coast of Vancouver Island, he lies in a sun-filled room at Victoria General Hospital. While doctors discuss various pathologies, brain cancer devours his brain. Fear devours me.

2 September 2007. To St Bees, Cumbria, England.
I sit in seat 52A on a train speeding north from Manchester to Carlisle. I'm travelling with Mum as a recent addition to a trip she and six of her hiking friends have been planning for a couple of years. Six months after Mike's death from brain cancer, I'm still staggering under a burden of anguish, so they've invited me to join them. Perhaps the weight of a backpack will ease my agony.

Mum, Sandy, Kay, Barb, Sandra, Joan, Mary and I will walk eastward from St Bees on the Irish Sea to Robin Hood's Bay on the North Sea. The 313 kilometre route – created by famed British fellwalker and guidebook author Alfred Wainwright in 1973 – links several long-established walking paths through the Lake District, Yorkshire Dales and North York Moors National Parks.

Changing trains in Carlisle, we continue north to Whitehaven. A grey sky presses down on green and gold fields quilted by dry-stone walls. Black-faced sheep gaze up as we rattle by. From Whitehaven a short taxi ride brings us into the village of St Bees cuddled between pastoral slopes and the windy shore.

3 September. Around St Bees.
We clamber down a steep path to the wide sand beach for a toe-dipping ceremony in the glittering sea. The chill water brings a vivid recollection of being with Mike at Spring Island. He had piggybacked me out to a waiting float plane, then standing in knee-deep water, had waved as we taxied across the bay. That was the

last time I'd seen him as a well man. Laughing and splashing now with Mum and her friends, my heart lurches. Guilt overrides my momentary joy.

Leaving the beach, we climb a red limestone headland towering above St Bees. From the top we look west to the Isle of Man and Ireland, north to Scotland and south along the English coast. Turning east we see the distant Lake District hills and settle our minds to the walk ahead.

We meet a local historian who, delighting in the curiosity of eight Canadian women, regales us with stories. Evidence shows, he tells us, that Mesolithic and Bronze Age people lived here, and probably the Romans too, although there are no artifacts to support that theory. Popular legend has it that in the 9th century, an Irish princess – who became St Bega – fled to St Bees to escape an arranged marriage to a Viking. When the Normans arrived, they built a priory here that thrived as the monks farmed and fished. After Henry VIII's Dissolution of the Monasteries in 1539, the buildings were plundered and fell into ruin. During the reign of Elizabeth I, one of Canterbury's archbishops hailed from St Bees.

At this point, with thanks for the tour through time, we continue our own explorations before we, too, become the stuff of history.

4 September. To Cleator.

This journey will be one of discovery rather than a race against time. Even though we arrive in Cleator by lunch, and we've already been passed by several people rushing along – all stating their determination to complete the walk in less time than someone else – we stay for the night.

I want to shout, "Don't rush. Life should not be hurried."

While washing down our lunch with beer at the Three Tuns pub, the proprietor entertains us with tales of ascending the Dent.

5 September. To Ennerdale Bridge.

Huffing up this formidable hill the next morning, we understand that her tall tales weren't exaggerated. From the summit, we see the

Irish Sea as a dim silver line in the distance. Later, we picnic below Raven Crag at the bottom of Flat Fell. There is nothing flat about the fell and raucous ravens soar above us. When we move on, they land and peck our dropped morsels.

That night we rest weary bodies at the Shepherd's Arms. We're in the Lake District now. This region of thirty-one lakes was once home to friends Samuel Taylor Coleridge and William Wordsworth, as well as to Beatrix Potter and Arthur Ransome. Mum recites a few lines from the *The Rime of the Ancient Mariner*:

> *Like one, that on a lonesome road*
> *Doth walk in fear and dread,*
> *And having once turned round walks on,*
> *And turns no more his head;*
> *Because he knows, a frightful fiend*
> *Doth close behind him tread.*

I pick a lighthearted Wordsworth quote:

> *I wandered lonely as a cloud*
> *That floats on high o'er vales and hills,*
> *When all at once I saw a crowd,*
> *A host, of golden daffodils;*

Recalling *The Tale of Peter Rabbit* and *Swallows and Amazons* – first read to me by Mum and then by myself as I learned to make sense of squiggles crossing the pages – I smile, surrounded with the memories of a magical childhood.

6 September. To the Black Sail Youth Hostel.

We walk along the shore of Ennerdale Water, so morning-still it's hard to tell where the reflections begin and end. Will my widowhood become this serene? A wind gust crumbles the images. As fragile and transient as the lost reflection, I could crumble just as easily.

Leaving the shore, we climb into the fells. Fells – from the Norse word for a barren mountain above the treeline. The fells are intercut by burbling becks. Beck – derived from the Norse word for brook.

We spend the afternoon and night at the Black Sail Youth Hostel. Other walkers stride on while we enjoy the sun and discuss philosophy with the resident sheep. The hostel is advertised as being remote and only accessible by foot. The staff and supplies, however, arrive by Land Rover. Regardless, in a country as densely populated as England, the relative isolation is precious. Once the through-walkers are long gone, it's just us, the two staff, the many sheep and the pink glow of a setting sun.

7 September. To Stonethwaite and Gillercombe.
Mum, Sandra and I leave before the others as Mum is worried about the morning's steep climb. Her arrival yesterday, more than two hours after most of us, has disturbed her. Her friends offer reassurance, but I am alarmed by a vulnerability she tries to hide with vehement denial that she is struggling. Despite her slow pace, Mum relishes her time on the trail. Surrounded by supportive, enthusiastic friends, she radiates happiness.

Gasping up the slope on this fog-bound morning, she quips, "I guess I can't make an excuse of taking a picture."

"Take your time, Mum. There's no rush," I assure her from several feet above.

She leans over her trekking poles, wheezing and sweating with exertion. I'm shivering for the lack of it. I've climbed slowly, pausing every ten steps. Mum's breathlessness frightens me. The rest catch up as we level off onto a long craggy ridge. Crag – derived from Gaelic for high outcrop. These rock formations are the remains left after glacial ice, then wind and rain eroded the softer surrounding rock.

Today, dense fog muffles sound and shrouds landmarks. Swirling eddies disorient all sense of direction. Jagged cliffs lurk nearby. Multitudes of wending sheep trails obscure the one safe path we seek between the crags and along the ridge. The way-marking cairns are spaced too far apart to be visible in the murk. We discuss a plan for safe passage, consulting compasses, maps and the GPS. A competent wayfinder, I offer to lead.

Focusing on my compass bearing and counting paces, I tread across the treeless rock-strewn highland and the eight of us spread out, each a faint shadow to the woman before and after. Next in line, Mum calls out just before I disappear into the grey. I wait. Once beside me, she confers with her GPS. It and my compass are in agreement, so we all continue on the same trajectory, spongy grass tussock to lichened outcrop, through knee-deep heather, past elusive cairns crouched among erratic remains of ancient glaciers. We and they, indistinct as ghosts.

Pink blossoms of dew-dripping heather soak our legs as we brush through. Dew gathers on our clothing in soft white streaks. The slope dips and I feel a moment of vertigo before my boots scrabble onto a wide gravel path.

"Found it," I call.

Descending beneath the cloud, we look down across a dim, monochromatic landscape. Far below, a narrow road ribbons through Honister Pass. Spotting a distant coffee shop by the landscape-scarring Honister slate mine, we chatter about how nice it will be to sip a warming cup of tea and maybe nibble on fresh hot-buttered scones.

Emerging from underground shafts, tiny, straining rail carts haul massive slabs of green slate. To the discordant din of industry drifting up the slope, our trekking poles clicking and rain pants swishing, we hike down from the desolate crags onto Honister Pass where we celebrate our adventure with the worst cup of tea ever brewed in Britain. No scones available.

Down we walk along the River Derwent, into the sun and on to Gillercombe where Mum and five others stay. Sandra and I walk further to Stonethwaite because Gillercombe is too small to accommodate all of us. We return for dinner with the others.

"How's Tad doing?" Sandra asks as we walk in the twilight.

I shake my head, unable to articulate my fear. "She's in her element," I say. "Surrounded by friends. Being here. She loves England. She loves walking."

Sandra nods. "She is happy. No doubt about that."

The spectre of Mum's physical decline casts an insidious shadow.

8 September. To Grasmere.

Sandra and I return to Gillercombe, and our walk continues. As we ply the trails, I watch Mum kibitz and laugh with her friends and am mesmerized by the brightness of her joy. She and I often walk together, she always breathless on the many uphill sections and sucking Ricola in a vain effort to calm her persistent cough.

"Tad usually leaves us in the dust," Mary comments.

"I guess she's had that cough for a while," Barb muses.

Her friends gather to her, taking turns walking slowly and waiting while she catches her breath. They encourage breaks, proclaiming they're admiring the view until Mum's breathing eases. I don't comment, knowing she will not welcome implied criticism. Her lungs are filling with fluid and Ricola will not cure the resulting cough, which has worsened since 2004. She has her reasons for not seeking medical treatment, but I do not know what they are. As Mum struggles up another hill, I think about Mike's horrible death from brain cancer and wonder how I will bear losing my mother to an early death as well. Anger simmers. I am unable to separate my need that she be well from her denial that she is ill. Despite my worry, Mum's infectious joy chips away at my sorrow.

As we near Grasmere, I contemplate the act of walking, this most ancient way of travelling. Although I've backbacked many times, longdistance walking is new to me. I discover a kinship with the hairy, naked humanoids who first walked out of the African continent. It feels right to heed this human predisposition to walk from one place to another. Migrations. Explorations. Quests.

My quests? Discover what Widow Kim does without her husband as a compass. Figure out how Daughter Kim honours her ailing mother. From this moment, what do I do? From this place, where do I go? One response – my only response – is to just walk forward. One step followed by another.

Kilometre after kilometre unfolds under the tread of my boots. Vistas open and close. I catch the scents of late-summer alyssum and lavender spilling over cottage garden walls. My fingers and lips redden with juicy, ripe blackberries plucked from hedgerows. Himalayan orchid seedpods burst in the sun, their popcorn scent drifting with each tiny explosion. Sleepy birds discuss winter migration.

Walking ahead of the others through the desolate stretches of Greenup Edge, I sense no other humans, but turning, I see seven small bodies crossing the rugged fell. I am not alone. The tiny specks we each create in the expanse of rock, bog and heath set me to thinking about our insignificant duration on this planet. I sit and gaze. One by one the women join me until, eventually, Sandra and Mum arrive. We all rest a little longer so they, too, can take in the wonder.

9 September. To Patterdale.

After Grasmere, we hike towards Patterdale. On the way, four of us want to hike up Helvellyn – England's third-highest peak – via the dramatic Striding Edge route. Disappointed at not being up to the strenuous ascent, Mum will take the low route with the others. They will be in Patterdale before us.

As we climb, a thick blanket of cloud descends. We hunker down, hoping it will clear, but rangers close the precipitous trail to the summit due to the inclement weather. With zero visibility and high winds in the forecast, hopeful hikers and climbers are told to turn around, so it is not long before we all join up again near Patterdale.

After returning home, Mum notes in her scrapbook: *How much I love these fells ... How I regret all the wasted time. If only I had been able to do this kind of walk 20 years ago.*

That would have been 1987. Mum and Dad lived in Sidney, near Victoria. Dad was retired and spending his summers sailing on the

West Coast. Mum didn't enjoy sailing, and stayed home tending her vegetable garden, but I wonder why she hadn't followed more of her own bliss. Although Mike died with no regrets, Mum's evident disappointments sadden me. They also remind me to live like Mike had – for today.

10 September. In Patterdale.

Making use of one of Patterdale Youth Hostel's washing machines, we deal with a pile of dirty socks and sweaty shirts, then spend the rest of the morning in the tourist-laden village, postcard writing and tea sipping. The traffic and bustle jar senses now comfortable with more solitude, so during the afternoon we wander in the nearby hills. This is what our legs and minds want to do. Because the White Lion pub welcomed us yesterday, we return there for another wholesome dinner. Mary and I have been ordering appetizers or soup to leave room for delicious desserts. This evening we indulge in massive servings of sticky toffee pudding.

11 September. To Shap.

Leaving Patterdale, we rest for a moment at an iron bench with the inscription "18**VR**97" in commemoration of Queen Victoria's Diamond Jubilee. Many bottoms have sat on this bench in the intervening one hundred and ten years, and I wonder what tales it might tell of secret trysts, romantic proposals, or solitary contemplations. I'm sure Wainright also sat here while he worked on the guidebook in my pack. So, I sit, too, and revel in views back to sun-soaked Ullswater.

Now our route climbs up to Boredale Hause. Hause – derived from the Norse or Anglo-Saxon word for a stream flowing through a mountain pass. Later we picnic by the indigo waters of Angle Tarn. Tarn – derived from the Norse word for mountain pond. The clear view of Helvellyn and Striding Edge make it difficult not to pine for the unattainable.

Mum chooses this moment to announce that this will be her last hike. Her words are greeted first with silence, then kind murmurs from these friends who have been hiking with her for years. I see how sad they are, but none argue. I turn my head so they can't see my tears. A bright torch has been extinguished. Mum's love of high places will remain fierce, and I fear for her wellbeing when she can no longer hike to the landscapes she holds dear.

We continue up to 780-metre Kidsty Pike. Pike – derived from the Norse word for a steep-peaked summit. Sharing Mum's exuberance at the summit makes up for not having been able to hike Helvellyn. Dancing around on the highest point, we watch cloud shadows chase across the fells, and mountain breezes stir sunlit tarns.

Kay, Sandra, Mary and Mum on the summit of Kidsty Pike.

"Mike, this is for you," I offer, imagining him dancing with me, the way we did during the Nijmegen Marches.

Mum brings me back to the present by pointing out a Roman road slicing across the countryside in the distance. I recall that Nijmegen was acknowledged by the Romans as being the oldest city in what is now the Netherlands. The connectivity of different places through time offers comfort. I feel Mike here. On the trail for a week, I experience a sense of transformation, becoming a different woman. Now, I am happy for more moments than I am sad, grief loosening its terrible grip.

We descend towards Haweswater reservoir. Today's steep ascent and the equally steep descent saps all Mum's reserves. As we creep along the shoreline towards Burnbanks, she struggles to put one foot in front of the other. It is my turn to walk with her, and I drop behind her so she doesn't feel pressure to keep up. Stumbling, shuffling, wheezing and gasping, she inches forward. I'm wondering if we'll make it before dark, when I see a couple of her friends heading back towards us. Having been worried that one of us had been injured, they're relieved to see we're both still standing.

Our accommodation for the night is in Shap, another eight kilometres past Burnbanks where the rest have been waiting. When we arrive, they announce that they are all much too tired to walk any further so we phone our B&B host who comes to pick us up. If Mum realizes the subterfuge, she doesn't let on.

We pile into a car too small to handle all of us, Mum and I folded into a small luggage space in the back, our heads squished against our knees. The fells fall behind as our host drives us through gentle undulating farmland, taking care to miss the larger potholes. Passing the stark ruins of Shap Abbey, she tells us it was built in 1199. Closed in 1540 during the Dissolution of the Monasteries, its fallen walls have since provided building material for the surrounding farms. Our B&B – The Hermitage – was built in 1691 and I expect we are, in part, sheltered by the ancient Abbey walls.

12 September. To Orton.

The Lake District behind us now, we cross Cumbrian farmlands into Yorkshire Dales National Park, sauntering through pastures and clambering over stiles. The styles of stiles seem limitless: wooden ladder steps up and over stone walls, or flat stone steps incorporated into stone walls, or small raised spaces – too narrow for a sheep – through stone walls.

A footbridge takes us over the roar of the six-lane M6 highway. A muddy stretch of path leads us past a smoking granite works industrial site. A rocky trail traces up onto Crosby Ravensworth

Fell and past the Neolithic stone circle of Oddendale. We pause. Were it not for the circular placement, it would be easy not to notice the stones, resting boulder-like in the heath.

Tumuli rise as small mounds, testaments to ancient burials. We stop for lunch, surrounded by a landscape etched by 8000 years of human endeavour. A nearby cairn, known as Robin Hood's Grave, may be an ancient burial site and has nothing to do with the outlaw. One theory postulates that nut harvesters used to drop a rock on the mound for good luck:

> *Robin Hood, Robin Hood, here lie thy bones;*
> *Load me with nuts as I load thee with stones.*
>
> Source: Dawn Robertson and Peter Koronka,
> Secrets and Legends of Old Westmoreland, *1992*

Adding a stone of my own, I consider the connectivity between my acts of walking and discovery and the acts of others, past and present. I seek an understanding of my place in the spectrum of human existence. Walking allows me to sense the larger world in concert with exploring my inner self. Since I am a product of ancestors, history, place and experience, Mike remains a part of who I am becoming. Our love, our children, our challenges and our triumphs – are me.

Over the next hill, we see the faint outline of a Roman road cutting arrow-straight across our route and heading north towards Hadrian's Wall. These northern reaches of the Roman Empire were never colonized to the same extent as southern England. Local inhabitants were loyal to whomever was in the best position to offer protection – whether Roman or northern invaders. Incursions were a persistent problem for the Roman soldiers and commanders, so building the wall offered six years of gainful employment, a sense of security and improved prosperity to local herdsmen and farmers.

We spend the night at the cozy George Inn in Orton. There, we discover that an early Quaker preacher, George Whitehead, was born near here in 1636. He initially lobbied Charles II, then James II and lastly William III and Mary II for the right to religious freedom. The resultant 1689 Bill of Rights established many of the civil rights most members of the Commonwealth nations take for granted today.

Mum and I share a room, and as we climb into bed, she tells me about the dream she had as she went into labour with me. "Just before I had you," she begins, "I was reading *Kim*. I had a vivid dream. A ragged boy, Kim, saved me from armed men on horseback ..."

Fascinated by the meaning of dreams, Mum records them in her journals, and they are an important aspect of how she perceives the metaphysical world. I tell her I've been dreaming about Mike and she assures me her father still visits her dreams. I don't tell her that in my dreams Mike is always turned away, and at a distance. I don't admit that I never manage to see his face.

13 September. To Kirkby Stephen.

As we walk, I consider Mum's dream and hope she will seek medical help because, once again, her life needs saving. We have made a habit of leaving each morning before the others. She's annoyed that everyone takes turns walking her slow pace, so getting a head start forestalls that daily argument for a couple of hours.

Today when she sees the rest catching up, she grumbles, "I wish you people would just leave me alone to walk the speed I want."

"The speed you *want* or the speed you *can*?" I ask. "Mum, it would be irresponsible to leave you behind. These are your friends. This is what friends do."

She sputters, "Oh, don't be so stupid." Her long-used phrase to deflect anything she disagrees with.

"Mum! Don't spoil this. Don't deny us the honour of walking with you. Be gracious."

She glowers. The others arrive, their cheerful greetings cutting the frigid air between us. We continue as a group for a few metres, then string out along the trail. Barb is walking with Mum this morning. I turn before dropping over a rise. Now far behind, they are tiny bright flecks against the muted bronze bracken and blush heathers.

"You okay?" Kay asks.

"I'm worried about her."

"We all are. But your mum will do things her own way."

As we walk, Kay reveals her relationship with Mum and I'm introduced to a woman who is an expert, a confidante, the group's matriarch. During our conversation, it becomes apparent that Kay does not know Mum is a grandmother of two adult grandsons.

"She never told you about her grandchildren? My boys?"

Kay shakes her head. "I don't think any of us knew that you have children."

Crossing a wild dale – a broad shallow valley – is fraught with the possibility of becoming mired in a bog. Following a string of marker posts across the treacherous ground, I wish I had similar markers to lead me to an understanding of Mum. She knit the boys sweaters when they were young. She bought them books. She seemed interested in their lives. For twenty-three years, she has not told her friends that she is a grandmother.

We eat our picnic lunch, sitting among faint mounds of several large prehistoric settlements while the ghosts of distant civilizations prowl our periphery.

"Such historic trampling has this bit of ground felt," Mum intones in her best imitation of Shakespeare.

I love this game. "I shall but leave an impermanent impression in the grass," I respond, inventing another line.

Mum passes me a biscuit. "Time is ours but to borrow, until we shuffle off this mortal coil," she challenges.

"Oh, Mother, the time of life is short," I offer, stunned by how close we're circling to the conversation she will not have, and also by the spectre of Mike hovering nearby.

Needing a moment, I lie back to watch the scudding clouds and to time travel. It is 8000 BCE. Britain is connected to Europe by a land bridge – Doggerland. It is an area of rich resources, first for Paleolithic and then Mesolithic hunter-gatherers. As the climate warms, the oceans to the north and south rise and some inhabitants migrate further west to settle in the area where we are now eating lunch.

Within a few hundred years, continued seawater rise redefines Doggerland as an area of marshes and lagoons, its population living well in a shrinking world. Then, around 6200 BCE a subsurface chunk of the Norwegian coast subsides – the Storegga Slide – causing a five-metre tsunami to flood Doggerland, drowning all still living there. Descendants of the tribes who had migrated further west are now isolated until boatbuilders create craft capable of venturing far enough off-shore to reach distant lands.

I imagine a group of Paleolithics or Mesolithics hunting the resident mammoths, maybe killing one just where we are now munching our bacon sandwiches.

The climate continues to warm, forests grow, and the inhabitants evolve and thrive. Neolithics develop agriculture and chop down some of the forests to create arable land. Through the epochs, the people of the Stone, Bronze and Iron Ages develop, each civilization marking the land with traces of their occupation. By 500 BCE the Iron Age Celts arrive at our picnic spot, having crossed the sea from Central Europe. In 71 CE, the Romans come marching through the land, today's major highways following the routes of their well-engineered roads. Germanic Angles come next, attacking defenceless voids left by departing Romans. The Vikings invade in 865 CE, and the last succesful invasion of this land from across the sea is the Norman conquest in 1066. The Normans themselves are descendants of Vikings – Norse men – who had raided and settled along the northern coast of France two hundred years previously. All of us with ancestral roots in Britain are a product of migrating, invading and subsequent settling and colonizing.

This is what humans have always done. It is what we will continue to do. But, despite all our contrivances to make movement quicker and easier, we must now adhere to national borders and physical barriers. We continue to distrust all who are Other.

Meanwhile, our climate is warming once again. I consider how much of the global population lives less than a metre above current sea levels and wonder where and when the next Doggerland will disappear. Given the Sumas Prairie flooding in mid-November 2021, I think we'll not have to wait very long to find out.

14 September. To Keld, North Yorkshire.
We continue up and over the Pennine mountains. As usual, Mum and I set off before the others. Kay's revelation about Mum's grandchildren secrecy still rankles.

"Mum, why have you never told your friends about Brian and Kyle?"

"What do you mean?"

"They don't know you're a grandmother."

"Well, what's that got to do with anything?"

"Isn't it part of who you are? Didn't you ever want to tell your friends about something they did? They're both accomplished young men."

"Well, I suppose they are. But no one would be interested. Why would they be?" She walks a little further. "Being a grandmother is *not* who I am." Her tone slams the door on the subject.

Our high point of the day is the summit of Hartley Fell, across which march nine tall cairns known as the Nine Standards Rigg. Here we pause, despite a gale, to muse on their origin. Some say they mark the boundary between Cumbria and North Yorkshire. They do. Another theory is that the Romans built them to appear like troops from a distance. They do. We've watched them, sentinels on their hilltop, for more than a day. Their truth remains shrouded by time.

Into the Yorkshire Moors we trudge, where more bogs await to suck down the unwary traveller. A wailing wind races low slate clouds across the sky. The gloom brings to mind the tortured ghost of Emily Bronte's Heathcliff striding across the moors cursing in vain as he seeks his Catherine in the afterlife. I shiver.

15 September. To Reeth.

The map promises a short walk along Swaledale – the valley of the River Swale – so we depart Keld as a group. Enjoying a calm sunny morning, we begin by following Swaledale as planned; however, this is where the Pennine Way intersects with the Coast to Coast. Although the valley path is easier, Wainwright recommends a higher moorland route past the atmopheric ruins of smelting mills and defunct lead mines.

All goes well until we come to a spot where the Coast to Coast markers direct us up out of the valley. No amount of persuasion convinces Mum that we should stay low. The open moors call. We fall in line and climb. At first Mum sets a steady pace, but as the day progresses her stamina dwindles. I watch the sun lower behind us. Her friends glance at their watches and most walk on, soon to be long out of sight. Mum's too exhausted to notice. A walk that should have taken four hours takes us more than eight.

While all her friends are loyal and supportive, over the past couple of days it has fallen to Kay, Sandra and me to take turns being Tail-end Charlie with Mum. The rest find it too difficult to be on the trail so long. I don't begrudge them. I have not commented, but hear the others make suggestions that she might like a day off, or that perhaps we share her backpack load.

Mum denies having any difficulties. "I don't know why everyone keeps fussing so much," she says.

"They're used to scampering to keep up with you. We're worried."

"How many times have I said for you to not wait for me?"

"Touché."

She gives us no choice but to leave her or to see her through. We will, of course, see her through as she has done for slower hikers in the past.

Shortly before arriving at our night's stop in Reeth, we descend again into the valley. The trail comes to a gate bearing a large "Beware of Bull" sign. Mum is not a fan of cattle, bulls in particular. We slip through the kissing gate and scan the field. No sign of the bull. We've almost reached the far side when we see the beast. Mum's journal describes it as obscene.

She pauses. "Hells bells. I can't walk past that thing."

"As long as you don't run or make noise everything will be fine," I lie.

We walk steadily, me leading until Mum zips past me, moving faster than she has for days. I trot along behind her and we clamber over the stile with fear-induced speed.

"Guess that got my legs moving." She leans against the far side of the stile, beaming, gasping and coughing.

Reeth offers no accommodation capable of hosting all eight of us, so four stay at Springfield House B&B and the other four go to The Old Temperance B&B above a bookshop selling Christian books and curios. There is nothing temperate about our dinner at the Kings Arms next door where the Yorkshire puddings are the size of dinner plates. No one leaves a morsel uneaten.

16 September. To Richmond.

We tramp past the ruins of 12th-century Marrick Priory and climb stone steps laid by nuns onto the hill above. Our walk through farmland includes the usual array of sheep-stopping gates and stiles. While the public right-of-way rules in England are nuanced, they're entrenched in a walking-for-leisure culture that developed with the Industrial Revolution in the 18th century. The public enjoys a legal right to walk on footpaths that have been in undisputed use for at least twenty years, including paths through private land. Many of the routes have existed for hundreds of years and most are annotated on the country's comprehensive Ordnance Survey mapping system. This right to walk does not, however, include cycling or horse riding.

We arrive on the outskirts of Richmond and are soon thumping single file along sidewalks, stopping at crosswalks to await lights and dodging folks out for Sunday strolls. Being Sunday, pubs have only served lunches and are closing for dinner. We end up at a North American-style restaurant, which doesn't really suit our style at all.

17 September. In Richmond.

A rest day means a laundry day. Joan and I take turns supervising the machines and sorting whose smalls belong to whom. Laundry done, we enjoy a wander through the historic town centre and tour through the the best preserved Norman castle in England. Built in 1071, just five years after the Norman Conquest, it is mentioned in the 1086 Domesday Book as "a castlery." Then we relax, write postcards, catch up on journalling, drink tea and find a proper pub for dinner.

18 September. To Danby Wiske.

Continuing our journey, we walk through the hedged farmland of the Vale of Mowbray. A dank underpass takes us under the A1 highway, the ground shuddering as trucks rush by overhead. Most of our walk traces along the edges of fields: some empty meadows, others occupied by cattle, some already harvested and ploughed, others laden with ripening grain. We walk through a few farmyards, stepping around machinery and cow patties, ducking laundry on a line and dodging a few curious hens. An overall-clad farmer under his tractor twists a wrench; another, wearing a tweed cap, unloads boxes from the back of a Land Rover. They smile and bid us good day, no one perturbed by eight women tramping through their yards.

In Danby Wiske, we again stay in two places: Mum and Joan – besides me, the two shortest of our group – at the Old Manor, the rest of us at the White Swan Inn. The Old Manor offers rooms with normal-height ceilings. Those of us at the White Swan negotiate roof rafters. I only bang my head a few times, but the others, especially statuesque Kay and Sandra, can't stand up straight. The White Swan makes up for cramped rooms and lumpy beds with a terrific pub menu.

19 September. To Osmotherley.

Through the Vale of Mowbray we continue to the A19 highway where there is no under or over crossing. We study our various maps and guidebooks. One of the books states: *The crossing of A19 ... is extremely dangerous and requires great care. Cars and trucks travel at high speed ....* None of our guidebooks offers an alternative. Stepping to the verge, we strategize.

"Wait. Wait. Now. Run. Stop!"

We all make it to the centre verge – which is much too narrow for comfort – then repeat the mad dash.

A small road, with more traffic than we are used to, brings us into Ingleby Arncliffe. This might have been a logical place to end our day. But Mum and a couple of the others walked in this area a few years previously, and they're excited about returning to a hostel at Osmotherley, a little further east.

We leave the vale and begin climbing up into the Cleveland Hills. Mum has found the gentle terrain through dale and vale easier walking and seems to have regained some energy, and I recognize her desire to achieve high ground again. Her will gets her to the hostel, but once again she lags behind as the terrain steepens.

"I don't recall it being so far," is her only concession.

No one says a word about how slowly she walks and how quickly she loses her breath.

20 September. To Clay Bank.

At breakfast Mum says she will catch a ride to our next stop. "This is part of the Cleveland Way," she says by way of explanation. "I've already walked it."

We accept this decision, but I'm torn to see her raising a forlorn hand at our backs when we set off. In her scrapbook, beside a couple of pictures of us waving and walking away, Mum wrote:

> *I had done this section before; there was lots of climbing; I was slow on the ups and I knew they would wait and not let me come in my own time. I decided to give the rest a rest and did not walk today. Not a good day for me, but a wonderful one for the rest.*

Kay and I take a high route, up and over five moors. The

cultivated Vale of Mowbray shrinks as we ascend into wild heather country: Scarth Wood Moor, Live Moor, Carlton Moor, Cringle Moor, and finally up to the summit of Hasty Bank on which perch the Wainstones. This towering outcrop of weather-sculpted sandstone was apparently held in high regard by Bronze Age people who left numerous carvings in the surrounding rocks.

The wind, sun and stiff pace are invigorating. I climb up, then stand, leaning into the wind on one of the stones, wild as the moorland, free as the hawks that soar in the wind above it. There, I leave a little more of my burden of sadness in a patch of heather.

At day's end, an abrupt descent brings us down towards Clay Bank where Mum awaits on the trail with a brave smile. She tells us how tonight's host, Gerry, has loaned her binoculars, so she's been able to watch us clambering around on the Wainstones, then she leads us on down to Malt Kiln House.

Gerry and Wendy host us for dinner, and while Wendy labours in the kitchen with final touches to our feast, Gerry recounts the history of the jet stone found in this area. While considered a gem, it is not mineral. Rather, it is created from wood decomposing over millions of years. Hard jet results from decomposed wood being compressed in salt water. Soft jet is formed in fresh water. Like coal, jet burns. Queen Victoria wore jet jewellery while she was in mourning.

21 September. To Blakey.

The first day of fall and our first day of rain. Gerry shows us a shortcut up onto Urra Moor right outside his back door. Slithering and scrambling in the mud, then trudging in squelching silence, we each engage in private thoughts while discovering the violence of rain on the Yorkshire moors. Arriving from all directions, it sneaks under cuffs, into boots, through hoods, and blurs eyesight.

The long-disused railway track across Farndale Moor provides easy walking. Rain drips off my hood onto my breath-fogged glasses. Coming towards me, a man materializes from the mist. He has a certain stride and body build. I recognize Mike and smile at him. His face turns towards me.

"Might rain today," he grins.

I reach out my hand, but he seems not to notice as he continues out of sight. The others emerge from the mist behind me.

"Did you see that man?" I ask.

"What man?" asks Kay.

"Did a tall man pass you just now?" I persist.

No one saw anyone.

"Did you see a man?" Mum asks.

"I saw Mike," I say.

"Well, I suppose that's possible," she agrees. "But he picked a hell of a wet day to visit."

"He liked the rain," I say, glad for Mum's acceptance of the visitation.

Dripping into the Red Lion Pub in time for lunch, we decide to get a ride to our B&B. The phone lines are down, but a message is relayed to our host. He comes to pick us up later in the afternoon after we've enjoyed lunch and have steamed dry by the fire.

22 September. To Grosmont.

Sun shines on our walk across the moors to Grosmont. On the way we catch our first glimpses of the North Sea. We don't in truth see the sea, but spotting the superstructure of a large ocean tanker moving along the horizon, we trust it is floating on an unseen sea.

We amble into Grosmont all atwitter to visit the railway station. As we arrive, a steam-train puffs alongside a platform recognizable as Aidensfield of the TV series *Heartbeat*, Hogsmead in the *Harry Potter* movies and Mannerton in *All Creatures Great and Small*. Today, however, it is just tourist-thronged Grosmont, and we look grubby in our mud-caked boots.

We stay in stately but shabby Grosmont House. Our host frowns at our boots as she invites us in through a side door. Unlike Gerry and Wendy, this woman isn't welcoming of her travel-worn guests. Cobwebbed antlers ring a gallery above the dining room. Mum is sure the place is haunted.

23 September. To High Hawkster.

In the flag-festooned manorial dining room, not one of the breakfasts we ordered last night arrives as requested. At first we try sorting out who ordered what and pass the plates around but that proves ineffective because there is no match up. So we just pass each other food items.

"Omelette? Anyone?" I ask. There are no takers. No one ordered omelettes.

I don't like omelettes, but eat it anyway because it occupies the plate in my possession. The cold bacon is glued to the plates in congealed grease, the tomatoes are tinned. As is normal in England, the thin toast sits in cooling racks. A dusty suit of armour regards us with reproach as we spirit bacon and toast into paper napkins for lunchtime sandwiches.

From Grosmont, we climb up and cross another bleak, windblown moor, then down into a mysterious elf-infested forest where we ford May Beck before heading up onto Sneaton Low Moor. Here the wind is so strong Mum risks being blown away.

Across the Greystone Hills, the muddy path is often indistinct, so we frequently refer to map and compass. All of us are capable route finders, so there is never doubt as to which way we should head. I enjoy the community of these skilled hiking women. They tell me that Mum has been their mentor over the years and on many hikes.

In High Hawkster, we stay at the Old Blacksmiths Arms, a 17th-century blacksmith's workshop converted into a B&B. We eat yet another delicious pub dinner, this one at the Hare and Hounds. Pudding this evening is spotted dick – steamed currant-filled pudding topped with rich hot custard.

24 September. To Robin Hood's Bay.

The final day of our cross-country odyssey begins in pouring rain. Arriving on cliff tops overlooking the North Sea, we turn south as the route rounds a couple of headlands, then sends us tramping down the steep path into Robin Hood's Bay.

We run onto the sand to dip well-worn boot soles into the

rain-dimpled North Sea. Out there, under the waves, lies sunken Doggerland. How quickly a violent act of nature wiped it out.

The sun returns shortly after our arrival, and a man takes a group photo. Mum tries to slip to the back, but her friends place her front and centre, a position she has earned and deserves.

Sandy, Kay, Barb, Mum, Sandra(back), Joan, Me(back), Mary
The sun shines in Robin Hood's Bay for the last moments of our Coast to Coast Walk.

18 March 2013. In Saanich, BC.

My sister and I sit by Mum's bed in the Saanich Peninsula Hospital. She nears death from congestive heart failure. Her weak, rail-thin body struggles against drowning in fluid building in her lungs. I've just returned from three and a half months in Nepal and am horrified by this husk of my once-vibrant mother.

"Take me to your mountains," she whispers between body-racking coughing fits.

"We are climbing high above the treeline," I begin. "All around us, towering, snow-covered peaks rise sharp against an azure sky. The scent of almond blossoms fills the air. Yak bells ring along the path ahead. Far below, small farms dot the landscape, their terraced fields lush with ripe rice...."

She opens faded blue eyes one last time, then dies, our warm hands in each of hers as they still and grow cold.

This is where I like to imagine Mum. She's tramping through a traquil countryside of lakes, woodlands and fells. In these places, she was happiest.

Chapter Two

Becoming a Pilgrim on a Portuguese Camino

Pilgrimage unites belief with action, thinking with doing, and it makes sense that this harmony is achieved when the sacred has material presence and location.

Rebecca Solnit, Wanderlust: A History of Walking, *2001*

The many faces of Camino way markers. All have the scallop symbol.

23 October 2016. Porto, Norte region, Portugal.
It's been over three years since Mum died. The joy of walking the Coast to Coast with her has stayed with me, but now, about to embark on my first pilgrimage, I wonder if without a religious affiliation, I possess the right credentials to become a pilgrim. James Harpur offers assurance:

> ... *categories such as "pilgrim" and "traveller" are fluid. The membrane between the sacred and the secular is porous. ... only the pilgrim knows whether he or she is on a pilgrimage ...*
>
> *James Harpur,* The Pilgrim Journey – A History of Pilgrimage in the Western World, *2016*

My friend Pat agrees with Harpur. "Anyone can be a pilgrim," she says. "It's a way of thinking."

A public health nurse whom I met in 1996 while ski patrolling on Mount Washington and with whom I shared kayak adventures and a trek in Nepal, Pat is an intrepid long-distance walker. Twice she followed Camino routes through Spain, and in 2014, she walked part of the Via Francigena from Besançon to Rome.

One spring day in 2015, while we sipped wine on the patio in my garden, Pat asked if I'd like to go on a walk. I knew she didn't mean along one of our local trails.

"Where?"

"The Via Egnatia."

"What's the Via Egnatia?"

"It's a Roman road across the Balkans from the west coast of Albania to Istanbul." She paused to gauge my reaction and added, "About a thousand kilometres."

"Why not?" I answered and we began to plan.

On 15 July 2016, five weeks before our departure, there was an attempted coup in Turkey, so we altered the plan. We'd walk as far as the Greek-Turkish border. Then what? We tossed our non-refundable Turkish visas, applied for Camino Pilgrim passports and researched the short 250-kilometre route. When we left home in August 2016, we each carried a six-kilogram pack. On 23 October, we completed that epic journey which, in the end, did see us to Istanbul.

Pat and I now fly from Thessaloniki in northern Greece through Munich on to Lisbon and then to Porto, Portugal. Thessaloniki's airport security requires that we check our trekking poles as they are considered too hazardous for cabin baggage. Despite three plane changes, their tiny bundle, resting in an enormous plastic bin, slides down onto the carousel within moments of our arrival. However, Pat's pocketknife, packaged in the same bundle, has disappeared during transit.

Only four Metro ticket machines – with inadequate instructions – service throngs of passengers heading into Porto from the airport. Two Metro staff help confused foreigners, but the laborious process creates long lineups. Once aboard the crowded subway, we count stops and emerge within a couple of blocks of our Rivoli Cinema Hostel. With the aid of the Pocket Earth navigation app on our iPads, and easy-to-follow directions from the hostel's website, we find the iconic red-door entrance and check in a couple of hours after clearing customs. Our tiny room is jammed with two bunk beds, a sleeping bag and wrinkled T-shirt occupying one of the bottom bunks. We are assigned the two top beds.

After an early dinner in a busy nearby restaurant, we wander to stretch our legs, and watch black-robed university students strolling, laughing, playing musical instruments and singing. Their traditional attire dates from mediaeval academic traditions. Drizzle begins, then switches to a slicing rain, sending the students rushing into bright-lit bars and us scurrying back to the hostel.

We spend the evening reviewing distances and plotting *albergue* locations into Pocket Earth. Three young men sprawled across the lounge couches do the same thing on their cell phones. I wonder how much company we'll have over the next ten days as we walk north into Spain to Santiago de Compostela.

"I'm skeptical about this pilgrimage thing," I admit to Pat. The

Via Egnatia was hard, but it wasn't busy with other walkers. There was much about our solitude that I had liked.

"Kim, keep an open mind. We don't need to wrap this in any spiritual quest, and it will be a cake walk after the Via Egnatia. The Camino Francés is really crowded these days, but I'm sure this lesser-known Camino will suit our style."

We've covered enough distance together for me to trust her judgment. Rivoli Cinema Hostel has a ten o'clock quiet-time policy, so my worries appeased, we head to our room and climb into our top bunks. We've fallen asleep when the light flicks on and a rain-soaked woman bustles in, bumping her pack against the bed.

"Sorry. Late flight," she whispers.

24 October. To Vilar de Pinheiro.

At breakfast, Pat and I squeeze into spaces at a table cluttered with French, Italian and Russian Camino guidebooks propped against sugar bowls and milk jugs. We eat bread and yoghurt, then pack lunches. Checking out at the same time as a crowd of other pack-laden pilgrims, we clomp down narrow stairs to the street-level door. Delayed behind two young women who stop in the doorway to discuss where they want to go, I squeeze by and look south. No Pat. Looking north, I see her, and several others, cross an intersection seconds before the walking light blinks red. I wait, toe tapping, as traffic streams past. Pat and I had planned to walk 700 metres south to the cathedral to receive the first stamp in our pilgrim's credential passport. Now, headed in the opposite direction, I feel a prick of annoyance.

The light changes, and trying to catch up, I dodge around slower pedestrians. A block further, Pat and one of our young hostel mates pause. When I catch up, the young woman begins introducing us to the art of spying the scallop-shell symbols that mark the route to Santiago de Compostela. We will find some carved into stone buildings; others will be bright tiles embedded into walls. Etchings in glass, brass plaques in sidewalks, paintings on signposts: once our eyes become attuned, the markers will be easy to spot.

Pat already knows this, so has pulled out her guidebook. I nod to the enthusiastic assault of information. The sunshine, the rain-washed streets and the old-city architecture beg a photo moment, so I take a picture while Pat continues flipping through her guidebook and the other woman's instructions drone on. Vehicles rush by in a roar of wheels rumbling over the cobbled street.

Tucking my camera away and digging out my iPad, I interrupt the lecture. "Pat, the cathedral is behind us. We're going the wrong way."

"No. The route heads north." Standing between us, the other woman remains determined to continue explaining all things Camino. She points north to emphasize her point and my idiocy.

"We planned to get our credentials stamped at the cathedral. It's south." Christ, I sound whiney.

Over the traffic din, Pat hasn't heard. The woman turns north and hurries to catch up with the others who are now far ahead. Pat follows. Shoving my iPad back into its pouch, I follow them. Irritated, I note that Pat's long stride easily keeps up with the blistering pace the youngsters set.

A block further, Pat pauses again. She grins. "Oh. Gee. What are we doing? No way we can last at this pace. Shouldn't we be at the cathedral by now?"

"It's behind us. The cathedral is south of the hostel. We're going north."

"Shit. We talked about that didn't we? How far?"

I open Pocket Earth. "Two kilometres. More. Going back now will add four or five to our day. I think we should skip it."

"Yeah. Too far," agrees Pat.

It's difficult to hear each other over the traffic-on-cobble din, so we walk on together, the sun shining, my equanimity restored, our young hostel mates long gone. Over the course of the day, we walk back past the airport and chuckle that a half-hour Metro ride now takes several hours on foot.

Porto's buildings present façades of white, blue, yellow, green or brown Azulejo tiles. Some are monochrome but most are intricately patterned. Some are cracked and worn, others shine new, indicating a continued pride in this wall-tiling tradition that dates from the 13th century. Nowadays, the tiles serve a decorative function, but the concept originated as a method of insulating buildings from fierce summer heat and chilling winter winds whipping off the Atlantic. Sometimes a careful scan is needed to identify the Way of Saint James scallop shell symbol tucked into the kaleidoscopes of pattern and colour.

Like the tiles, cobbled streets and sidewalks enhance Porto's historic appearance, but our trekking poles create an annoying click with every arm swing, and the tips sometimes get stuck in the cracks. We pay near-constant attention to our feet so as not to trip over the uneven bits prevalent at the road's edges. Nice as the cobbles look, we'll be grateful when we're walking on a quieter, softer surface.

We enjoy our picnic lunch by Ponte de Dom Goimil, possibly built in the 13th century to replace an older Roman bridge over the River Leça. Too narrow for modern traffic, the bridge, now hidden among farm fields, serves as a pedestrian way. Snoozing in the sun for a few minutes after lunch, I consider the tread of soldiers, traders, farmers and pilgrims tramping and scuffing over its stone surface throughout its history and feel familiar and comforting connections. Packing up, we continue and add our footsteps to the fabric of that story.

Arriving in Vilar de Pinheiro, just north of the airport, we stay in a private home providing accommodation to pilgrims – Residencial Santa Marinha. The bedding hasn't been washed after previous guests, so we haul out our sleeping bags. A dysfunctional TV sits under a layer of dust. Damp towels – straight off the line – only provide a partial drying after our hot showers in a scuzzy bathroom. I like paying just €15.00 for the room but hope for cleaner digs in coming nights.

Dinner at a cozy family-owned restaurant across the street consists of enormous plates of fried cod and chips washed down with excellent wine. The bottle of wine costs €3.00. After spending

€30.00 per bottle in Istanbul, Pat and I relish the idea of enjoying lots more cheap Portuguese wine.

Before falling asleep, I revisit my morning's upset about not visiting the cathedral. I'd wanted to acknowledge the beginning of our sojourn as pilgrims. I'd wanted to see the cathedral. The speed with which the young people walked had reminded me of the fallibility of my aging body and my imagination conjures their disdain. I want to tell them that Pat and I have just walked across the bloody Balkans. With deep breaths, I let the disappointment go. Then sleep.

25 October. To Póvoa de Varzim.

The room's one light bulb burns out when we flip the switch, so we pack up with the aid of our headlamps. Today's route, while still along unyielding cobbles, leads us through the less populated hinterland of Porto.

As we clatter through a village, a woman calls out, *"Bom Caminho."* Later another and then more.

We wave and smile, revelling in a culture that understands walkers – pilgrims – and welcomes them. Every time we hear the greeting, our stride quickens and we walk a little taller.

Pilgrims have been walking this and several other routes to Santiago de Compostela since the 11th century. Following roads first laid during Roman occupation in the 1st century CE, they sought divine healing and blessing through visiting the shrine of Saint James the Apostle, known in Spanish as Santiago. The legend of how his relics came to be interred in a remote northwest corner of present-day Spain invites imaginative speculation.

Known as James the Greater, Saint James is thought by some scholars to have travelled and spread the gospel throughout the Iberian Peninsula after the crucifixion of Jesus, which took place sometime between 30 and 36 CE. Upon return to Jerusalem in 44 CE, he became the first Christian apostle to be martyred when King Herod Agrippa I of Judaea ordered his beheading.

The story contends that two of his disciples spirited the headless body out of Judaea and brought it by boat to the Roman village of Iria Flavia – modern Padrón – on the Iberian coast at the western extremity of the Roman world. This journey might have taken close to a year, by which time the body may have been decomposed to little more than bones. According to legend, Queen Lupa helped the disciples bury their friend within the confines of her palace.

With the 460 CE collapse of Roman control in Iberia, the territory was fought over and occupied by several warring factions, and it is possible the remains were removed for safekeeping. While Christian King Alfonso II of Asturias – present-day northern Spain – was on the throne between 818 and 842, remains of three men were discovered buried in a crypt under a woodland about thirty kilometres north of Iria Flavia. With support of Pope Leo III and King Charlemagne, credence was given to the claim that these were the lost relics of Saint James and his two disciples.

During the 10th and 11th centuries, pilgrims from as far as Naples and Rome, Budapest and Kraków, Gdańsk and Aarhus thronged to Santiago de Compostela, a site that would come to rival Jerusalem and Rome. Over the years churches were built to accommodate the ever-increasing number of pilgrims, with the Cathedral de Santiago de Compostela being consecrated in 1211.

Modern Santiago pilgrims tramp the same routes across Europe as those followed by pilgrims past. Some come in faith. Some come seeking answers to inner questions. Some people start walking for the sense of adventure but become pilgrims as they journey. We are all united by mode of travel and destination. We are all greeted and welcomed by a culture that has grown up around this ancient form of tourism.

> In the twenty-first century, pilgrimage in the West is enjoying a boom, ... At the heart of this attraction is a spiritual impulse that has existed from time immemorial. It is a desire that connects us with our medieval forebearers and, indeed, ancient ancestors, ... Pilgrims of every era and every faith are bonded by comparable aspirations, hopes, doubts, physical endeavors ...

James Harpur, The Pilgrim Journey –
A History of Pilgrimage in the Western World, *2016*

By early afternoon, we walk into Póvoa de Varzim where we stay, by donation, at parish owned Albergue de Peregrinos de São José de Ribamar. Entering an unlocked main door, we find our way upstairs to a four-bunk room, spread out sleeping bags to claim our territory on bottom bunks, then inspect the modern, industrial kitchen. Spotless, it seems to offer every pot and utensil imaginable to create dinner. There are no signs of staff or other guests. While we're wondering about security, another pilgrim arrives, escorted by a chattering woman. When she sees us, she stops in mid-sentence and frowns.

"Do you speak English? *Você fala inglês?*" I try.

She does speak English, but she's not happy about our unannounced appearance.

"You have to phone first," she says, wagging her finger.

"We don't have a phone," says Pat, flashing her pilgrim credential.

I grab mine too. "We're *peregrino*."

All is forgiven. She launches into a torrent of Portuguese as she shows the three of us around the kitchen with instructions to clean up after ourselves and to be gone by nine the following morning. She stamps our credentials, shows the man into his room, hands over some keys and trundles back downstairs.

"Joe," says the other pilgrim by way of introduction.

He's perhaps a little younger than us, greying temples and the wiry build of an athletic walker. His smile reaches his eyes. From León, Spain, he speaks excellent English and likes walking this Camino because it's not as busy as some of the others. Joe heads off to the restaurants. We walk to a nearby grocery store and shop for dinner, a bottle of Portuguese wine, breakfast and lunch supplies. The bill is €11.00. We check our receipt. There must be some mistake, but every item is accounted for. The prices here are less than half what we were paying in Greece for similar items.

Back at the *albergue*, we hand wash our smalls and string our clotheslines between the beds.

"Bunk beds are useful for something," Pat admits.

She's tall, so when sitting on a lower bunk, she needs to bend forward.

Opening the wine before preparing our simple pasta meal presents a problem. The kitchen doesn't contain a corkscrew. Pat's pocketknife had one, but now gracing some airport worker's pocket, it's no help. I go to work bashing a pointed knife into the cork with a meat hammer, then twist and pull and twist and pull. Bit by bit the cork emerges with only a few cork crumbs escaping into the wine.

While we eat, Joe returns, and close behind a couple of American women limp in. They seem overwhelmed by the rigours of the trail and their enormous packs. Speaking laborious Spanish to the same woman who welcomed us earlier, they aren't making themselves understood.

She keeps interrupting them. "Speak English. I speak English."

"Why don't they understand we are in Portugal?" whispers Joe. "Almost everyone here speaks English. Not so many speak Spanish. I tried telling those two yesterday. I guess I didn't make myself clear."

Now we pause to listen. Voices rise, the women continuing to struggle with Spanish.

"I'll try to help," says Joe. "Their Spanish is unbearable." He winks and goes out into the hall where his soft voice sorts things out.

After a few minutes all three women retreat down the stairs.

"They don't want to sleep in a dorm or bunk beds," Joe says. "She's going to show them the nearest hotel. I begged them to speak English."

From the door downstairs we hear, "*Gracias*."

Joe groans. We laugh and pour him a glass of wine.

"*Obrigada*," he says.

After washing up and putting everything away, we sit with our feet up and study tomorrow's route.

"How are you enjoying this?" asks Pat.

"So fun. I feel myself becoming a pilgrim."

She smiles. "Meaning?"

"Finding a purpose to the journey. Expecting the journey itself to reveal the purpose."

I don't enjoy the cold shower before bed, so decide my donation to the church will only be €6.00. The booklet we received with our credentials explains that €6.00 is standard and up to €10.00 per bed is a generous donation for a dorm room bed when no meal is included.

26 October. To Marinhas.

Departing Póvoa de Varzim, we swing west to the coast. Soon we're marching along a wide boardwalk through sand dunes while the Atlantic thumps against the shore a few metres away. Thousands of gulls soar and screech. Hundreds of neoprene-clad surfers catch the curling waves. The sun beats down on the back of our heads and we sweat.

We enjoy the freedom from city noise as we walk through small villages, past thatched windmills and between stone walled kitchen gardens. Always we hear, "*Bom Caminho*."

"*Obrigada*. Thank you," we call back in a unison mirrored by our cadenced pace.

I take a picture every time I see a new version of the scallop shell signs. Most are the now-familiar stylized yellow shells on blue backgrounds with arrows indicating turns. Others are brass plaques engraved with the shell and Caminhos de San✝iago – with the red cross of Saint James replacing the t in Santiago.

This guidance is in stark contrast to the challenges Pat and I experienced while walking the Via Egnatia across the Balkans. Here, a tremendous amount of funding, interest and a long history have created community support, acknowledgment and acceptance. I imagine this might be what the Via Egnatia Foundation is trying to establish, but they will need their project to be embraced by the local population before the sense of camaraderie we feel here will be achieved.

In Marinhas our credentials are checked and stamped at the town's fire hall. We're given a key and directed to atmospheric Albergue São Miguel. Through a grey stone gateway, we discover a flagstone courtyard and old building repurposed to welcome pilgrims. This *albergue* is operated by the municipality and again, payment is by donation. The accommodation offers a large mixed-gender dorm, small ill-equipped kitchen and access to a washing machine.

Our clothes have only seen one other washing machine since we left home at the end of August. Diving into our packs, we dig out everything washable except what we're wearing, then decide to risk a few hours of commando living. I take on washing duties while Pat walks back into town for groceries.

As the machine agitates our clothes, I sit in the sun and chat with a Belgian couple on a yearlong cycling trip with their two young children. They have custom outfitted two bikes with small front wheels and tandem seats low in front of the handlebars. Sitting in those seats, the kids are encouraged to pedal as much as they can manage. Both bikes tow small trailers. Their luggage includes camping gear and schoolbooks. Staying in hostels is an occasional treat.

While we chat, I hang laundry in the sun and discover an extra pair of socks.

"These yours?" I ask the parents.

They shake their heads. I examine the socks – like-new, quality, merino wool.

"Anyone else staying here?"

Again, they shake their heads.

The socks are my size and I begin considering miracles. During our Via Egnatia walk, someone had stolen a pair of my merino socks. Unable to find a good quality replacement pair, I ended up with a series of painful under-heel blisters from wearing poorly made cotton/polyester socks. My heel remains tender, and I still only have one pair of socks suitable for walking. This find feels like divine intervention.

"Thank you, Saint James. Gift accepted with gratitude."

Joe and Pat arrive with shopping bags of groceries.

"Look who I found," says Pat.

They squeeze into the kitchen, and a few moments later Pat re-emerges with two glasses of wine.

She hands me one. "Joe says he loves to cook. He's making dinner for us. I donated our dinner groceries to the effort."

Soon the smell of roasting chicken wafts from the kitchen and my stomach rumbles as Pat helps me shift the laden laundry rack into a retreating patch of sun. We shiver as the day's warmth fades. Our fleece jackets are still too damp to wear, so we wrap sleeping bags over our shoulders.

Joe's delicious dinner includes roasted eggplant and salad. We eat the chicken to the bone. Our clothes are dry by the time we're ready to roll into our bottom bunks. Pat notices my new socks.

"Divine intervention," I say, laying them on my boots.

I fall asleep to Joe's snores and the murmur of the Belgian dad reading his children a story.

27 October. To Viana do Castelo.

My new-to-me, machine-washed socks wrap my feet in luxury, hugging my toes and fitting snug around my feet with no stiff wrinkles to tug and smooth. We stuff properly clean clothes into our packs, gobble bowls of fruit and yoghurt, gulp Nescafé, grab lunches from the fridge, wave goodbye to the family and to Joe, then head out into the sunrise.

Soon our trail traces through a hillier landscape and into a woodland: bracken browning, leaves falling, squirrels foraging, the sound of nearby Rio Neiva hurrying to the ocean. We cross the river on a one-metre wide, concrete slab bridge supported by a series of pillars. Water flows inches below and there is no railing. Although we aren't treading on ancient stone slabs, the bridge has a timeless feel. The river is wide here but not very deep. I imagine pilgrims removing sandals and lifting their robes to wade through the chilly water and am pleased with the ease of our crossing.

Upon entering the next village, we stop to visit the parish Church of St Tiago de Castelo do Neiva. A previous church built here in 862 CE was dedicated to Saint Tiago the Greater, providing evidence of the oldest known dedication to Saint James outside present-day Spain.

We receive our mid-day credential stamp here. Once we reach Santiago de Compostela, our credential passport will be checked for these stamps. To be granted our pilgrim certificate, we will need two stamps from each day to prove that we walked the route. During the day, we pop into a church, café or shop to receive the first. Whether our stamps are delivered by clergy or a shop or café owner, they are provided with warmth and genuine interest in where we are from and a warm "*Bom Caminho*" following us out the door and on our way. We always receive our second daily stamp when we check into an *albergue*.

This aspect of our walk invites me to consider the meaning of a pilgrim's journey. Experiencing a gentle but profound shift in perception of self and place, I recognize this transformation as an essential element in my expanding worldview. The heaviness of the xenophobia we experienced and the refugee smuggling we witnessed in the Balkans begins to lift. It will take me four years to figure out how to bear witness to those events. When I do, I write *In the Footsteps of a Roman Legion – Walking the Via Egnatia* as testament.

Exiting the woodland, we continue along narrow lanes between tall stone walls. Were it not for the blue and yellow Camino signs, it would be like walking through a maze. Pausing for a sip of water, I get a peculiar feeling of being watched from above. Looking, I see long, upturned horns bobbing along the top of a three-metre-high wall. Then another set and a third.

"What do you suppose those belong to?" I ask Pat, pointing up at the horns.

"Jesus – whatever they are – they're huge."

The lane slopes up and away from the wall. We walk a little further, and turning back, discover three Cachena cattle peering over the wall from a raised pasture. Their side of the wall is a metre high and except for their sharp-pointed horns, the little brown beasts with cream-ringed eyes and long lashes look friendly. Their large ears and wet dark noses twitch with curiosity.

We cross the wide mouth of the Lima River via Ponte Eiffel on a sidewalk separated from vehicle traffic by a low guardrail. The long metal bridge hums and vibrates as vehicles rush by. The far side delivers us into the city of Viana do Castelo where we stay at parish-run Albergue de Peregrinos São João da Cruz dos Caminhos. The usual €6.00 pays for a bed in a damp basement dorm with thirty-two bunk beds.

The mattresses and pillows have rustling plastic coverings. We recognize Joe's backpack and sleeping bag, and while we're hand washing our smalls, he appears. The communal shower is hot. A couple of old bedsprings supported on sturdy posts offer an excellent opportunity to dry clothes in the wind and sun. Two fellows from Hungary arrive and politely take bunk beds near Joe's at the far end of the basement.

"The kitchen here is not so good," Joe says. "I am going to visit a friend, but there are great restaurants close by."

He points out a couple on Pat's iPad. We take his advice and go out for dinner, fumbling home by headlamp in the early nightfall.

28 October. To Caminha.

It doesn't take us long to leave the city behind, then our journey continues through productive farmland and charming villages. All the villages we've seen in Portugal are clean and well kept. Unlike in Greece, where a skulking spectre of menace shadowed our steps, here streets are swept, no graffiti mars the walls, shops are open, buildings are in good repair. Here, a sense of prosperity and pride prevails. People smile, men don't loiter and stare. Behind intricate wrought iron gates set into the stone walls, leaves have been raked and spent vegetation trimmed from manicured gardens. Sparkly swimming pools surrounded by patios and palm trees grace palatial homes set within grand expanses of landscaped grounds.

Churches and chapels abound, often white stucco and stone with one ornate bell tower and Portuguese Renaissance or Baroque façades and rooflines. Stone crosses rise from many crossroads. Some, weathered and lichen-scarred, attest to centuries of watching over pilgrims tramping past.

After lunch, our route swings back to a trail along the ocean. We catch up with an elderly man we've seen a few times. He strides past us in the mornings with a firm swift step, then we pass him in the afternoons when his body tires and slows. Today he leans forward over his trekking poles, seeming to struggle up a hill in the afternoon heat. We slow our pace and walk with him because offering friendship and support is what pilgrims do. Although a quiet man, he doesn't seem to mind our chattering intrusion on his peaceful journey.

Thirsty, we stop for a beer at an outside bar in the heart of Caminha before heading to find accommodation. We invite the tired man to join us. He pauses momentarily, then, thinking better of mid-afternoon imbibing, continues his solitary journey.

Like last night, our evening's Albergue Peregrinos is an uninspiring church basement dorm. But here we are also offered a €6.00 pilgrim's meal including a generous glass of wine. We present ourselves to the nearby dining hall and are soon enjoying an excellent meal and the company of several other pilgrims.

Most are familiar faces and the multilingual conversation swirls: where folks come from, how many Caminos they've bagged, how to treat blisters and sore knees, what footwear they are wearing and what gear they are carrying. Pat and I notice a boastful phenomenon between some of the young men who discuss how far and how fast they walk. We're proud of our six-kilo packs, but two teenage pilgrims from Italy carry much less. Pat and I, in our early sixties, are among the oldest people at the tables, but there are a few with more age-weathered bodies than ours. A couple of white-haired women smile at us over the heads of the two young Americans flirting with the Hungarians and raise their glasses in silent salute. We smile and raise ours in solidarity.

29 October. To Mougás, Galicia region, Spain.

Our food acquisition and consumption have taken on a predictable pattern. We eat a picnic breakfast of yoghurt and Nescafé, then begin walking by eight. When cafés open in mid-morning, we stop for coffee. An Americano for Pat and sweet cappuccino for me. We also indulge in fresh, sticky bakery treats, sometimes chocolate or fruit filled, often icing drizzled. This is when we pick up fresh buns for picnic lunches. We buy our breakfast yoghurts, lunch cheese, cucumbers and tomatoes and sometimes dinner supplies each evening. This pattern ensures our food is always fresh and our packs never overburdened with extra supplies.

The ability to resupply so frequently is the result of the local population – shop owners – embracing the custom pilgrims bring to the region. Less well-travelled routes, such as the Via Egnatia, recently completed, and the Via Francigena, not yet on our radar, do not offer such reliable or frequent services. Here on the Portuguese Camino, we're grateful for the ease of travel through welcoming and supportive communities.

Today, our routine is the same, although we must wait until 10 AM for the day's first ferry from Caminha to A Guarda, Spain. The Santa Rita de Cássia ferry operates on a flexible schedule because it crosses the tidal estuary of the Ria Minho. A couple of cars board with us, but most of the passengers are fellow pilgrims. On the far side, the crowd dissipates as fast walkers surge ahead and slower folk drop behind. Very soon we once again have the trail to ourselves.

Having not wanted to dangle our still-damp smalls in people's faces while on the ferry, Pat and I pause to pull out socks, underwear, shirts and trek towels, and pin them to our packs where the sun and wind make quick work of the drying process.

Our walk hugs the shore, climbs rocky headlands, meanders through villages. When we pass farmers and shoppers, they call out, *"Buen Camino"*

"Gracias," we call in return.

The landscape is wilder here, the tidy villages more rustic. Windmills perch on the headlands. On some, the blades have been removed, and the buildings appear to have been repurposed as homes. Others present blades to the wind, and a couple still bear white canvas sails.

As in Portugal, people seem busy with their daily tasks. Old stone-faced churches sport red-tiled roofs. Weathered stone crosses occupy many crossroads. Gnarled trees lean away from the prevailing Atlantic winds. White-capped waves pound against the rocky shore. Small brown birds scuff around for bugs and seeds, chirping and fluttering away as we trudge past. Far ahead and in the distance behind, the bright jackets and packs of pilgrims bob along between low stone walls, sun glinting on their trekking poles.

A warm sun-pocket, protected from the constant wind and overlooking the ocean, invites us to enjoy our picnic lunch. We're making good time, so take a few extra minutes for a siesta because in Spain this seems appropriate.

The route, tucked between the rugged coastline and a busy highway, sometimes takes us along a bike/pedestrian lane along that road. The hard surface and traffic noise detract from our enjoyment, but the road stretches are short, and effort has been made to guide us pilgrims through forest paths and byways as much as possible. While never far from the road, we are often unaware of its proximity.

Family-owned Albergue Aguncheiro in Mougás overlooks the ocean and offers thick mattresses with sheets, blankets and pillows with cases. The owner will cook us dinner because there's nowhere nearby that's open. This is our first private *albergue*, and although the beds are expensive at €10.00, the smaller dorm and added comfort of a hot private shower is well worthwhile. We're invited to hang our clothes on lines strung in a huge greenhouse in the back yard.

When she unpacks, Pat has a scary moment. Her clean underwear has vanished. She thought she had put them away with her other laundry, but somewhere back on the twenty-five-kilometre trail, the wind must have blown them off her pack. We each carry two pairs, one to wear and one for spare. She dumps out her pack, scattering multi-coloured packing pouches across her bed. No underwear. She shakes the pack again, and out they slide, with the pin from today's drying still attached. Presumably, they had been busy working their way to the bottom while she walked.

This calls for a celebratory beer. We sit on the bench outside the door in the warmth of the evening sun and watch it dip below the Atlantic horizon. As spicy dinner smells drift out the door, Joe arrives and enters.

Beer in hand, he comes back out to join us. "*Salud.*" He raises his bottle.

"*Salud.*"

We chat about life after our Caminos. Joe will return to family and work in León. We will travel to Morocco.

"The food there is terrible," he says.

Despite his spare frame, food is important to Joe. He goes on to explain how the advent of mass tourism has diluted the delights of real Moroccan cuisine. We will soon have ample opportunity to test his theory and will come to the same conclusion.

Later, Joe and another pilgrim join Pat and me for a delicious home-cooked Spanish dinner of fresh pan-fried fish, mounds of potatoes dug from the back field and vegetables harvested from the family's garden. They make wine with grapes from a nearby vineyard.

30 October. To Vigo.

We set off with the dawn and continue along a quiet coastal road with minimal local traffic. Tramping through village after village, we notice many gardens have stone coffin-like structures sitting up on stilts. Curious, we ask what they are and are told they are for corn storage, the small decorative holes in the sides providing air circulation, and the stilts keeping rats out of the corn. Pat and I dub them rat houses and soon discover they come in a variety of sizes and designs. Most are made of stone or concrete, some are utilitarian, but others are ornate, more for show than function. Many have crosses on top.

We cross the Rio Miñor via the 13th-century Ramallosa bridge. About three metres wide, it once accommodated carts and wagons. Small pullouts along its length would have enabled pedestrians to hop out of the way of hooves and wheels. Today, pedestrians have it to themselves. Pat and I tuck our trekking poles away to avoid the annoying click of their tips against the ancient stone surface as we cross. I imagine clopping horse hooves, rumbling hay wagons and carts laden with farm produce coming into market. Among them, sandaled pilgrims carrying their staffs and shoulder bags walk, perhaps praying, perhaps considering a stop for beer and bread at the next tavern.

Due to an ill-conceived decision, today we walk a challenging thirty-five kilometres. A couple of evenings ago, we read a posted notice that the only parish *albergue* on this next section of the route had closed for the season, so we decided to stay at a private one three kilometres off the route. Despite the detour, this seems like a good option, and after our pleasant experience last night, we look forward to the more comfortable accommodation.

We're close to the turnoff when another pilgrim assures us that there is a municipal *albergue* just a few kilometres further along the route. We carry a comprehensive list of the *albergues* and don't see this place listed, and our instincts usually keep us from making dumb mistakes. But in a moment of laziness, we decide not to make the detour and continue to the recommended *albergue*.

No *albergue*, municipal or otherwise, exists. We ask at a couple of shops and cafés and are assured there never has been one. Not too worried, we're confident of finding a guesthouse or hotel in the next village. We've seen several over the past week, but not today. We leave the trail and march, weary, along the busy road in the hope of coming across a roadside hotel. Nothing. We loathe road walking. For the first time on our Camino journey, we aren't happy pilgrims, but Pat and I have been in worse spots. We're strong. We have the energy to keep walking even if we do two days in one.

"What were we thinking?"

"We weren't thinking."

Traffic gets heavier and noisier as we approach the city of Vigo. Tired, and now half a day ahead of schedule, we trudge along a wide boulevard in the heart of town. Pat looks up and sees a huge modern hotel across the street. It looks expensive. She looks at me, I look at her. We press the walk button. Traffic stops. We cross and step through revolving glass doors into a large reception area.

"*Hola.* Do you have a twin room?" Pat asks a suited woman at the counter.

"*Si. Peregrinas?*" She doesn't seem put off by our bedraggled appearance.

We nod.

"Would you like a stamp?"

We grin and push our credentials across the counter. Pat peeks into the hotel bar, while I see to pilgrim stamps and registration details.

"You want a beer?" she calls.

I nod, then turn back to the receptionist and ask where we can find the nearest restaurant. There are several around the square, but they won't open until eight thirty.

"We Spaniards don't like to eat too early, but you can order take-out pizza."

I pop into the bar. "Hey, Pat, how does take-out pizza sound?"

She agrees. The receptionist phones in our order, we take our key card and two beers, then head up an elevator to our huge room with big bouncy beds and a private bathroom. When I pop down to retrieve the pizza, I bring up two more beers. By eight thirty we have dined and are in bed.

31 October. To Redondela.

A shorter seventeen-kilometre walk provides needed recovery time after yesterday's efforts. Even so, it takes three hours – eleven kilometres – to escape Vigo's urban sprawl. City walking is accompanied by constant traffic noise, exhaust, people-dodging and the unrelenting pounding of our feet against hot hard pavement. For the first time since beginning our Camino, the way markers are often hard to spot and inadequate. In some cases, they appear to be missing, but sometimes it's a matter of a delivery vehicle being parked in front of a sign, or arrays of streetlights obscuring sightlines. Even so, we navigate our way out of the city maze with only a couple of short detours.

Breaking into the countryside again, we hear the silence, but for most of this day one village or town blends with the next offering only a few moments of rural tranquility. At a festive market, we stop to buy some bright jelly candies. I pick one of every colour: red, pink, purple, blue, yellow, orange and various shades between.

Pat takes a bite of one of hers and frowns. "This isn't dried fruit. It's candy."

Pat's not a candy eater. She looks at me chomping away on my second piece and hands over her bag. I am, of course, delighted and over the course of the day, will devour both bags.

A few stalls after the not-dried-fruit stall, a woman deep-fries *buñuelos*. We each buy a bag of those as well. When we're in towns, we collapse and stow our poles, so hands free, we walk and munch, burning our greasy fingers and spilling icing sugar on our shirts.

We notice many more casual day-walkers than usual and discover that this is the first of a three-day celebration and that tomorrow is a national holiday. In this part of Spain – Galicia – many Celtic traditions continue to be celebrated. Samhain – end of summer – was an important Celtic festival marking the start of the dark months. Romans also celebrated this time of year, honouring Pomona, their harvest goddess. Then came Christianity and a vain attempt to co-opt and stamp out earlier belief systems.

Today is *Día de las Brujas* – Day of the Witches. Our first mission when we walk into Redondela is to stock up on a few extra groceries in case stores are closed tomorrow.

Our evening's municipal *albergue* is a repurposed 16th-century mansion in the old part of Redondela. The repurposing has dispensed with past grandeur but there's a washing machine, which we take advantage of, sharing our load with three women from Barcelona.

The fourteen bunk beds in our mixed-gender dorm are occupied by five other women when we arrive: three Barcelonans, an Athenian and a Hanoverian who appears to be directing newly arriving men to the other dorm. It only takes us a moment to discover why she's determined to establish gender segregation. A troop of noisy Boy Scouts will be allowed to occupy beds in either room if there is any space after the pilgrim check-in time of up to four o'clock.

When the two laughing Italian teenagers we'd seen at the pilgrims' dinner in Caminha and another German woman arrive, we encourage them to stake out as much territory as possible. Recognizing the imminent threat of boy invasion, they comply. We are now twelve women, all in possession of a bottom bunk and united in our determination to defend our territory. Although there are only two spare bunk beds, there is still space for sixteen more people.

At four o'clock the *albergue* manager comes in and counts. Then goes next door and counts. The men haven't been strategic. There are more of them than us, but there are more spare bunk beds in their dorm than ours. The boys are sent next door.

Dining out in Spain is difficult for anyone wanting to eat before eight thirty in the evening. Pat and I wander up and down several streets looking for a meal before finding an Irish bar doing a roaring business. We squeeze in the door to be drowned by racket but are shown to a small table in a corner. The Guinness is cold and cheap. The tapas are generous and tasty. We are content.

That night, when I get up for my nightly visit to the washroom, I sit on the seat, then leap up. It is wet. It stinks. I peer at the floor. It's wet too. The bathroom door opens, and someone bumps into the next cubical, not shutting the door. I exit to the sight of an underwear-clad, tousle-haired teenager directing his stream just about everywhere except in the bowl.

"You disgusting little brat," I mutter.

He jumps, splatters pee against the flush handle, then scuttles back to his dorm without flushing and without washing his hands.

I grab some paper towel, run warm water and go back into a less defiled cubicle to scrub myself clean. My sandals leave a trail of boy-pee footprints back to my bed.

1 November. To Pontevedra.

In the morning, the scout leaders and the *albergue* staff get an earful from twelve irate women, Pat and me included. The men also complain that the boys were disruptive during the night, jumping around on the bunk beds and being obnoxious. The leaders, who were in the same room but apparently oblivious, apologize, but no one forgives the boys' revolting behaviour. Staff armed with cleaning supplies take on the bathroom, and the boys are sent outside to eat their breakfasts. Pat and I wash our sandals under a utility-room tap and wrap them in paper towel before packing them.

It seems that we've only just left Redondela when we're walking through the next town, Arcade, where we cross the Rio Verdugo estuary on Ponte Sampaio. The tide is out, so we have a good view of the sturdy foundation piers between each of the ten arches. Skilled mediaeval engineers and builders have enabled this bridge to withstand centuries of rushing tidal flow, an endless stream of traffic and even an armed struggle for independence. On this bridge – in June 1809 – Galician forces defeated Napoleon in a battle that marked the end of French occupation in Galicia.

Today is *Día de Todos los Santos* – All Saints' Day – and families, dressed in their best, crowd into cemeteries to lay flowers on the tombs. As the day progresses, the tombs become buried in mounds of colourful blooms.

By lunch time, we arrive in Pontevedra, another large city. Our municipal Albergue Virxe Peregrina is new and bright. However, it is in a seedy high-rise residential part of town with few amenities. We end up enjoying our afternoon beers at the nearby railway station, then later have the worst meal of the trip at a dingy Indian fast-food restaurant. As we eat, we realize this is a predominantly immigrant community, and the people living in the neighbouring tenements are probably struggling with under- and un-employment.

During the afternoon, the Boy Scouts had arrived, but their reputation preceded them, so we saw the leaders and boys get a firm lecture on hostel etiquette. No need to understand Spanish to get the drift. The boys had been ushered into their own room and denied access to the main lounge area. When two tried to sneak over to the vending machines, the *albergue* staff had directed them back into their own space.

"Are we sharing a bathroom with those boys?" I ask one of the staff, before we turn in.

He shakes his head, "Don't worry. Their dorm has its own bathroom. They are forbidden from using any other."

2 November. To Caldas de Reis.

Today is *Día de los Muertos* – Day of the Dead or All Souls' Day – and tradition holds that the dead will be offered food. We wonder if the graveyards will now fill with edible offerings, but it seems that the dead are supposed to visit their relatives and enjoy private feasts at home.

As we walk through Pontevedra, we pass the unique Capela da Virxe Peregrina – Chapel of Pilgrims. I run up the steps to the arched portico, anticipating a credential stamp, but we are too early, and the door is locked. No cafés are open, so there is no place to wait. Spain stays up late and doesn't get going until the mornings are nearly over. While I take a picture of the tall Baroque structure, two other pilgrims march by without so much as a glance at the chapel. But they stop and ask if we are lost because Pat is studying Pocket Earth.

"No, but we were hoping to pop into the chapel," she says, pointing.

They look and shrug, "It's just another building. Nothing special."

I recognize them as one of the speed-conscious duos and wonder what they miss by putting their heads down and counting hurried hours instead of savouring the odd dawdle. Their trekking poles hammer and clack at the cobbled pavement as they rush on.

They are wrong about the chapel, though. It is special. Built in 1778, its footprint is scallop-shell shaped. It was built for pilgrims. For us. This is our chapel, and it is as unique as the pilgrims who pass it by or visit. We walk on, disappointed to have not been able to see inside.

A few minutes later, we cross Rio Lérez via the 12th-century Puente del Burgo, its graceful arches reflected in the morning-still water. This bridge was built on the site of an earlier Roman bridge, its clean lines bearing just one embellishment over the cutwater piers – the pilgrim's scallop.

We leave the city behind without finding a café open for breakfast, but as we pass a village shop, the happy Italian teenagers call out. Stopping to greet them, we notice the shop has a small table and serves coffee. The shop also serves beer which the teens are drinking. Tattooed and pierced, they look fierce, but they are full of light banter and good humour. Enjoying a gap year between high school and university, they are walking the length and breadth of Europe on a shoestring budget.

They leave as we drink our coffees, but later in the day, we pass them again as they indulge in another beer. They walk fast, but take frequent breaks, so in the end we arrive at our destinations about the same time.

Upon our arrival in Caldas de Reis, we head to a municipal *albergue*, but it is filthy and appears to be a flop house for degenerate drunks sprawled on stained mattresses. We spin on our heels and bump into the Italians. They'd found a nicer private *albergue*, then seeing us walk by, have come to point us in the right direction. We thank them for their thoughtfulness and walk back through town.

Checking into Albergue a Queimada, we discover modern décor and a well-appointed shared kitchen. There are also twin rooms. The idea of privacy appeals, so we each pay €8.00, then go out to grocery shop. A stir-fry with a bottle of cheap Spanish wine wraps up another day of pilgrimage. While we eat, we chat with several of our fellow pilgrims. We come from a variety of experiences and countries, our ages range from eighteen to eighty, we speak seven different languages, yet all of us are united in the one simple goal of walking to Santiago. No one we speak with is walking for specific religious reasons, but we all identify as pilgrims.

3 November. To Padrón.

We wend our way through the gentle Galician countryside, enjoying the return of rural walking. Small attractive villages – each one with a church. Shady forested lanes, rolling hills, fall blooms. Always the scallop-shell way markers and calls of "*Buen Camino.*"

Stopping in Padrón, we pop into the tourist kiosk to get information about *albergues* in the next couple of villages. We are now twenty-five kilometres from Santiago and would like to add a few more kilometres to shorten tomorrow's distance. Pat leans her trekking poles against the wall while we talk with the tourist woman who is unable to help. There are a couple of *albergues* here, but one is already closed for the season. Between here and Santiago there are several *pensions* but no *albergues*.

We thank the tourist woman, leave, then sit on a nearby bench in the sun to eat our lunch. Packing up to carry on, Pat realizes she doesn't have her poles. We go back to the tourist kiosk. It is locked for the two-hour Spanish lunch break, but we see Pat's poles inside.

"So, we stay at the *albergue* here tonight."

The *albergue* door is locked, and a sign informs us that pilgrims must wait to check in at 4 PM. Worse, we see the Boy Scouts milling around. Pat checks. They plan to stay at this *albergue*. Neither of us feels like aimless wandering with our packs for the next three hours, and we do not want to risk sharing a dorm with these obnoxious boys, so we check out a couple of Padrón's *pensions*.

At a crooked old house, the proprietor offers a pilgrim rate of €18.00 for a small twin-bed room with ensuite bathroom. We accept. Our tiny room has a sloped floor, white lace curtains, hand-embroidered doilies on a polished antique dresser and crisp fresh bedding. We don't put our travel-soiled packs on the beds when we unpack. After days of smearing water around our wet bodies with tiny, quick-dry trek towels, we relish drying ourselves with fluffy terry towels. Bodies showered and dried, laundry washed and hung in the sunny window, we head out to retrieve Pat's poles and enjoy cold beer by the river.

The boat carrying the bones of Saint James, escorted by his two disciples, is said to have landed near here. Legend suggests the disciples moored the boat to a Roman altar stone called the Pedrón. Pat and I go to the Church of Santiago where the stone is now kept in an open crypt under the altar. I see a certain humour in a pagan Roman altar stone now being housed with such care under the altar of a Christian church.

We buy a couple of premade salads for dinner and take them back to our cozy room with a bottle of wine, which we ask the store salesperson to open for us to save a fight with the cork. Wanting an early start and excited about real bedding and thick pillows, we're both in bed by dark to read and soon to sleep.

4 November. To Santiago de Compostela.

Our days have been sunny and warm, but this morning we wake to low cloud and an ominous threat of rain, so pack rain jackets and ponchos at the top and hurry away, wanting to get as many kilometres as possible under our boots before rainfall. We don't get far before we're pulling on fleeces and raingear.

The rain pours with November intensity. The temperature drops, and we shiver as we trudge. Today it is we who keep our heads down and count the hours. I don't pull my camera out, and we don't pause for water breaks. We do stop for a hasty lunch, standing to eat by a stone wall serving as a makeshift table. Pat pulls a small tetra pack of red wine from her pack to celebrate our last pilgrimage lunch. Rain plops off the brim of my hat into my cup while I sip.

As we enter town, more and more pilgrims fill the streets as various other Caminos converge: Camino Francés, Camino del Norte, Camino Primitivo, Camino Inglés and others. One count lists 281 Camino routes. Another concept suggests that the journey to Santiago begins at a pilgrim's home. What is clear is that the popular North American concept of *The* Camino as a singularity is false.

Soon we are a multi-national, backpack-carrying throng swarming onto the expansive square at the foot of the imposing cathedral of Santiago de Compostela. After circumnavigating the cathedral, each façade offering ornate blends of Romanesque and Baroque architectural styles, we find the administrative building where we join a queue to receive our certificates.

Like a row of tellers at a bank, certificate-issuing clerks examine each pilgrim's credentials to confirm the correct number of stamps from appropriate locations. Then comes the interview. This, I was not expecting.

"Why have you completed this Camino?"

"Umm. Well. ... My friend asked if I wanted to. ... For fun."

A scowl. "Fun?"

"Yes. It was fun. And easy. All the scallop-shells make it easy."

The scowl deepens. "You walked a Camino for easy fun?"

I have no idea how to get myself out of this mess and glance over at Pat. Her interview seems to be going much better. Her clerk is smiling. I look back at mine. "Yes. The walk was easy, and I had fun. Meeting people, learning about them. Learning about being a pilgrim."

"So, you learned something while you were having fun?"

I don't like this character's tone. "Oh yes. I learned a great deal." I smile with my teeth.

"Like what?"

I want to say that I learned that I like Portuguese and Spanish wine. That I don't like sleeping in a dorm. That I like sunny days more than rainy ones. But that's not what he has in mind. I look him in the eye. "I learned that humanity requires compassion, empathy and generosity. I learned that each one of us has the power and obligation to behave well as members of the human community. I learned that we should use caution when passing judgement on others."

He pulls a certificate from one of his certificate piles, signs it and shoves it at me without a smile.

"*Gracias*," I say before running for the exit.

Pat waits outside. She had a more pleasing response for her inquisitor so has a fancier certificate. She told him she came seeking answers. Why hadn't I thought of that?

As we walk back up to the cathedral, I tell her about my interview, and she howls. At the entry, we are rejected by a guard and sign. "No backpacks in the cathedral."

"Seriously?"

"*Hola*. Kim. Pat."

We turn to see Joe waving at us. He arrived yesterday and now offers to mind our packs while we go inside. We thank him, and he settles down with his cell phone while we enter.

Despite not being a Christian, I'm in awe of cathedrals and this one does not disappoint. The towering Romanesque nave and transepts rise pillar upon pillar, gallery upon gallery to a graceful barrel-vaulted ceiling. In contrast to the clean lines of stone, the gold magnificence of the altars and organ are an assault of glitter and opulence. We join other pilgrims and tourists, craning our heads to admire a cornucopia of baroque plaster statuary, ornate chandeliers, huge thuribles, elaborate reredos and grand pulpits. A central column incorporates a statue of Saint James. So many pilgrims have rubbed their fingers across his left foot that a hollow has been worn in the stone. After adding our touch to the traditional conclusion of a Camino pilgrimage, we descend into the crypt, where the foundations of the 9th-century church are still evident.

We see the silver coffin said to contain the bones of Saint James since Pope Leo XIII authenticated the relics in 1884. Despite my skepticism, I realize that it is what people want to believe that is important. My pilgrimage has been rewarding – and fun – regardless of whose bones rest beneath the altar.

Before leaving, I find a donation box tucked into a corner and drop in the dime given to me by a friend before I left home in August. I have thus fulfilled my promise that I would leave it here in the Cathedral of Santiago de Compostela.

We exit, relieve Joe of our packs, say "*adios,*" and head to the train station where we buy tickets for the morning train to Lisbon.

Our plan had been to spend our last night in a seminary up a hill above the city, but as we walk past a pleasant looking hotel, we decide to skip bunk beds and stay closer to the station instead. We go out for dinner, toast a successful pilgrimage and turn our sights to our next adventure.

A scenic coastal journey brings us to the Cathedral of Santiago de Compostela .

Chapter Three

In the Company of Chaucer on the Pilgrims' Way

*When the sweet showers of April have pierced
The drought of March, and pierced it to the root, …
Then people long to go on pilgrimages, …
And most especially, from all the shires
Of England, to Canterbury they come …*

Geoffrey Chaucer, "General Prologue," The Canterbury Tales, *1387
David Wright, translator, 1985*

Marianne, Pat, Sally and me, a cheerful company of pilgrims outside a pub.

**29 December 1170. Canterbury Cathedral, Kent, England.
A Murderous Tale.**

*Death threatens at all ages, and will strike
All ranks of men, for escape there is none; ...*

"The Clerk's Tale"

Within the hallowed transept of Canterbury Cathedral, footsteps echo from the shadows as four knights approach Archbishop Thomas Becket with swords drawn.

"Willingly I die in the name of Jesus and in defence of the Church," gasps Becket, as his blood and brains spill across the floor.

King Henry II had tried in vain to elicit Becket's support for a new law, so after years of dispute, he is said to have railed, "Will no one rid me of this turbulent priest?"

The knights, taking their king at his word, rode to Canterbury and by murdering the archbishop, created a martyr. Becket was buried in the cathedral crypt and the two monks appointed to guard the site soon recorded 703 healing miracles attributed to visits to the tomb. In response, in 1173, Pope Alexander III canonized Becket. The following year, the now penitent king made a pilgrimage from his capital of Winchester to Canterbury, the cathedral having become one of the most important pilgrimage sites in the European world.

**18 April 2018. To Winchester, Hampshire.
A Traveller's Tale.**

*You're off to Canterbury – so Godspeed!
And I'll be bound, that while you're on your way,
You'll be telling tales, and making holiday: ...*

"General Prologue"

Two forgettable Air Canada meals and nine hours after departing Vancouver, Marianne, Pat and I gaze down on the hedge-rowed fields and lane-linked villages of England, the fairy-tale landscape belying England's population of fifty-six million.

Marianne, a mutual friend, who also enjoys a good long walk is joining Pat and me on another walking adventure. We alight in Heathrow to stand in a ninety-minute immigration queue where a rumour circulates that the delay is due to extra security checks to catch migrants sneaking into the country. When Pat, Marianne and I step up to the counter, we're only subjected to a few cursory questions.

"Why are you visiting?"

"To walk."

"How long will you be here?

"Six weeks."

"Where will you be staying?"

I flash our eight-page itinerary at the agent.

He holds up his hand. "Have a nice stay." Stamp. Stamp. Stamp. Three passports slide back at us. "Next."

In the meeting area beyond, hundreds of faces scan arrivals as we in turn hunt for someone familiar. Liz, who has come to meet us, and I spot each other right away. We went to school together while I lived in Sundridge, Kent from 1968 to 1970, then reconnected in 2016. Marianne and Pat introduce themselves while Liz leads us to her car. The aggressive nature of English driving – tailgating and speeding – keeps us three jet-lagged travellers wide awake during the hour-long drive to Winchester.

After dumping our packs in our four-storey Designers Guild Annex apartment, we cross the road to the Old Vine pub where a round of beer chases our sketchy airline breakfast and aids in recovery from the terrifying drive. Liz orders a coffee.

While we visit, Liz and I discuss details of our other friends – Mel, Kate and Mary – coming to Kent and everyone meeting up at Liz's home on the evening the Pilgrims' Way takes us through Kemsing.

"We'll be tired and hungry after walking all day, so will want an early dinner." I explain. "Might be easier if we meet at a pub."

"No. No. I want everyone at my place. I'll pick you up at five o'clock," Liz promises.

Another friend from the Comox Valley, Sally, who has already been in England for four days visiting with her son, arrives to complete our company of pilgrims. We catch up on each other's recent adventures, then see Liz off with thanks for the drive and promises to see her in a few days.

Wandering across the road and along an avenue of blooming magnolia and cherry trees, past beds of colourful tulips, we come to the cathedral. The spring sun offers soothing warmth, and we're told that this is one of the first nice days of the year. At the cathedral, however, there is no one who can issue our pilgrim credentials, and we're asked to return in the morning.

Pat, Marianne and I struggle not to fall asleep over a delicious dinner at the Old Vine. Already over her jet lag, Sally goes for an evening stroll while the rest of us climb up to our rooms where Pat and I share a sloped-ceiling attic. Before crawling into our beds, I open the window to the glorious sounds of pealing cathedral bells reverberating across the rooftops.

19 April – In Winchester.
Historic Tales.

In the old days, the days of King Arthur,
He whom the Britons hold in great honour,
All of this land was full of magic then. ...

"The Wife of Bath's Tale"

After an English breakfast of thick back bacon, runny eggs, fried tomatoes and fried bread, we set out for the cathedral where we are forgiven the £10.00 tourist fee and receive our pilgrim credential passports and the first stamps. The cathedral wraps us in the mysterious essence of filtered light, echoes and murmurs that prevail in such places.

Winchester had been a centre of Pagan worship since 164 CE,

with the first Christian church being built in 648 CE on command of the King of Wessex. The Normans began building the cathedral in 1079. When it was consecrated in 1093, the many tombs of Saxon kings were moved into its crypt. In 1905, inspection revealed that not only were the walls cracking, bulging and leaning, but the southeast corner was also sinking.

An engineer discovered that the Normans had created a platform from a raft of beech trees layered one upon the other under the entire building. While some of the trunks were still solid, others had rotted away. Further excavations revealed that seven metres below the surface, a layer of gravel could provide a firm base for new foundations.

Workers began digging trenches through layers of soil, peat moss and clay to the gravel bed. But when they broke through the peat moss, they discovered it had been acting as a seal to keep the water table from rising. The seal broken, water rose and filled the trenches. A pump was employed to solve this problem, but the cathedral continued to sink with water filling the trenches.

A diver named Walker was hired to remove the remaining peat moss and to lay down bags of cement to stop the rising water. His monumental task was hampered by the bulk and weight of his diving suit, the dark confined spaces, as well as bodies and coffins that kept floating into the trenches. He dove under the cathedral, laying bags and blocks of concrete and bricks for six or seven hours every day for six years. When he was finished, the pumps started up again and flying buttresses were added to stabilize the cathedral.

We read this incredible story in a brochure while standing on steps leading into a crypt half filled with water.

"It's always like this after the rains," a chaplain explains.

Back on the main floor, we tread upon the largest collection of mediaeval floor tiles in the country, admire lofty Gothic arches, painted ceilings, stained glass windows, Jane Austen's tomb and St. Swithun's shrine – the official start point for the Pilgrims' Way.

The cathedral well visited, we stroll along the Itchen River where an empty table on a riverside terrace invites us to enjoy cold beer.

Fortified, our next stop is the Great Hall. Dating from 1067, it is the only remnant of William the Conqueror's Winchester Castle. His Domesday Book, an instrument of Norman colonial power, was once housed here, but today it's the huge replica of King Arthur's round table hanging at the end of the hall that invites speculation.

When Sir Thomas Malory wrote *Le Morte d'Arthur* in 1485, he proposed Winchester as the site of legendary Camelot. Malory's reasoning may have been inspired by this 13th-century Winchester Round Table, but the truth behind the Arthurian legend lurks somewhere in the mists of time, and the real location of Camelot remains a mystery.

I pull out my camera to take a picture and tap the on/off button. No click-whir. Dead battery? Impossible. It was fully charged this morning. Always with a spare battery on hand, I swap and try again. Still no click-whir. This makes no sense.

"My camera's not working."

"I saw a camera store near our apartment," offers Marianne.

We walk over, but the shop is closed for the day.

Sally reads the sign on the door. "Opens at 9 AM."

"Too late. We want to be walking by eight thirty," I say.

"That's too early for me," says Marianne. "I'd like a relaxed breakfast."

Pat and Sally agree that there's no need to rush.

"Let's get that camera looked at before we leave," says Pat.

20 April. To New Alresford.
A Trail's Tale.

> *I have to warn all in this company*
> *A fourth part of the day's already gone.*
> *Now, for the love of God and of St John,*
> *Lose no more time than you can help, I say ...*

"Introduction to the Man of Law's Tale"

After breakfast, Pat and I rush to the camera store where the clerk sells me an expensive new battery. I'm sure that the battery charger not liking 220 voltage is the real problem, but the shop has no compatible chargers. Noticing cameras priced at little more than the just-purchased battery, I buy one of those as well. Pat had been planning on using her iPad to take pictures, but after just one day is tired of the slow and cumbersome process, so she buys a camera too. The entire exchange takes us less than ten minutes.

Equipped with new cameras, we hurry back to collect Sally and Marianne who have just finished their breakfasts. The four of us now need to buy lunch supplies before heading on our way. Pat and I have done this so many times on previous trips that we can shop for a good picnic within a couple of minutes. Four women seeking consensus about two cucumbers or three, this tomato or that one, apples or pears, takes longer than buying cameras.

"Let's just each buy our own lunch," says Pat. "This will take all day otherwise."

In our usual way, Pat and I buy to share, without discussion, then wait on the sidewalk until first Sally then Marianne emerges to tuck assorted groceries into their packs.

"Let's make a habit of buying lunch supplies in the evenings," I suggest, then berate myself for the implied impatience. They are new at this.

Pat and I open Pocket Earth and the app guides us out of the city as the cathedral spires drop behind rooflines and treetops. Our names and footsteps are now added to the host of pilgrims who have trodden this historic route over the past millennium.

The sun shines on the gentle countryside, colouring budding blossoms, encouraging unfurling leaves, and warming four modern pilgrims. For five hours, we tread hushed pathways and a few short stretches of quiet single-track lanes. We walk through pedestrian tunnels beneath a couple of motorways. We stop at two quaint village churches to receive pilgrims' stamps. At one, a deacon greets us. At the other, the stamp is attached with a chain to a desk, and we serve ourselves. There, we eat our picnic lunch amongst the gravestones and English daisies. In a nearby pasture, lambs leap and nudge their mothers, bleating and tumbling on wobbly legs.

Pat reads the printed instructions in our Cicerone guidebook, I read the paper map. We refer to our iPads from time to time to confirm our actual location. It's more time consuming than we'd anticipated. Sally, who is just walking, asks what's taking so long. Marianne, who doesn't mind the pauses, enjoys them to use her iPad to take pictures of fancy estates with sleek horses grazing in white-fenced paddocks.

We arrive at the Cricketers Pub in New Alresford as thirst begins to demand more than sips of the tepid water remaining in our water bottles. We settle at a table in the pub's garden and order beer. Sally phones her brother-in-law, Tim. He duly arrives and we pile into his car for the drive to Farnham. We are staying with Sally's sister and brother-in-law, Gail and Tim, for the next four nights. Welcomed into their beautiful home, we enjoy a delicious dinner, drink a bit too much wine and tumble into beds as the sun sets.

21 April. To Chawton.
St Swithun's Tale.

> *I've got relics and pardons in my bag*
> *As good as anybody's in England,*
> *All given to me by the Pope's own hand.*

> "The Pardoner's Tale"

After breakfast, Tim drives us back to New Alresford where we pick up our trail. Wanting to take part in navigating responsibilities, Sally interprets the guidebook instructions. I continue map reading. Pat keeps an eye on our location with Pocket Earth. Few of the numerous trail signs indicate the Pilgrims' Way, but the more ancient and well-marked St Swithun's Way follows our desired route.

Anglo-Saxon bishop of Winchester from 852 until his death in 862 CE, Swithun had been a trusted royal advisor, with some documents suggesting that he accompanied Alfred the Great on a pilgrimage to Rome when Alfred was a child. The only miracle attributed to Swithun during his lifetime was his repair of a basket of broken eggs. However, as posthumous miracles accumulated, pilgrimage to his shrine in Winchester became popular with both monks and lay people seeking redemption from sin or healing from illness and disabilities. In 971 CE, St Swithun was appointed patron saint of Winchester, thus displacing saints Peter and Paul from that honour. Little else is known about Swithun, although superstition holds that if it rains on St Swithun's Day – 15 July – it will rain for the next forty days.

We give thanks to the countless St Swithun pilgrims for creating the pathways and the rights of common way that we now enjoy as we follow the intricate network of England's walking trails.

Today's walk takes us through a pastoral landscape of gentle rolling hills, along paths and narrow lanes between hawthorn hedgerows. In a woodland, we walk along a sun-dappled path bounded on both sides by a sea of bluebells. Time collapses and I'm transported to the bluebell wood at the bottom of our Groom's Cottage garden when we lived in Sundridge. This was a magical place where my sister and I spent hours in the spring chasing bluebell fairies and in the summer hunting gnomes in towering bracken. Fifty-five years later, the magic of that time and place continues to enchant me.

While we eat lunch, foreboding clouds gather, so we hurry on, stepping inside Jane Austen's house in the village of Chawton as the first raindrops fall. Wandering through the little house, now converted to a museum, we read notices telling us that this is where Austen penned *Mansfield Park*, *Emma* and *Persuasion*. This was her home until she moved to Winchester shortly before her death – at age forty-one – in 1817.

Next, we scurry across the road to the Greyfriars Pub and bundle inside without getting soaked. A table found, beer ordered, Sally phones Tim and he soon joins us for a pint before we head home for dinner.

22 April. To Farnham, Surrey.
Sunday Tales.

> *Before the bishop caught them with his crook,*
> *They'd be put down in the archdeacon's book,*
> *Whereupon being in his jurisdiction,*
> *He had it in his power to penalize them.*
>
> "The Friar's Tale"

I sleep soundly so miss the excitement of a raging thunderstorm. Dawn arrives to a cloudless sky, just glistening puddles telling the tale of last night's deluge. Marianne's knee is bothering her, so she decides to take the day off and enjoy Gail and Tim's garden. Tim drives Pat, Sally and me back to the Greyfriars where we set off for our day's walk.

We're keeping our daily distances to around fifteen kilometres to ensure time to dawdle, take pictures, enjoy lunchtime snoozes, pop into churches and, of course, indulge in afternoon beer at the end of the day.

Today we continue through the same undulating countryside. Straight across farm fields, along hedgerows, through enchanted bluebell woods of ancient oak and beech, along sleepy lanes, past thatched cottages and grand gated estates. Over stiles, through kissing gates, past lambing sheep and skittish horses. Wherever we cross a road or walk along one for a short distance, we feel the pressure of rushing vehicle traffic, but for most of the day we have the route – and our slow-moving universe – to ourselves.

Stopping at a church, wanting a stamp for our pilgrim's credential, we discover the place locked up tight.

"On a Sunday?" we chime in unbelieving unison.

Grumbling, we carry on. As we pass another church, we see a woman coming out the door so hail her. She comes to the gate and hearing our request, signs our credentials, explaining that her church committee is looking into getting a stamp. As we chat, we discover that although the place had once been a church and a school, it is now her private home. We thank her for taking the time to provide signatures. She assures us she'll encourage the committee to move forward on stamp acquisition.

At another church in the next village, the service has ended, and tea and cakes are being served. We enter, accept refreshment and ask the frock-coated minister for a stamp. Although aware of the Winchester to Canterbury pilgrimage, he seems flummoxed as he studies our credentials.

"Never seen these before," he says while signing. His church doesn't have an official stamp. We suggest he might like to get one for his lovely church.

He peers at us, askance. "I don't imagine we'd have much call for such a thing," he says.

We carry on, happy to have the two required acknowledgements of our passing. From the guidebook, we read that this village has a pub worthy of a stop – The Star. The day is warm. It's almost lunchtime. We read the directions and head off on a short detour to the pub for a refreshing beer. Upon arrival, we find it locked up tight. However, the gate to the garden behind the pub is open, so we enter and enjoy our picnic – washed down with water. There's a car parked outside and we're certain *someone* is within. We hope that *someone* will pop out and offer us beer, but this does not happen.

"Probably the cleaner," suggests Sally.

"You think a cleaner can't draw a pint?" asks Pat.

We giggle at the thought of a toilet-brush-wielding cleaner chasing us off the premises for trespassing on private pub property.

Walking into Farnham a short time later, we stop at an open pub for a belated beer, then continue to Tim and Gail's home. We spend the rest of the afternoon sitting in the garden, enjoying a second beer while Tim entertains us with stories about piloting the rich and famous – members of the royal family and, to his chagrin, Trump – without giving away any secrets of course.

23 April. To Guildford.
A Miraculous Tale.

> Our Host gave each and all a warm welcome,
> And set us down to supper there and then.
> The edibles he served were of the best; ...
>
> "General Prologue"

A cooler day greets us, but it remains dry and pleasant for walking. Marianne takes another day off to give her knee more rest. Tomorrow night we will stay at a walk-in, self-catering youth hostel reported to be three and a half kilometres from amenities, so over breakfast the four of us collaborate on a grocery list for tomorrow's lunch and dinner and the next day's breakfast and lunch. Marianne offers to shop at a grocery store near to Tim and Gail's.

Pat, Sally and I then set off, now along the North Downs Way. We've discovered that much of the original Pilgrims' Way has been paved and become part of the modern road network. But, like St Swithun's Way, the North Downs Way runs almost parallel, the routes sometimes intersecting and blending into one. While Pilgrims' Way markers have been few, ample signposts mark the North Downs Way, thus navigation today is easy. Part of that ease is sharing the task among three people. Pat and I thank Sally for contributing to the route-finding process and not just following along.

"Why would I just want to follow?" she asks, "Navigating is part of the fun, don't you think?"

We laugh. Over the last three days Sally has embraced the role of co-navigator, first reading the book's instructions, which still confuse me. Then she's learned to read the map, which still confuses Pat. Today she's using Pocket Earth on her iPhone.

Sally also sets a blistering pace. She is older than the rest of us by several years, but her energy and walking speed have us scurrying to keep up. She always reaches a hilltop well ahead of us. There she'll wait with a quizzical look. A courteous woman, she doesn't comment, but I can see that she wonders what's the matter with the rest of us.

We haven't gone far when we need to cross a road busy with speeding commuter traffic. The road is narrow and windy with no verge. Vehicles come round the nearby corner at tremendous speeds while hugging the hedges on either side. We watch from the bank above. There is no room for stray walkers. We plan our assault and dash across during a four-second lull. As we're ducking into a wooded trail on the other side, a grey car comes honking and speeding towards us, the driver yelling, "Water. Water."

Pat and I have no idea what's happening, but Sally turns, sticks out her arm and snatches her water bottle from none other than Tim, the driver of the vehicle.

She smiles at us with a sheepish shrug. "I guess he noticed I forgot it on the table," she says.

"Now how could he have known where we'd be?" I ask.

"Oh, he and Gail walk this way all the time. He'd have worked it out."

Sally takes this miracle in stride, but Pat and I are impressed. That evening, Tim confirms that he had indeed calculated our crossing time and planned the hand-off to the second.

We tramp through woods, farmland and a couple of tiny villages. At one village we notice a golf course. It's ten o'clock and we've been walking since seven-thirty. Time for a comfort break and refreshment. Pat and I are used to pausing behind the occasional bush, and as leave-no-trace walkers, we tuck used tissue into small biffy bags we carry for that purpose. Today there have been few bushes offering much in the way of privacy, so we hurry into the golf club, secure a table then rush to the ladies' room.

The club's waitress accepts our invasion with cautious grace. "This is a private club, but would you care for the menu?"

We order toasted tea cakes and cappuccinos, and she warms to us three oddly dressed characters, although the idea of walking from Winchester to Canterbury seems like a dubious activity.

"Like Chaucer's *Canterbury Tales*," I offer.

"Well," says our waitress, "those pilgrims walked from The Tabard Inn in Southwark. That's London, not Winchester."

"True, but we're following Henry II's route when he went to Canterbury in penance after Becket's murder."

"Would you like strawberry jam or marmalade with your tea cakes, then?" she asks.

An hour after our arrival, we return to the task of pilgrimage, the waitress wishing us the best on our journey. In the next village, we stop at an arts and crafts store – a place of great temptation where Pat buys a pheasant-feather-adorned hat.

Meanwhile, Marianne has enlisted Tim's assistance in driving her to the grocery store where she spends a couple of hours choosing the groceries on the list and adding a few extra just-in-case items. Upon our return to Tim and Gail's – again via Tim's pickup service – we divide an enormous mound of food and squirrel it away in our backpacks. This daunting task accomplished, Marianne, Pat, and I join Tim for an evening of sampling craft beer while Sally and Gail attend a yoga class.

24 April. To Tanners Hatch Youth Hostel.
Pilgrims and Soldiers' Tales.

> *"Bring not every man into thine house,"*
> *He said; and it's a pretty risky business,*
> *This giving a night's lodging; you can't be*
> *Too careful about sharing privacy.*
>
> *"The Cook's Prologue"*

As we heave our too-heavy packs into the back of Tim's car and climb in to be ferried back to Guildford, Marianne realizes the risk of aggravating her knee by carrying the extra weight. Tim drops Sally, Pat and me as planned, and after we thank him again for the drives and hospitality, he continues with Marianne to a carpark near the youth hostel. Cars aren't allowed access to the private road without permission, so Marianne is on foot for the last couple of kilometres.

It doesn't take us three walkers long to leave Guilford behind as we cross the River Wey and we begin climbing up to St Martha's Hill. We stop for a rest to admire the view from the top, leaning against the sun-warmed stone wall of St Martha's Church. A sign tells us that it has been here since 1100. We're disappointed that there's no stamp but are no longer surprised.

"I guess they'll have to strike a committee to study the idea," says Pat.

"For a country with so many walking paths, it seems odd that there's little acknowledgment of this one. It's historic. Everyone seems to know about the Pilgrims' Way, but people walking it – well not so much," I grumble.

"We tend to take our history for granted. It's everywhere here, really," says Sally.

Even though she's lived in Canada for over twenty years, Sally hasn't lost her Englishness.

I, however, remain disgruntled. Having embraced the purposeful walking of pilgrimage, I enjoy the conversations generated when we stop for those stamps. By feeling the world unfold beneath our feet, by talking with people we meet, by listening to what those people tell us, modern pilgrims become part of a connective fabric that contributes to global miracles of generosity, patience and understanding.

We march along the ridge and into the charming village of Shere. The Domesday Book recorded Shere as having one church, two mills and fourteen ploughs. Today there's no sign of the ploughs or the mills, but the church – dedicated to St James the Greater – still stands, surrounded by tombstones, which in turn are encircled by daisy-filled grass. The church is locked.

We soon climb back up the ridge. Along Hackhurst Downs and the White Downs, we tramp, passing some red brick WWII pillboxes tucked into the hillside and overlooking the valley below. I can't imagine this little line of fortifications providing an adequate wall of defence had the Germans managed to land. The last successful invasion of this island was secured at the Battle of

Hastings in 1066, about one hundred kilometres to the south.

Since that Norman colonization, Britain surpassed nations such as Spain, Portugal and France to become the most rampant colonizer in human history. Does a history of being colonized create a people more likely to inflict the same pain on other nations? What is the connection? Perhaps humans are predisposed to hunger for power, to desire more territory, to subjugate Others. Even though the UN now regards colonization to be an international crime, civil wars and invasions continue. Those crumbling brick pillboxes symbolize inclinations towards conflict.

We've been walking for six and a half hours as we enter the peaceful National Trust woodlands of Ranmore Common and connect with the three-kilometre track to Tanners Hatch Youth Hostel. Just before our arrival, an energetic Marianne meets us on the trail.

"Beer," we call out. "Please tell us you've found some beer."

Marianne hasn't found the path into Westhumble, three and a half kilometres distant, so no beer awaits. Instead, she puts the kettle on for tea while we unload food from our packs and rub aching shoulders. The well-equipped kitchen provides everything we need to create a delicious dinner. The hostel's manager, Andrew, lights the fire against the evening chill and we soon collapse on comfy couches, resting tired feet on the coffee table. We ask Andrew to join us for dinner, and when he sees how much we've carted, he agrees to help us lighten tomorrow's load.

A retired Royal Logistics Core Sergeant Major is also here, supervising a school group of teenage boys.

"Don't worry. They're camping outside and will not defile the ladies' room," he says, when Pat and I tell him about our Boy Scout encounter in Spain.

In his role of supervisor, he's been granted permission to park his vehicle outside, so Marianne wastes no time in commandeering his services to drive her into Westhumble to pick up some wine for dinner.

We ask Andrew if he has a stamp he could use for our pilgrim credentials, and he produces a beautiful one. Dinner prepared and consumed, and wine finished, we wash dishes and tidy the kitchen, packing leftovers into the fridge for Andrew, who insists he won't have to cook for the rest of the week.

25 April. To Redhill.
Hospitality Tales.

> *He found the miller sitting by the fire.*
> *For night was come; as they could go no further,*
> *They begged him for God's sake to give them shelter,*
> *A room to sleep in; and they offered money.*
>
> *"The Reeve's Tale"*

The four of us set off from cozy Tanners Hatch on a crisp, blue-skied morning. Our route takes us through a woodland, across a couple of fields, along a lane and into Westhumble in little more than half an hour. The village, too distant to walk to yesterday, isn't so far on rested legs. From the village, we pick up our hybrid North Downs/Pilgrims' Way route and climb up to the spectacular viewpoints of Box Hill.

While admiring the view, I lean against one of Britain's more than 7000 trig points, which sits atop a concrete pillar. Long before the advent of the Global Positioning System, these points were used by the Ordnance Survey Agency to map the country. The process requires line-of-sight between at least three triangulation – trig – points.

The agency was created to map Scotland after England quashed the 1745 Jacobite uprising and the work continued into England as the country mobilized to repel potential invasion during the 1803 to 1815 Napoleonic Wars. The result is that Britain has some of the most detailed and accurate maps in the world. Strips of Ordnance Survey maps grace both our North Downs and Pilgrims' Way guidebooks.

At a nearby kiosk, we buy coffee and tea biscuits, then settle at a sunny picnic bench, before an increasing wind hurries us along. Later, we stop for lunch near a weed-infested brick chimney of a disused lime works. We've settled in a warm sunny spot and started eating when huge black clouds race over, delivering a vicious rain squall. We shove our picnic back into our packs, pull on our ponchos and carry on. A while later the sun returns, so we stop at another scenic lookout, spread wet gear on the ground and pull out our lunches. We've only taken a few bites when even blacker clouds, a stronger, colder wind and more driving rain interrupt us. Leaping up, we pack in haste and struggle back into flapping ponchos.

Marianne's knee gives her no trouble until our steep descent off the Downs at day's end. Now, after three days off, she finds her pack heavy. Pat and I use Pocket Earth to guide us the last three kilometres through Reigate and to a Travelodge – that still retains old-world charm – next door to the train station in Redhill.

We're staying in town because accommodation in this part of England is very expensive. With listed prices of between £500 to £1000 per night for a twin room, the more attractive rural places nearer the route are out of our price range.

"Oh my, aren't we on the wrong side of the tracks?" jokes Sally.

The bits of rain-sodden garbage and the swath of industrial clutter contrast with the charming villages and rural landscape. Wrong side of the tracks or not, we're welcomed into warm, quiet rooms with plenty of space to dry wet gear, and pub downstairs offers good dinner fare.

26 April. To Oxted.
Oning and Offing, Donning and Doffing Tales.

Some say that we
Love best to have our own way and be free, …
And others say that we take great delight
In being thought dependable and discreet,
Able to hold steadfastly to one purpose, …

"*The Wife of Bath's Tale*"

At breakfast, Marianne tells us that she needs to take another day off, as her knee is worse again after yesterday's walk. Leaving her to enjoy a second cup of tea while she studies bus and train schedules, Sally, Pat and I pop into the train station next door. Within moments we're aboard a crowded commuter train headed for London. During our three-minute trip, we feel the curious eyes of the suited, brief-case-carrying commuters – who aren't focussed on their cell phones – scrutinizing our boots and packs. Maybe they're jealous, wishing they were free from jobs in tight little offices, wanting to tramp around the countryside. Hopping off in Merstham, we link up with our route.

"Marianne can't be having much fun," says Sally.

"Once she sorts out what to do about the weight of her pack, she'll be able to join us," Pat offers.

I'm worried about Marianne, too. After the Pilgrims' Way, we have two more walks planned. Having only joined us for three of seven days, it looks like she may not be able to continue.

As we head out of Merstham, I read the guidebook and change the subject to local trivia. "Merstham is recorded in the Domesday Book as having one church, one mill and ten ploughs."

"What did they want all that information for?" asks Sally.

"Collecting taxes. In 1086, the village paid £12.00."

As we ponder Norman tax collection methods, we walk through a pedestrian tunnel under the M23 motorway. Overhead, vehicles rush by in a muffled roar. On the far side, we lean into our climb back onto the North Downs.

Past rolling fields, lambs hiding behind their mothers. By orchards, young trees in tidy rows and buds swelling. Through idyllic villages tucked into sheltered valleys. Into bluebell- carpeted woods, with chartreuse leaves bursting. Beneath chestnut and cherry trees, blossoming cream, white and pink.

A constant roar reminds us that a kilometre away, but hidden by trees, the M25 motorway runs parallel to our route. We cross over two intersecting motorways via pedestrian overpasses. Despite the swath of exhaust and noise that the motorways blast across the country, our ancient path manages to continue uninterrupted.

Even though the day begins sunny, we're wearing our fleece jackets because yesterday's cold front has brought much cooler temperatures. By noon the wind picks up and rain threatens. Chilly, we don our rain jackets. The wind drops, the sun returns, we remove jackets and fleece. An hour later clouds pile up and rain begins. We layer up again. Moments later the sun is back, so we stop and disrobe.

Despite the numerous stops to adjust our attire to suit the weather of the minute, we're making good time, so detour up a hill to a vineyard. An afternoon glass of wine will be just the thing on this blustery day. The place is closed. We march back down again and continue to Oxted where we stop at the Old Bell Pub as we enter the village. The barkeep serves us refreshing draft beer and signs our credentials.

Half an hour after leaving the pub, we knock at our B&B and the host greets us with his fly unzipped, but without concern about our arrival time or the condition of our attire. Judging from the dirty rooms, we gather that cleanliness isn't top of mind here. When Marianne arrives shortly afterwards, having spent the day at a church concert and exploring the Redhill shopping mall, the host's fly is appropriately zipped.

Sally's long-time friends Keith and Liz live nearby, so she's called them and arranged for us to meet at a local pub for dinner and animated conversation. When we crawl into bed that night, we all use our sleep sheets because the bedding looks as if it hasn't been laundered since the previous guests, maybe the previous several guests.

27 April. To Kemsing, Kent.
Fifty Years to Make a Tale.

> *They saw a carter with a load of hay*
> *Driving his cart along the public way.*
> *The road was deep in mud; so the cart stuck.*

"The Friar's Tale"

We wake to a grey day and set off into steady rain. Instead of tramping twenty-three kilometres, Marianne again decides to explore the countryside by bus.

We stop for coffee at a golf course clubhouse, entering during a men-only meeting. The host pulls a small table off to one side and produces menus. Although most of the men remain oblivious to our intrusion, a couple frown in our direction. We aren't sure if they disapprove of our gender or our dress. Both? We don't care. Packets of biscuits come with our coffee. As Pat opens hers, a biscuit flies out and lands under one of the men's polished shoes.

Good-bye biscuit. We dissolve into ill-stifled giggles, causing more frowns from the men, one of whom doesn't realize how close he came to being knocked in the head.

"You should have shouted, 'Fore' to warn him," I say.

"They have the same packets at their table," Sally adds. "The waitress will just think that man dropped his own biscuit."

We take turns visiting a posh ladies' room before rustling into our ponchos, swinging packs to our shoulders and returning to the rain.

Thanks to that relentless deluge, we slosh through muddy quagmires and slide down slopes as slippery as skating rinks. Our boots become encased in pontoons of slimy heavy clay. We stop every four or five hundred metres and use our trekking poles to clear treads so we can continue walking.

We pass through more bluebell woods. Every day, the woods' floors become bluer as the blossoms open. Today the blooms nod beneath the weight of raindrops. Muted light creates stained glass effects as it plays with the blue woodland carpet and chartreuse branch-arched ceiling. Eating our picnic lunch in semi-sunshine under an ancient spreading oak, we take care to find spots where we won't squish the bluebells. Bees, butterflies and magical creatures buzz, flutter and work their enchantments.

As we pack up to carry on, Sally asks Pat and me to leave our iPads in their pouches. "I want to navigate on my own," she announces, waving her iPhone at us.

With gratitude, we comply. "We're in your capable hands, Sally."

For this reason, it comes as a surprise when I look across a stretch of valley and realize it's familiar. Although the new M26 now scars the scene, having walked here with my parents, I'm overwhelmed by the powerful sense of homecoming.

"Knockholt is just over there," I point north. "And soon we'll see Chevening Park. The House too."

A few minutes later, Chevening House comes into view below us. The red brick façade doesn't look too impressive, huddled in the gloom. It's raining too hard to take a photo. We plod on, but I'm warm with memories.

We walk down into Dunton Green where The Rose and Crown Pub invites us in to enjoy deep comfortable chairs and beer. As we drink the last drops, Pat looks out the steamy window, and considering her already-dry pants and poncho, decides to end her day here and grab a taxi for the last little bit to Kemsing.

Sally and I walk on for another ninety minutes and get drenched in the hardest downpour of the day. As we walk the last bit of trail, Marianne meets us. She's coming from our B&B where, despite the rain, she has been denied entry.

When the three of us drip in a short time later – just after the prearranged check-in time – the host insists that we leave our wet boots in his unheated, damp vestibule. We pull off our boots, set them beside Pat's, tiptoe across a spotless floor and up carpeted stairs. My wet socks leave a trail of footprints. The host frowns. While showering and scrubbing my socks, I wonder why my feet got so soaked today. My boots are new and Gortex. They shouldn't leak.

This is the evening we're having dinner with my four school friends – Liz, Mary, Kate and Mel. Back in Winchester, Liz and I had arranged that she would pick us up at five o'clock, so we crowd into the chilly entry to wait. Our B&B host is anxious that we leave because he has somewhere he needs to go and doesn't trust us to lock the door. We ignore his impatience and wait inside, opening one of the bottles of wine we've bought for Liz. We wait. We finish the bottle of wine. We're hungry.

An hour later, Kate – who has driven from her home in Somerset – picks us up, apologizing for the delay. We arrive at Liz's to find Mary – who has come up from near Brighton – helping with dinner preparation. Mel had arrived earlier off the train from Manchester.

"Goodness," says Sally. "We've only walked from Oxted."

Liz, who has been at work all day, shoos us into the living room while she and Mary finish cooking.

Realizing that our request for an early dinner has been sidelined, we hug rumbling stomachs, drink more wine and share stories. Used to being on the trail early and in bed before nine, we're tired beyond the point of hunger by the time we all crowd into the dining room to enjoy delicious chili and lasagna – which rekindles our appetites – amid laugher, more wine and remember-when stories.

Mel is staying at a B&B close to ours, and as no one is fit to drive, the five of us bundle into a taxi. Falling into bed a short time later, I realize that it's almost tomorrow and am glad we've decided to take a break from walking and to enjoy a day with our four English friends instead.

28 April. To Rochester.
A Wet-Footed Tale.

> *And high above, depicted in a tower,*
> *Sat Conquest, robed in majesty and power,*
> *Under a sword that swung above his head,*
> *Sharp-edged and hanging by a subtle thread.*
>
> *"The Knight's Tale"*

A bit of a sleep-in and strong coffee helps deal with foggy heads. The radio informs us that the temperature on this low-cloud day will only rise to 8°C. We shudder.

"At least it's not pouring yet," says Sally.

"Is there more coffee?" asks Pat.

We're in the entry with our packs at the appointed time of nine o'clock. Mel walks over and joins us. We bump into each other in the cramped space as we haul on cold damp boots. I lean out the door and pour out the puddles from the bottom of mine.

"What the hell?" says Pat.

I shrug. "They started leaking yesterday."

"Aren't they waterproof?" asks Marianne.

"Well, they're supposed to be. But apparently – no. More like sponges."

In that moment, we all begin calling my boots the sponges. Once back in Canada, I return them to the store where they are warrantied, and I receive a new pair. That, however, does nothing to ease the misery of several cold-wet-footed days to come.

Mary and Kate arrive in two cars to pick us up. We stow our packs, pick up Liz who is tidying up from last night's feast, then drive over to visit Combe Bank School where Mel, Kate, Mary, Liz and I first met.

Built in the 18th century as the estate home for Baron Sundridge, the grand house still sits shining white, on a rise in a manicured lawn, surrounded by rhodos, azaleas and parkland trees. Over the years, people such as Charles Darwin and Oscar Wilde have visited, the sweeping gravel drive crunching under the wheels of their horse-drawn carriages as it now crunches under our car tires. It was a convalescent centre for wounded soldiers during both World Wars, cots lined up in the ballroom where we had our assemblies, nurses and doctors easing pain, patients healing where we struggled with Pythagoras and Shakespeare. When I was a student here, it was a Catholic girls' boarding and day school. Today it is called Radnor House and is an independent day school for boys and girls.

Our next stop is Hever Castle, Anne Boleyn's home until she married Henry VIII. This is where Mum and Dad brought friends who visited while we lived in nearby Groom's Cottage, and where, roaming tapestry-hung rooms, I imagined myself dressed in a long gown and being courted by a handsome king. My king was always a young man, never corpulent, ulcerated or prone to wife-beheading urges. Innocent childhood me. Had I lived in those times, I'd probably have been the chamber pot cleaner or a farm peasant.

The engine light of Kate's car flashes ominous warnings, so she calls the AA and waits with the car. Meanwhile, the rest of us enter the grounds, then cross the drawbridge into the courtyard, where we're welcomed by an actor playing Thomas Boleyn. We explore the house, admiring rooms furnished in period pieces, and peopled by costumed wax figures onto which light filters through mullioned stained-glass windows. Next, we wander through the Italian garden, the topiary, the rose garden, past the lake, fountains and grottoes, along pathways, and under pergolas, my chilled feet sloshing with every step.

Our visit complete, we meet Kate, car now repaired, and cross the road for a leisurely late lunch at the Henry VIII Pub before being driven back to Sevenoaks where Pat, Sally, Marianne and I catch a train onward to Rochester.

Our hotel rooms here are above a vibrant pub, but up on the third floor, we can't hear the din coming from the bar. I turn my sodden sponges upside down on a hot water radiator and turn the heat up. By the time I've showered, they're dripping and steaming. We go down into the fray below for a terrific pub dinner.

29 April. To Aylesford Priory.
A Potatoes and Tea Cakes Tale.

> *But, seriously, dear Host, all Aah's asking's*
> *Get us some food and drink, and do us well:*
> *We'll pay for all, cash down, reet on the nail, ...*
>
> "The Reeve's Tale"

My first act of the day is to examine the sponges. The toes are still damp, but when I pull them on, warm and damp feels much better than cold and wet.

We arrive downstairs to a silent pub, sticky floor and smell of spilled beer, the only indication of yesterday evening's revelry. An artery-clogging English breakfast provides enough leftovers for us to make bacon and toast sandwiches for lunch. While we're eating, a rough-dressed, grey-whiskered man wanders in and leans on the bar. The odour of damp wool and unwashed body follows him through the door. He greets the barkeep who pours him a coffee. His eyes roam across our plates as he asks us where we're from and where we are going.

Pat and I recognize homelessness when we smell it. She shoves a pound coin across the table towards me and jerks her head. I scoop the same from my pouch.

"Shall we buy him some breakfast?" I whisper to Sally and Marianne when the man turns back to the bar.

They don't catch on.

"He's homeless," Pat mouths.

Now understanding, Marianne and Sally contribute, and I take the coins to the bar.

"May we buy you breakfast?" I ask.

His smile reveals a blackening front tooth. "Thank you."

I reach over the bar and pop the coins into the barkeep's hand. "Breakfast for our friend, please."

A few minutes later, as we step into the rain, I notice the man's breakfast being handed to him in a paper bag and feel a twinge of disappointment that he's not been invited to enjoy it in the dry warmth of the pub.

Rochester Cathedral's bells begin their Sunday pealing, so we walk up High Street to join well-dressed worshippers. A couple of deacons at either side of the entrance greet parishioners and by our boots and packs, recognize our status as pilgrims. One of the deacons takes us aside, stamps our credentials, then shows us the Pilgrims Steps. Although now covered by new wooden treads, the original stone is worn into deep scoops from centuries of pilgrims coming to pay their respects. When the deacon invites us to stay for the matins service, we explain that we need to get walking and can only stay for a short time. Even so, the welcome remains warm and several other cathedral personages come to say hello and ask about our journey.

Packs at our feet, we settle into a row of chairs near the door and give ourselves up to the thunderous organ and glorious choir. Cathedral acoustics enhance every whisper, and the music resonates from the vaults and into our bones. The second oldest in England, Rochester Cathedral was first consecrated in 604 CE. Since then, it has suffered fire, plunder, desecration and neglect. With each restoration, another architectural style was incorporated, so the cathedral now presents a harmonious blend of Romanesque, Norman and Gothic styles. Just before the liturgy begins, we slip back out into the chill day.

Having organized a taxi to transport her pack, Marianne joins us today as we only have an eleven-kilometre walk. She's hopeful that because there are no hills and that by not carrying any extra weight, her painful knee will give her less trouble.

Leaving the cathedral, we stride past the walls of Rochester Castle, then down onto the esplanade along the south bank of the River Medway. Close to its mouth, this reach of the river is tidal so as we walk, we watch moored boats strain at their lines as the tide rises. A couple of river barges await enough water to float them from where they rest in the mudflats. Gulls and other shore birds squabble and soar as they feed on tiny crabs.

Our route turns away from the river and for a while leads us along a bridleway. Like city crosswalks with designated pedestrian lights, here there are designated horse lights, the buttons placed high enough on the poles that riders don't have to lean down to press. We share the chilly wind-blown path with no horses, bikes or other walkers but are pleased to have pedestrian buttons to press when the route leads us across busy roads.

Neither the drizzle nor the route is conducive to picnicking, so we pop into a down-at-the-heels pub and order beer and crisps. We had hoped for a hot meal, but lunch isn't served at this pub on Sundays, and no one seems to mind us munching our napkin-wrapped sandwiches.

A short time later, we slosh into Aylesford Priory amid a deluge. Founded in 1242 by Carmelites, the priory has been providing hospitality to Canterbury pilgrims for centuries. Today, however, no dinner is available.

"It's Sunday," says the receptionist by way of explanation as she stamps our credentials. "You can just drive over to Ditton across the river."

"We're on foot," Pat reminds her.

"Oh right. Of course. Well, The Chequers is just down a ways. In the village."

I check Pocket Earth and see the pub less than a kilometre away.

"Maybe the rain will have let up by then," Marianne says. Shivering as she picks up her pack from where it sits by the counter, she continues, "This wasn't a great day to rejoin you. Should have taken the bus."

As pilgrims, we receive a discount, then are given directions to cross the quadrangle, enter the small door on the left, turn right, climb the stairs and proceed down the hall to our little unheated attic rooms. Draughty toilets and showers lurk further down the hall.

Appetizing tea cakes, with a sign designating them for a yoga group, occupy a table in the lounge. There is no sign of the yoga group and our stomachs rumble. Deciding that marauding tea cakes while we are guests at a priory might invite divine retribution, we remove ourselves from temptation and brave a chilly meander through the immaculate, historic grounds.

Walking into the village a while later, we look forward to a hot dinner at the Chequers. The pub has been in operation one way or another since the 1500s; however, dinner is not served on Sundays. We stand dumbfounded at the bar, then order four beer and four bags of crisps.

"What's that bowl of potatoes for?" I ask the barkeep of a large ceramic serving bowl containing several roast potato chunks.

"Oh, that's leftovers from lunch."

"Can we have them?"

Looking alarmed, he pauses in drawing a beer. "They're cold. We generally toss leftovers into the pig bucket."

"We're hungry. Cold is fine." I try not to worry about the pigs missing roast potatoes from their evening's slop.

The barkeep shoves our beer, crisps, the bowl and four forks across the counter. We pay for our drinks and crisps, grab the lot, hurry to a table and dive in. A few patrons raise their brows, but most don't seem to notice our uncouth gobbling. No doubt; in its five hundred years of operation, the Chequers has seen stranger things than four grey-haired women sharing a bowl of cold potatoes.

The beer eases our disappointment. By the time we depart, dusk has fallen, and the rain has stopped. Back in our attic, we discover the yoga group has not touched their tea cakes. We circle the table. We stare. Eight hands remove eight tea cakes. Pat rearranges the plate to disguise our theft. We sneak back to our rooms. Sally and Marianne are sharing one, Pat and I another. The bible on our bedside table offers reproach.

"Kim, put a blanket over that bible," suggests Pat as she takes a bite of ill-gotten tea cake.

"No way, it's too cold in here." I wrap the blanket around my shoulders.

Pat reaches over and tucks the bible into a drawer, then we continue munching without remorse.

30 April. To Harrietsham.
A Stormy Tale.

> *It's there our Host began to crack his jokes:*
> *'Well, gentlemen! It looks as if we're stuck.*
> *Dun's in the mire! Who's to pull him out?*
>
> "The Manciple's Prologue"

We wake to the sound of rain drumming on the slate roof. The tea cakes remain as we left them, on the table, which now also hosts a couple of mouse droppings. The shower water never runs warm. We shiver, wash, pack, tromp downstairs, cross the quadrangle and enter the massive high-beamed Pilgrims' Hall. Built in 1280, it has in turn been a dining hall, barn, brewery, almshouse. Today, an extensive buffet is laid out on a side counter. A large table is set with ten places and another set with four. We help ourselves to bacon and eggs from a chafing dish, yoghurt, cold toast, tiny packets of marmalade, coffee from an urn, and arrange ourselves at the table for four.

We're well into our meal when a woman bustles out from the kitchen and marches over to our table. "That breakfast isn't for you," she says.

"Who's it for then?" asks Marianne.

"The yoga group."

"Well, where's our breakfast?" asks Pat.

"You have the pilgrim discount. No breakfast with the discount."

"Well, you offered the discount without mention that you figured we should walk on empty stomachs," I grumble.

"And there was no dinner last night. Either here or at the pub," Sally adds. "So, we are quite hungry." She pops a forkful of egg into her mouth.

"We've seen no sign of the yoga group," says Marianne. "Maybe they left already."

Pat sets two rashers of bacon between two slices of toast, wraps the sandwich in a paper napkin and tucks it into her pack.

While I surreptitiously add a fried egg to the two slices of bacon already on my toast-to-be-sandwich, the woman glowers at Pat, then huffs back into the kitchen, where she sounds the alarm that there are foreign marauders in the dining hall.

We finish breakfast without repentance, rustle into all our raingear, swing packs onto our backs and head out into a gale. The rain drives sideways, tree branches sway and crack, a wall thermometer reads 5°C, our rain ponchos whip around our legs and Sally's hat sails into a bush.

"I think this is too dangerous for walking," yells Pat over the din.

Sally retrieves her hat, and we all squeeze back into the priory.

"Train?" I suggest.

"Why?" Sally asks.

Leaving Sally to reach her own conclusions, Pat and I get out our iPads to check schedules, only to discover that the four Wi-Fi passwords assigned to us on check-in yesterday have expired. Watching puddles spreading beneath our feet on her clean flagstone floor, the receptionist offers to look up the schedule. It's easier, she assures us, than issuing more passwords. Given the rigmarole we went through to receive yesterday's passwords, we agree.

"Where are you going?" she asks.

"Harrietsham," I say.

She taps at her computer. "A train will be along in an hour," she tells us. "But you'll have to change in Maidstone."

Since we're no longer walking today, Marianne decides to carry her pack instead of having it moved by taxi. She asks the receptionist to phone and cancel the pickup, then we exit again into the storm. Across a humped mediaeval stone bridge, we splash. Along a road, where racing vehicles hurl puddle-sluicing muddy showers, we scurry. We stand for several chilly minutes at the rail crossing until an express train howls through and the barriers rise.

At the station, we purchase tickets, then wait, shivering on the platform, until our train arrives. We climb on, shake ourselves like dogs, pull off dripping ponchos and settle into seats. The train remains huffing in the station. An announcement informs us that due to flooding and electrical problems at the crossing, the bars won't come down again, and we can't leave until they do.

"Can't someone just pull them down by hand?" suggests Sally.

We decide that the lights might also need to flash so people don't just drive smashing through. We've noticed English drivers tend to drive over the speed limit and do not follow what we consider "normal" rules of safe driving etiquette. The mud drying on all four of our faces attests to their lack of concern for pedestrians.

The gate problem resolved, the train clunks forward only to grind to a halt a couple of moments later, our rear carriage still in the crossing. Another announcement informs us that there are wind-blown branches on the tracks, but the train engineer will get out and remove them. We peer from foggy windows at scowling car drivers tapping steering wheels with impatience. Up ahead, we catch glimpses of the branch removal effort. That done, we again lurch into motion. One of the drivers held at the crossing blasts his horn to hurry us on our way.

At the exchange stop in Maidstone, we dash through the storm to another station where we huddle in a heated waiting room. Our next train arrives on time, and after a few minutes we clamber off in Harrietsham. A short walk through more foot-soaking puddles in even heavier, driving rain brings us dripping to the Roebuck Inn, where we're invited to check into our rooms early. Returning to the bar, we look forward to a hot lunch. This being April, the central heating has been turned off for the season. The bar is chilly, but we're dry.

"No lunch on Mondays, dearies. Sup's at six," the barkeep informs us.

We stare at him.

"We serve lunch every other day though," he says into our blistering silence.

"Is there another pub in town?" I ask.

"Well, there is. But it's closed on Mondays."

"Of course it is," says Pat.

"That might have been planned a little better, don't you think?" Sally asks.

We order four beer and while the barkeep draws them, he explains that many pubs in England are closed for various reasons – not making a go of it being the most common.

"No wonder," I mutter.

While sipping beer, we eat our picnic sandwiches. Unconcerned, the barkeep goes about his business. By late afternoon the smells of roasting and frying set our stomachs rumbling. We're the first served and the meal restores our faith in English pub hospitality.

1 May. To Wye.
A Sad Pub and Empty Church Tale.

> *I can tell a story with a moral to it:*
> *Here's one I preach to bring the money in.*
> *Now if you'll all be quiet, I'll begin.*

"The Pardoner's Prologue"

I roll over in bed and listen. No wind howling around the building. No rain beating against the window. Cracking open my eyes, I realize the room is glowing with dawn sunshine. Sliding out of bed, I look out onto a world sparkling clean and inviting.

We're all up, dressed and downstairs in record time. Our packs are full again and heavier with all the wet-weather gear stored inside. We gobble a hot English breakfast of greasy eggs, sausage, hash browns, fried tomatoes, racked toast and bitter coffee. I sip the coffee and ask for tea instead.

Waving good-bye to our hosts, we're walking before eight-thirty. Marianne finds walking without her pack eases her knee pain so has once again arranged for a taxi to pick it up and take it to our accommodation in Wye.

Over more of Kent's pastoral hills, we walk through and around and up and down field and forest and wind-swept grasslands. Past large apple orchards, boughs heavy with blooms. Past fancy estates, long drives bordered by coifed shrubs and stately trees. The breeze keeps the day a perfect temperature for walking, and we enjoy a picnic on a patch of nearly dry grass by a farm gate.

Most landowners respect the right of common way, but at one estate, a lethal-looking electric fence blocking the path sends us on a long circuit around. Like most walkers, we respect the private lands we cross; however, we feel distain for the owner of this unfriendly fence.

The rural landscape is so domestic compared to our Canadian West Coast. Here, we never walk far without seeing a farmhouse or tiny village, but due to the stormy weather, some of the trail leads us through quagmires of slimy mud. In other places, we slosh through impressive puddles that would make our West Coast proud. On private land, it would not be appropriate to create detours into fresh ploughed fields or to trample new spring growth, so leaping, splashing and sliding, we're soon muddy and wet to the knees.

Many villages of this part of England have a pub, often across the street from a church. However, many pubs are closed as they can't make ends meet. So, too, churches are closed with few parishioners to support costs. Pubs and churches were once the heart and soul of village life, and we feel a creeping desolation in the shuttered windows, unkempt graveyards and empty streets.

At the New Flying Horse Inn in Wye, we're given a warm welcome, and while drawing our beer, the barkeep tells us that many people now drive to the bigger towns to work and shop so the villages are devolving into soulless bedroom communities.

While we've been chatting, Marianne has been looking around. "Has a taxi delivered my pack?" she asks.

The barkeep shakes his head. "No taxi. No pack."

As Marianne laments her missing pack, the barkeep makes a couple of phone calls to unravel the mystery. When the taxi driver had arrived at the inn in Harrietsham, he waited for his fare to come out the door. When no one appeared, he left. The dispatcher now sends another taxi with explicit instructions for the driver to retrieve the pack himself, put it in his taxi, then deliver it here at the New Flying Horse. A journey that has taken us the better part of the day takes Marianne's pack less than an hour.

2 May. To Canterbury.
Our Canterbury Tale.

> *As we were entering a village-end;*
> *And thereupon our Host ... spoke up like this:*
> *'Now, gentlemen and ladies,' he began,*
> *'We're short of only one more tale – just one.*

"The Parson's Prologue"

Forecasts call for a return of damaging winds and lots more rain starting around noon, so we decide to take a train for the first part of our walk with a view to arriving in Canterbury before the storm breaks. Alighting in Chilham, we congratulate ourselves as smart strategists. We only have twelve kilometres to go and the weather, though cool, is dry.

Before long, cool becomes chilly and dry becomes drizzly and the wind begins playing with grasses and small branches. Perched on a bench in a sheltered bus stop, we eat our lunch in one of the sad little villages with a pub and church that are both closed. The drizzle becomes rain. The wind snatches bedraggled blossoms from cherry trees, flings tree bits onto the roof of our shelter and moans around the steeple.

As we walk through dripping apple orchards, down puddled lanes, across muddy fields, past flattened bluebells, within creaking forests and up sodden hills, the rain becomes a deluge, the wind now roaring. Sideways. Stinging. Soaking. My feet, awash, are cold within the sponges.

Trusty Pocket Earth comes in handy once again to guide us through Canterbury's ancient city gates to the cathedral. Here queuing tourists huddle beneath ineffective umbrellas as they file forward to pay admission and enter. They turn alarmed eyes to us four bedraggled pilgrims as we ease past and step up to the wicket.

"We're pilgrims," I say, peering through my fogged, rain-smeared glasses.

"The four of you?"

"Yes."

"Please follow me," says a young man who pulls on his coat and exits the ticket booth.

We trot in his wake, sloshing to a kiosk window.

"These people will help you," says our guide before dashing back to shelter.

The kiosk resembles a New York food truck. Three dry, enthusiastic people crowd within its shelter. We stand outside in the deluge and shove our credentials across the counter.

"We walked from Winchester," I shout over the din of rain drumming on the roof.

"Would you like a blessing with this?" asks one of the dry people as she applies the final stamp.

Wiggling my toes and wondering if I'm developing trench foot, I find my brain slow to compute the question. A blessing? Did she say blessing or dressing? Mustard? Feeling I should be ordering a hot dog, not getting my pilgrim's credentials verified, I clarify. "A blessing?"

"Yes, if you wait here for a few minutes, we'll call the bishop over to bless you."

"She wants to know if we'd like a blessing with our stamps," I relay to the others who are standing behind me and can't hear.

They regard me, then the dry woman, with stupefied gazes.

"You want us to stand here in the rain waiting for blessings?" Pat hollers.

"Yes. I will call the bishop." The dry lady smiles.

"How about just the stamp for today and a blessing tomorrow?" I ask. "We're a bit too wet to be blessed right now."

The young woman regards us and agrees. "Tomorrow then?"

"Tomorrow sounds just perfect."

"Did she say she was calling a bishop?" asks Sally as I hand back our stamped credentials and we turn away.

"I think so. Hard to hear over the racket. Definitely a blessing though."

We drip along the last kilometre to our hostel, where we're invited to leave all our wet rainwear in the lounge.

"Will it be safe?" asks Marianne.

The receptionist thinks for a moment before answering. "Well, for now. It's too wet to take into your room."

She shows us our small room with a bunk bed, two twin beds, no chairs, no table and no hooks. Nowhere to even hang a towel.

"This is cozy," says Pat, dumping her pack on a bed because there's no other place to put it.

However, there is a beer fridge in the lobby, so we grab

refreshment, retrieve assorted items of left-over food from our packs, sit on our beds – Sally on mine because she drew the short straw and has the top bunk tonight – and begin the process of becoming dry.

3 May. In Canterbury.
Poohsticks and Wolfhound Tales.

And then with royal pomp they fetched the gifts,
That is to say, the sword and the mirror,
Which in due course were borne to the high tower
By officers appointed for the purpose; ...

"The Squire's Tale"

The storm has left clear skies in its wake. The hostel offers an inadequate breakfast, so before embarking on an exploration of Canterbury's historic wonders, our first mission is to find a café.

Crossing a pedestrian bridge over a tributary of the River Stour, we pause to chat with some punters bailing out a fleet of partially submerged, rain-filled punts. They tell us that the river is flowing twice as fast and twice as deep as usual due to all the rain.

Marianne's knee continues to bother her, so although we're just strolling around town, she's using her trekking poles. Wanting a picture, she leans her poles on the bridge railing and pulls out her iPad to go through the cumbersome process of using it as a camera. Leaning closer to the rail, she knocks her poles, and they fall through the bars into the torrent below. One of the punters leaps into action, scampering and hopping from wobbly boat to wobbly boat. Despite his valiant effort to save the poles, they spin away in the turbulent water.

While Sally, Pat and I continue with our café quest, Marianne heads off to find a sporting goods store and new set of poles. Coffee enjoyed and poles acquired, we visit St Dunstan's church where Henry II is said to have removed his boots to walk barefoot for the final kilometre of his penance pilgrimage. A couple of women in the church allow us to understand that we are intruding.

"We are cleaning," says one, her tone haughty.

"Pilgrims," says the other, her tone disparaging. The Hoover roars to life.

We are certain that, but for the cleaners, the place would be locked. Oblivious to the role this church plays in the Canterbury pilgrimage saga, they appear anxious that we be gone.

After meeting Liz at the train station, we enjoy lunch on a sunny terrace by the river, taking great care to not play any more Poohsticks with Marianne's new poles, then go to the cathedral.

Pat tells the ticket people that Liz is our support person, so she, too, enters for free. A step into the cloisters reveals yellow sunlit sandstone with carved roof finials rising slender above the surrounding galleries. Pillars worn by over nineteen centuries of weather support graceful, adorned arches. Whispers and footsteps echo. The hair stands up on my arms. Ghosts brush past, centuries of souls busy with their hauntings.

The original cathedral, founded in 597, was rebuilt from 1070 to 1077. After a fire in 1174, the next rendition was in the Gothic style and included expansion to accommodate all the pilgrims who flocked to the place where Thomas Becket was murdered. Upon arrival, those pilgrims bought badges commemorating their visits and in so doing, generated enough revenue to fund the new construction.

In 1538, Henry VIII accused Becket of treason and summoned him to face the charges. When the dead man didn't appear, Henry found him guilty and confiscated the shrine's treasures. It is said that the king's men removed two coffers and twenty-six carts of valuable goods. None have been recovered.

We visit Becket's treasureless shrine, our pilgrimage now complete, but it is an art installation that claims our attention. Circular arrays of clothing hang from the vaulted ceiling like vast chandeliers. The clothing was left in the Calais Jungle by refugees waiting there before crossing to the UK.

At first glance, I'm offended by the apparent hypocrisy. The owners of that black bra, the worn pair of socks, those little pink overalls, that tattered sweater, all waited in Calais because Britain refused them access. What questions do these sad lost clothes ask of us? Who were the humans who suffered? Are the people who once wore this clothing still alive? Do the clothes demand that we consider the harm that has been done? Maybe the idea is to encourage us to wonder and to question our humanity. I look at those clothes and am reminded of similar items Pat and I saw scattered along the Via Egnatia. Where are – how are – those people now?

A clergyman comes along – alerted by the entry people that there are pilgrims in the cathedral – and after welcoming us, he asks about the focus of our walk. Having sought and found myself as a pilgrim while walking the Portuguese Camino, I'm able to explain that I like walking with a purpose. We all have our own responses, but none of us claim religious motives. He respects our reasons, and we sit talking with him about the refugees, the decline of church attendance, closed churches – and pubs – and global humanitarian issues.

During the conversation, we tell him how, when we'd arrived in Winchester, the bells had pealed during bell-ringing practice. In Rochester, the cathedral bells had pealed for Sunday service. He asks a passing church warden if any bell ringing is imminent and is informed that no bells will ring until later this evening.

We express disappointment, but a few minutes after leaving the clergyman to his duties, the bells peal for a short sequence. We grin at each other, knowing that Canterbury's bells have been rung just for us. Our blessing.

On that note, we see Liz to the train, then set off to meet Sally's son Kindred and his dog Rintrah – a regal Irish Wolfhound. Kindred arrives with two large backpacks, and we climb a steep hill commanding a view of the cathedral. He unpacks five crystal champagne flutes, a bottle of vintage champagne and a loaf of bread. Kindred has made the bread from a special recipe, having folded into it surprises such as eggs, ham, cheese, olives, red peppers and other culinary delights. Rintrah lies, head on paws, regarding us with his thoughtful gaze and listening while we tell Kindred a Canterbury Tale that Chaucer, too, might have enjoyed. We sip the champagne, munch the bread and admire the tower of Canterbury Cathedral glowing in the setting sun.

We endure wind and rain, but on our last day the sun shines again when Sally's son Kindred and Rintrah meet us with champagne and a special celebratory loaf.

Chapter Four

Upping and Downing on the Cornish Coastal Path

Cornwall's overall economy during the medieval period relied on the sea, whether for trade, food, smuggling, piracy, or wrecking. Its ports had welcomed and feared the arrival of strangers for centuries ... Roman records ... indicate that the tin trade had long been in existence ...

Historians claim that plundering and wrecking continued because of Cornwall's relative isolation and lack of law enforcement on the coast. ... it was generally accepted that no Cornish jury would ever convict a fellow countryman on a wrecking charge, ...

Cathryn Pearce, Cornish Wrecking 1700 – 1860: Reality and Popular Myth, *2010*

Pat, me and Marianne upping and downing along the Cornish Coastal Path.

8 May. Between Tintagel and Port Isaac.
A Secret Liaison.

Pat stops in her tracks and I pile in behind her. Like a roofless tunnel, this section of the narrow path is cut deep into the soil and banked on both sides by thick gorse. I peer around Pat's billowing poncho to see a black male sheep hopping down from the back of a white female sheep.

Marianne arrives. "Why are we stopped?" she asks.

"Sheep," I say. "Two sheep having a liaison and blocking the path."

Marianne peers around us. "Liaison?"

"Sheep sex," explains Pat.

Their sheepish expressions tell all we need to know about the mischief.

"A Romeo and Juliet affair," I suggest.

"Go for it, dear, just dash by them," says the black to the white.

She takes a step forward and two back. "Oh. No. I can't. I'm too scared," she bleats.

We wait and murmur nice things to them, but the pair spin and gallop along the path ahead of us. Maybe not wanting to be too far from their field and the hole in their fence, they stop. When we catch up with them, they panic and take off again. With no desire to scare the silly creatures off the cliff, we pause while they try to find the courage to pass us, but for a third time they run ahead. Because we're worried that they will get lost or injured, and the path remains narrow and hemmed in by gorse, we all stop again.

The sheep turn and face us. Then the black sheep clambers over the white sheep.

"Let me go first. I'll run past and you follow," he instructs his sweetheart.

She agrees and both sheep dash towards us. We clamber to the side, pulling ourselves up off the trail by gripping the gorse and hoping we don't tumble into the sea far below. He barges past, bumping us with his soggy wool coat. As she draws level, she leaps and flies by, four feet off the ground. They are gone.

"When sheep fly," I quip.

We drop back to the path from our prickly perches, brush ourselves off and continue on our way, immersed within the confines of the fog, the gorse and our own thoughts.

4 May. From Canterbury, Kent to Bude, Cornwall.
Westward Ho.

Our Kipps Hostel breakfast is just as poor as yesterday's, but today we have no time to enjoy better fare at the café. Sally leaves us and will now visit with Kindred before flying home to Canada. Marianne, Pat and I walk to the station and hop on a train for an hour's trip from Canterbury to Victoria Station in London.

Instead of taking the Tube, we take advantage of the sunny morning to walk across Hyde Park to Paddington Station where we catch a train on to Exeter. From there, a third train takes us to Barnstaple where we catch a bus, arriving in Bude on the Cornish north coast in the late afternoon.

We check into the Brendon Arms Inn, owned by the Brendon family since it first opened in 1872. The inn sits beside a scenic inner harbour at the mouth of Bude Canal. Dug in 1823, the canal enabled shipping of coastal lime-rich sand to inland farms to enrich heavy clay soil. Canal depth is maintained, even at low tide, by a sea-lock at the canal's mouth where it enters the Celtic Sea.

Oddly tired after a day of doing very little, we're more interested in a good pub meal than the history and scenery of Bude, which we will have all day tomorrow to explore.

5 May. In Bude.
Limelight.

We spend a relaxed day preparing for our coastal walk. While Marianne makes arrangements with a luggage transport service, Pat and I explore the cliffs above the village and visit Bude's Castle Museum. Built in 1830 by Sir Goldsworthy Gurney, the castle has been a heritage visitor centre since 2007. As we take in the exhibits, I learn about the origin of the term "being in the limelight."

Sir Goldsworthy was a physician and inventor. One of his inventions involved using a blowpipe to direct a flame enriched by a mix of oxygen and hydrogen at a cylinder of quicklime. This produced a brighter light than that of a candle or oil lamp. His lights were called limes. Next, he invented the Bude light by oxygenating the flame of a standard oil lamp to create a bright light that was used to illuminate lighthouses and the British Parliament Buildings.

6 May. To St Gennys.
A Surprising Amount of Upping and Downing.

Weary, having been kept awake until the early hours of the morning by a raucous party in the pub right below our rooms, we climb out of beds for as early a breakfast as we could negotiate – seven thirty.

Given how late the staff were up dealing with the revellers, we understand they'd prefer to be in their beds rather than making us eggs and toast but we're anxious to get an early start on the trail. Pat and I like having the day's walk done by mid-afternoon to give us time to wash and dry laundry, rest tired feet and legs and enjoy wherever we've walked to. Marianne would prefer more leisurely mornings, but she bears with us and tries to be ready when we are.

Despite a massive fog bank off the coast, we walk under a sunny sky. In a couple of places, new housing construction obliterates the path. With no alternate routes marked, we make short road detours. For the rest of the day, we follow grass and clay pathways or clamber up and down very steep stairways. Walking along high cliff edges, climbing down into deep gulches, crossing open scrubland and tramping through wind-twisted, stunted woodlands, we see more sheep than people. At one point, we squeeze by a huge brown ram who will not budge off the path. Our route passes through a couple of fields occupied by curious, soft-eyed cows and in another, horses nod and gallop away.

Sixteen hard kilometres and six long hours after leaving Bude, we arrive at a B&B in St Gennys. It will remain nameless. A sleepy looking man answers our knock.

"Wife's away," he says. "Key's in the door. Bottom of the garden." He points.

We follow his finger and a little path to a chalet at the bottom of an unkempt garden. A peacock spreads his tail feathers and screeches. From the roof of the chalet a peahen replies.

When we open the door, the smell of must rushes out to greet us. The place is chilly and damp. There are two tiny bedrooms and a sitting area. Travelling with three people can be awkward for equitable sharing of room expenses, but Marianne has solved potential dilemmas by paying the extra and enjoying her own room wherever we've been unable to find a room with three beds. Because accommodations tend to be expensive in England, Pat and I are grateful for her generosity.

Marianne heads to her room. It has a saggy double bed. Pat and I enter ours: a saggy child-size bunkbed. Pat is taller than me. I'm not sure she's going to fit.

"I best take the top," I offer.

She nods. When we plop down on the mattresses, the bed wobbles and the tired bedsprings sound just like the peacocks. Three weary women giggle. The peacocks screech and scamper around on the roof. We shower in the dingy little bathroom, tiny mushrooms growing in the corners. At least there is ample hot water.

Socks washed and hung to dry in a patch of evening sun, we head off to a pub a kilometre further down the road. We buy supplies for tomorrow's lunch in a small shop and are soon settled at the pub, beer in hand and dinner ordered. As we eat, the sea fog roams around, sometimes brushing tendrils across the window before eddying away to sea again.

Later, my back propped by a lumpy pillow, feet tucked under the thin bedcovers, I reread what the guidebook says about the Bude to Crackington Haven stretch of path. The description includes phrases such as: *punishing ascent* and *testing beginnings*. I read these bits to Pat.

"I agree with that," she says before rolling over and falling asleep, her feet hanging over the end of the bed.

7 May. To Tintagel.
Fogginess and High Cliffs.

The peacocks sleep all night and begin their infernal racket the same time as my more pleasant alarm music begins. We pack and walk up through a mist-shrouded, dewy garden to the main house for our prearranged breakfast.

In the Alfred Hitchcock dining room, a brass peacock sits on a large porcelain egg from which sprouts a scrawny cactus. A freakish doll, Chucky's girlfriend perhaps, sits on a chair and a china spotted leopard glowers in a corner. A hideous stuffed monkey reclines on another chair. Dusty antique curiosities clutter every flat surface. Our plentiful and delicious breakfast is served at a table squashed into too small a space. We use sterling silver cutlery to slice bacon and scoop eggs off fine china made in Bavaria.

Yesterday introduced us to the upping and downing nature of the trail. Today's leg from Crackington Haven to Tintagel is described in the guidebook as an arduous nineteen-kilometre walk, using phrases such as: *the highest point on the coast path in Cornwall and the highest sea cliff in the country*.

All morning, we climb up, around and down, but for the most part, we're enveloped in fog so get little sense of how high the cliffs are other than through the pain in our legs. The downing is harder than the upping. Leaning on my trekking poles, I listen to my knee cartilage grate and creak with each jarring downward step.

A couple of times, the fog lifts just enough for us to glimpse the ocean churning away at the foot of rugged bays and headlands. During a sunny interval, we eat lunch washed down with beer at an outdoor pub.

The afternoon doesn't give us an easy time. The cliffs weren't as high but there are still endless steep ascents and descents. The steps seem to have been designed for giants, not for short me. Even tall-legged Pat and Marianne grumble.

Despite the fog, the rugged scenery is compelling. At one point, we round a corner near a cliff edge and there in the fog loom two enormous shaggy-haired, long-horned goats. Their appearance is so sudden, and they are so close that we all jump. The animals bound off the edge, their hooves clattering stones as they disappear.

As the afternoon progresses, the fog dissipates, and by the time we walk into Tintagel, the sun shines and the sea sparkles. The village throngs with bus-tour tourists swarming in bright dresses, floppy sun hats and pretty sandals. Purses slung across unburdened shoulders, they chatter and shop. We ease in among them, try not to jostle people with our packs and reach for tomorrow's snacks from shop shelves burdened with all kinds of rock candy sticks and foil-wrapped King Arthur chocolates. Plastic Excaliburs, starred Merlin hats, Pendragon-adorned shields – all made in China – clutter the sidewalks.

I have been anticipating visiting the castle again, to feel the touch of ancient wisdom and remember myself as a four-year-old being enchanted by the magic of this place. Not today. Tourist trappings and paraphernalia have destroyed the charm of the grey-stoned village. The Arthurian legend has been cheapened to the point of parody.

"What's the matter?" asks Pat.

"I don't know why I thought Tintagel wouldn't have changed in sixty years, but I didn't expect this … crassness."

"It's pretty awful. You still want to walk out to the castle?"

"No. I'll cherish a fond memory instead."

It's four o'clock. Our hostel is close by, but my request for earlier check-in had been rebuffed – 5 PM means 5 PM.

Tucked between the shops selling junk souvenirs, tables sit outside busy tea shops where Cornish cream teas are served.

"You guys ever had a Cornish cream tea?" I ask.

Marianne and Pat shake their heads.

"Well, come on then. Here would be the place and we have an hour."

Supervising our packs and trekking poles, I lay claim to a little table and three chairs while Marianne and Pat go inside to order. They are soon back, reporting that three cream teas will be delivered to our table. We wait in hungry anticipation.

A waitress soon arrives with pots of tea, then returns a minute later with three dinner plates each heaped with two enormous, sugared scones, a large dish of thick yellow cream – which looks like creamed butter – and a small pot of jam. We set about devouring the rich sweetness. Marianne quits halfway through. I throw in the towel with half a scone remaining. Pat does us proud by finishing.

The fog rolls back in as we stagger to our feet and walk the last kilometre along the coast to YHA Tintagel. I turn back several times.

"What are you looking at?" asks Marianne.

"The castle – it's just there in the mist," I say, remembering that day when I was four and I heard the baby cry. Seagulls, Mum had told me, but I knew better.

8 May. To Pendoggett.
Windy Wetness.

Due to the enormous cream tea we'd gobbled so late in the day, I had been unable to eat dinner but have regained my appetite. We eat our self-catered breakfast in the hostel's cozy dining room, then don jackets and gaiters to set out into a cool, cloudy day.

Although the sky is overcast, the visibility is improved from yesterday, so we can see as far as the next headland. The sea, surging against the shore, is a grey blanket, the horizon indistinct. We hear the constant whoosh followed by the clatter of millions of pebbles being rushed to and fro.

The repeated climbing over headlands soon warms our bodies against the chill, and we remove jackets and gaiters. The ups and downs aren't as high as yesterday's, but there are many more of them and they are steeper. Several times, I feel moments of vertigo. It's not bad when I'm climbing, with the security of the slope rising to one side, but where the trail hugs the cliff edge, or the descent is exposed and precipitous, I fight the sensation of spinning into the abyss by following close on Pat's heels, focusing on her legs and moving mine in unison.

An artist's palette. Jagged slate headlands rise out of the sea to meet the gentle slopes of viridian, sheep-filled pastures. Yellow blooms of wind-bent gorse. Pink foxgloves towering above rock-hugging stonecrop and bobbing heads of sea-thrift. Clusters of white violets and sea campion. All glowing jewel-like in the cloud-dimmed light.

Past rock walls. Over stiles and tiny bridges. Through farm gates. Treacherous, muddy, shale-strewn descents and breath-taking ascents mark our passage.

We stop for lunch in the lee of a rock wall. I devour a delicious Cornish pastie, my third since leaving Bude. Some historians claim these culinary masterpieces originated in Devon as early as the 11th century, and they had become synonymous with a Cornish tin miner's lunch by the 16th century. Wives and mothers would wrap vegetables – often potatoes, but sometimes meat – within pastry pouches, perhaps marking the miner's initials in the top. Descending and ascending into and out of the mines took such a long time that the miners would spend their entire shift underground, so they carried their pasties with them into the mine shafts. I'm pleased to be eating my plump meat-filled pastie under the vast dome of the sky.

As we pack up drizzle begins. Backed by a stiff sea breeze, it soon increases to a driving rain. We pull flapping ponchos over ourselves and our packs but do not pause long enough to put our gaiters back on. Our ponchos fill with wind and snap like errant sails as we walk along the exposed cliff edges. I add fear of being blown away to my struggles with vertigo.

My boots – which we now call sponges because they leak so much – had dried while we were in Bude, and I've enjoyed a couple of dry-footed days. But before long I feel the familiar slosh of walking in puddled boots. We put our heads down and concentrate on walking without slipping in the mud or being blown off the cliffs until we meet the love-crossed sheep.

Having seen the lustful sheep scurry off into the fog, we creep down the last knee-grinding descent to drip into Port Isaac – home of Doc Martin – and discover a pub at the bottom. Without discussion, we enter and order beer. As we sip, the sun comes out, so we order more beer and dash to the picnic tables outside. No one else is there, so we commandeer four tables, three of which we festoon with wet ponchos, socks and jackets. Marianne and Pat's feet are damp, but I ring out my socks and pour a stream of water from the sponges. Then we sit with our feet up on the benches to steam in the sun. The fellows behind the bar are accommodating of having their pub take on the appearance of a laundry facility. Given the weather in this part of the world, they must be used to this sort of behaviour from walkers.

Feeling we've walked further than the posted fifteen kilometres, we agree with the guidebook's comments about this rugged section of trail: *one of the most challenging legs of the whole walk.*

Our accommodation at The Cornish Arms B&B in Pendoggett is five kilometres off the route because we were unable to find reasonably priced rooms in this popular tourist town. Disinclined to walk the additional distance, especially along a narrow road, we will take a taxi, but first spend the afternoon wandering around scenic Port Isaac.

While visiting one of the various Doc Martin locations, we watch a crew set up to film a sequence. I try to spot Martin Clunes – Doc Martin – but there's just a crowd of lighting and sound techs moving equipment from one place to another. Not into standing around to await potential filming, we leave them to the mysteries of setting up for a shoot.

The ubiquitous Cornish pasties make shopping for tomorrow's lunch easy, then a taxi whisks us inland to The Cornish Arms, an atmospheric 16th-century inn. We settle into a pleasant room with three adult-sized twin beds. The owner is a cyclist and understands the concept of an early breakfast. He promises it will be ready by seven o'clock and that he'll drive us back into Port Isaac in the morning. We enjoy an early dinner and are asleep before the sun sets.

9 May. To Padstow.
A Podium Performance.

Following my habit of studying the guidebook description while eating breakfast, I read: *If medals were ever to be given out for the toughest section ... then the initial three miles of this winding 12-mile stage would certainly stand somewhere on the podium.*

"That's nearly five klicks," Pat says. "We best get on with it."

Marianne's pack transfer service has been working well, so as usual, she leaves her pack at the reception desk with tonight's address on the tag, then joins us outside in the salt-filled air where our ride awaits to take us back to the trail in Port Isaac.

"Ready?" asks Pat, as we alight at the harbour, swing packs onto our shoulders and extend our trekking poles to walking length.

Nodding, we begin our day by climbing a gruelling set of stairs up out of the village. Once at the top, we enjoy stunning views then descend a precipitous path to the next bay. As we continue, we discover that in a couple of places, ropes have been secured to enable walkers to pull themselves up and lower themselves down nearly vertical parts of the path. In other areas, railings have been installed where the path hugs so close to the cliff edge that a false step could result in a disastrous tumble.

The sea is a lumpy menacing grey. Swells rush ashore with a crashing force that reverberates through the cliffs and vibrates under our feet. We eat our lunchtime Cornish pasties while watching enormous breakers dash themselves against the rocky beach of a narrow inlet. Gulls soar, cry, wheel and dive. Sea arches echo with the boom of swells smashing themselves into narrow openings and surging through with the churning fury of a beast attacking again and again, whittling away at the land and sucking it into its maw.

Signs warn walkers to stay away from eroded cliff edges that periodically collapse to leave raw wounds of exposed rock and soil. From time to time the original trail has fallen away, and new routes cut further into pastures. Some farmers are amenable. Others resent the increasing trespass on their private land. Sturdy fencing along the landward side of the trail ensures walkers keep to the path. In these areas, our world is reduced to a narrow strip between sea and fence.

After the initial five kilometres, the trail becomes easier, or maybe we are getting used to its capricious nature. The scenery continues to astound us with its sense of remote and wild beauty, yet we are never far from a village and the farmland reaches to the sea. The contrast between the pastures of cows and sheep and the stark cliffs plunging into the untamed ocean is striking.

The villages we pass through tend to be at the heads of long narrow bays where breakwaters have been built to protect fishing fleets. It always feels odd to come off the rugged path into these bustling harbour villages filled with car-driving, bus-riding tourists.

Today we meet more walkers than usual. Most are day-tripping between the road-accessed villages. The first few metres from any car park are the most crowded with sandal-shod folk who are walking for a few minutes to take in the view.

Some people are through-walking like we are, staying in accommodations and carrying light packs. A few, camping at the trail-side campsites, carry significant loads. A couple claim to be wild camping, although I find that difficult to imagine given the amount of restricted-access private land and the narrow rocky shoreline. I wonder how the wild campers are dealing with their personal waste and hope they are disposing of it in some environmentally sensible manner. We see just enough toilet paper along the trail to know that not every trail user has respect for the area or other walkers.

In writing this chapter, I reflect on Raynor Winn's *The Salt Path* in which she relates her experiences with her husband Moth. Just after being told that Moth had a terminal illness, they were forced from their home and while packing up, Winn found a Coastal Path guidebook. Solution. Disguising their homelessness and seeking healing for Moth, they became through-hikers and wild campers. Many of their experiences mirror our own, but while we grumble about late check-ins, they waited until near dark to put up their tent in secret places. While I munch my daily lunch pasties, Winn and Moth counted their pennies and ate noodles. Leaving no trace, they hid their homeless state, walking this path burdened with heavy packs and worry, death stalking Moth's every step.

The headlands lower and soon we see the expanse of Padstow Bay. It was near here that poet Laurence Binyon penned the famous lines:

> *They shall grow not old, as we that are left grow old:*
> *Age shall not weary them, nor the years condemn.*
> *At the going down of the sun and in the morning*
> *We will remember them.*

Although Binyon was referring to the young men dying during the first months of WWI, the poem brings Mike to mind. We used to joke that I'd never be as old as him, yet here I am, just as grey, and eleven years older than he was when he died. I walk in silence for a while, feeling his presence at my side. Looking across the grey water, I imagine him paddling his kayak through the waves. Salt encrusting his paddling jacket, he's laughing into the wind as his kayak surges forward, arrow-straight and out of sight.

The tide is low, so we walk along the firm yellow sand, then into the sand dunes to arrive at the passenger ferry ramp where we catch the little Black Tor Ferry to cross the Camel Estuary to Padstow. Having tramped nineteen kilometres, we join dog walkers, cyclists and other through-walkers clustered at the shoreline. The ferry arrives, drops its bow ramp and we board, each paying £2.00. This service saves a twenty-kilometre walk around the inlet to Padstow by the nearest bridge, and there has been a ferry operating across this stretch of water since 1337.

Our Symply Padstow B&B host has assured us that we will not be welcome until after four o'clock, so we dawdle through the busy town, stopping for our groceries and scouting out a nice place for dinner on our way up the hill and along a residential street of large well-appointed homes. Our B&B is one of these, and having arrived at the correct time, we are welcomed by a pleasant woman and shown to two spacious rooms from which we have fabulous views across the rooftops, the harbour and bay.

After an early dinner, in a restaurant rather than pub, we buy a bottle of wine and spend the rest of the evening sipping Chardonnay in the comfort of our B&B while watching rain squalls smear veils across the bay.

10 May. To Treyarnon.
Bliss.

We're wrapping two short sections into one day, the guidebook assuring us that between here and Trevone is: *an easy and enjoyable eight kilometres with cliff-top scenery at its best without the sharp ascents and descents characteristic of the path up to now*. It goes on to describe the next section from Trevone to Treyarnon as *mostly flat with a lovely spot of beach walking*.

Our standard practice is to stop every hour for a short rest, and today our first stop is at the Stepper Point Coast Watch building where we chat with the two volunteers. Their job is to keep an eye out for trouble on the water, to record the passage of hikers and to make weather reports. By the time we climb the slope to their door, our descriptions have been noted in the log. They now add that we are Canadians.

Atop the nearby headland, forlorn Stepper Point Daymark Tower comes into view. Dominating the clifftop, it provides a tangible marker for our journey. Built in 1830 as a daytime navigation aid to guide seafarers into Camel Estuary, the grey stone tower is visible for up to twenty-eight nautical miles – forty-eight kilometres – from offshore.

The sun shines and a sea breeze keeps the temperature perfect for walking. With no gruelling ups or downs, the trail undulates along the cliffs, sometimes near the edge, other times through stretches of wind-stunted gorse, through gates and over stiles. Rimming a blue ocean, crashing waves rush in to meet the black-sided, green-capped cliffs. Prolific wildflowers nod among swaying grasses. Seagulls soar in the thermal updrafts. A mouse-seeking hawk hangs motionless over a crevasse. Black-snouted lambs nudge their mums with hungry intensity.

In Trevone, Pat and Marianne decide to take the bus on to Treyarnon. Pat spent most of the winter recovering from a lower leg stress fracture, so she couldn't train for the endurance aspect of the walk as much as she'd wished. Without the stamina developed through a prolonged training period, fatigue catches up with her today. Not for the first time on this walk, I notice that she's rubbing her Achilles. Even without her pack, Marianne is finding the route a challenge so is happy to have Pat's company on the bus.

I continue alone. The trail is well marked, the weather amenable. Pat and Marianne will report my absence if I don't show up at our hostel.

A large dark triangular shape in the deep water off a small bay catches my attention. It seems to align and move in unison with an enormous indistinct shadow beneath the surface. It looks and moves like I imagine a shark fin should. Shivering in the warm sun, the theme music from Jaws playing in my mind, I reach for my camera as the mysterious shape and shadow sink out of sight.

A few minutes later, some people, equipped with binoculars and telephoto cameras, tell me we've seen a basking shark. One of the men has a marine biology field guide from which he reads that this is the world's second-largest shark, that it is plankton-eating and that it can grow to eight metres long. The naturalists hurry on, excited to catch another sighting. I continue onto a wide, soft sandy beach for the last few kilometres of my walk.

I stop to talk to the lifeguards on duty. We have seen them on previous beaches but haven't had an opportunity yet to find out about their work. These lifeguards tell me that this area is a surfer's paradise, but that many come without the knowledge of where the rips are and how dangerous some of the surf conditions can be. In the summer, it is not unusual for them to conduct up to ten rescues per day. Today there is just one boogie boarder getting tossed around, and due to his evident lack of ability, they were keeping a close eye on him.

"This beach is never safe, anywhere, at any time," one of the men tells me.

Despite unsafe water, the beach is an inviting change from the trail, but walking in soft sand is tiring work. By the time I climb up to the firm path again, I'm glad to see Treyarnon Bay Hostel in the distance. A few minutes later, I stagger into the hostel garden to find Pat and Marianne enjoying beer in the sun – and join them in that pursuit.

They've found an excellent local bus service that connects all the small hamlets, villages and towns along the coast. Good information to keep in mind.

YHA Treyarnon, the epitome of a perfect hostel, is on the path, on the beach, has a bar and serves food. We have a large room to ourselves with an ensuite bathroom. We want for nothing.

11 May. To Newquay.
Welcome to *Poldark* Country.
After an excellent breakfast, we set off under a low-hung sky into a cold wind whipping off the ocean.

"What's it like here in the winter?" I wonder.

"Miserable," suggests Pat.

"Just like this," Marianne figures.

The scenery continues stark and wild, although the cliffs are less lofty along this section of the coast. We walk past the earthworks of an Iron Age fort, lumpier than normal lumps in the gorse, attesting to the ramparts of a fortified settlement where a Celtic tribe lived in a wealthy, organized society of skilled craftsmen, sailors, soldiers, farmers, builders and metal workers. The people who built this hill fort forged iron for tools and weapons, and crafted copper, bronze and even gold for their household goods and jewellery. They mined and shipped tin to trade with people living across the channel. Their small villages consisted of thatched, round houses either near or within the protective fort ramparts.

In Porthcothan, we come to a tiny café/shop beside the beach. Owned by an enterprising young couple, it is doing a thriving business before nine. This is the first place we've come across in the past three weeks that has been open for coffee at such an early hour, so we stop for caffeine, treats and conversation.

Having enjoyed our coffee break, we continue into the wind, after a while coming to a spectacular area known as Bedruthan Steps. *Poldark* fans would recognize this as one of many locations used in filming the series. A dejected busload of tourists, bundled up against the wind, wanders around taking in this popular *Poldark* site. Many have walked down the long flight of steps to the beach far below. Some are struggling back up again. We do not follow suit as rain is threatening, and we've already walked up and down more than enough steps in the past few days.

As we approach Mawgan Porth – *porth* means beach in Cornish – chilling sideways rain begins. We pop into a pub, but as it is not yet eleven, just have tea. Watching the foul weather beating against the windows, Pat asks the barkeep about a bus to Newquay. None of us feels like suffering more Cornish wind-lashing and another Cornish soaking.

After a cold wait on a windy corner, we're rewarded with the bus coming into view and stopping to admit three dejected walkers.

"Little late today," says the driver. "Road's bad due to all the puddling."

We're soon ten kilometres further along the rain-drenched coast and scurry the couple of blocks to our Backpackers Hostel. This odd collection of rooms carved out of two houses has morphed into a popular surfers' hostel. What might have once been a large living room is now surfboard storage. Various instructions are posted in the showers about not letting sand go down the drains. Sandy people must shower in the surfer's shower room before entering the rest of the hostel.

Several surfers with dreadlocks, worn tie-dyed clothes and calloused bare feet wander around looking like they spend most of their time on their boards. We do not fit the demographic. However, young Patrick, our Australian host, makes us comfortable, taking us next door where we have a cheery top-floor room all to ourselves.

Toilets and showers for un-sandy people, such as we, are down a steep flight of stairs.

Between rain deluges, we dash to the local Red Lion for an excellent middle-of-the-afternoon meal. While we're eating, the sky darkens. The rain buckets even harder, bouncing off the pavement and roaring down the road gutters. Within minutes, the clouds dissipate and the sun shines from a clear blue sky.

We shop for wine, snacks and tomorrow's lunch, then retire to our penthouse for a relaxed feet-up, wine-sipping, snack-munching evening. Our drying gear hangs from every chair back and door, and we wonder why hostels always seem to lack enough coat hooks.

12 May. To Perranporth.
Surfer Heaven.

We've been promised breakfast at seven o'clock. Included in the hostel's overnight price of £15.00 each, this makes our stay here the least expensive so far. The decor is another bonus. The ceiling of the barrel-vaulted dining room is painted in a colourful underwater motif, enabling diners to imagine themselves catching an epic ride within a curling wave. With a friendly smile, morning host Alex serves our bread, marmalade and instant coffee to the table in two battered cardboard boxes. While we eat, he mops the floors around us and keeps up a steady stream of stories about his surf exploits all over the world.

"You're up earlier than most of our guests," he finishes. "What is it that you are doing?"

"Walking the Coast Path," Pat says.

"Walking?"

We nod.

"Pat surfs," I say, seeking common ground.

Looking at Pat, his eyes betray doubt.

"On the West Coast of Vancouver Island," says Pat.

"Tofino?" he asks, now interested.

Pat nods. Alex is suitably impressed.

As we leave Newquay, our first challenge is crossing the tidal flats at the mouth of the River Gannel. Our options are to take a seasonal ferry when the tide is high, use a boardwalk when the tide is low, or walk inland to use a bridge. We've planned our crossing for low tide, so march across the estuary on the boardwalk – known as Penpol Footbridge – as it emerges from the ebbing tide.

Once again, the sun shines and the sea breeze keeps temperatures pleasant. The headlands continue to be lower along this part of the coast than they were where we started out. As we walk up, around and down, we enjoy the views and wildflowers. We walk through several stretches of sand dunes and past numerous sandy beaches.

Most of the beaches are populated by surfers revelling in the rising, cresting, curling, crashing procession of waves. The roar is a constant accompaniment to the occasional cry of a gull and whoop of a surfer catching and riding the perfect wave.

Our path takes us past collapsed tin mine shafts with signs warning of the dangers of falling into holes. Along a fenced military area, more signs warn walkers not to proceed when red flags are flying – red flags denoting live-fire practice. In another spot, we see just one sign warning that the path is precarious due to erosion below. We pass several holiday parks filled with cheek-by-jowl caravans, surrounded by fencing and, of course, No Trespassing signs. I start singing:

> *Sign, sign*
> *Everywhere a sign*
> *Blockin' out the scenery*
> *Breakin' my mind*
> *Do this, don't do that*
> *Can't you read the sign?*

Les Emmerson of Five Man Electrical Band, "Signs," 1971

We stop at a posh café for cappuccinos and cake, then carry on a few more kilometres to a pub where we buy take-out pasties straight from the oven. We continue over a headland and down onto a glorious wide stretch of golden beach, an excellent picnic spot for the best pastie yet – spicy steak and onion.

Resting in the sun, we watch a rain shower out at sea and comment on the turning tide. I read in the guidebook about the cliff we will have to walk around – Cotty's Point – before the tide comes in.

We watch the waves and enjoy midday laziness until ever-vigilant Pat says, "We better get going if we're planning to get around that headland."

Sure enough, the water has crept much closer. Up we jump to scurry the rest of the way along the beach. The headland is about two kilometres away, its cliffs dropping vertically to the sand. We walk faster and watch the water getting closer. The lifeguards drive around, keeping an eye on the Saturday strollers and the coastal walkers.

We make it around Cotty's Point by running and hopping away from the wash of incoming waves. Once, we leap onto some rocks as deepening water curls across the sand. A minute later, and we'd have been climbing a long steep path to walk around the clifftop.

As it is, we're in a pub garden in Perranporth, boots off, sipping beer by early afternoon. When clouds begin piling up, we head off to buy groceries for tomorrow's lunch and dinner at our self-catering hostel, then have another beer at another pub – inside this time. Unable to dawdle any longer, we walk up the hill to our clifftop hostel. From there, looking back across the beach we'd walked along earlier, we watch droves of surfers riding waves that are now dashing themselves against the headland and surging into the beach-rimmed bay.

We aren't supposed to check in at YHA Perranporth until five o'clock, but as we arrive at four thirty, earnest rain starts. There's no porch or other shelter, so trying the doors, we find one is unlocked. We enter and settle in the lounge.

The assistant manager – who has been out surfing – arrives and is surprised to see us in residence. "How did you get in?"

"The side door," I tell her. "Figured you left it unlocked, knowing we'd be arriving before five."

"I told you to wait outside," she says.

"Seemed stupid to stand outside in the rain." I smile.

She shrugs and assigns us a four-bed bunk room. Later, the manager arrives. She, too, has been surfing.

I hear them muttering about old foreign ladies not following the rules, so step around the corner into view.

"What troubles you most?" I ask. "That we're old or that we didn't stand outside and get soaked."

They fidget in red-faced silence.

"How about I drop a line to YHA's head office with your concerns."

"No need," the manager says, now looking anxious.

"Every need," I assure her.

I send an email. The response is immediate and apologetic. The two young women are courteous – pleasant – for the rest of our stay. Cozy in the lounge, we watch the clouds blacken, and the surfers leave the bay as massive waves break with violent plumes of spray. After our picnic dinner of salads, hummus, veggies, crisps, biscuits and wine, we sleep soundly, lulled by the sound of the storm kicking up a fuss outside.

13 May. To Portreath.
More Sun and More Ups and Downs.

Our nineteen-kilometre walk is once again up and over and down a series of rock headlands intersected by isolated sandy bays. Again, we pass many old mine shafts and ruins of the tin mines that populated this area in the late 1800s. Periodic signs continue to warn people to stay on the path due to dangerous unmarked holes in the surrounding heath.

The warm sun encourages us to enjoy an afternoon snooze with the second half of our picnic lunch. We've started splitting our lunches between two or three stops to revive our bodies with the constant fuel they crave and to mitigate the overstuffed feeling of eating too big a meal. Lying on the grass beside the path, we listen to the surf crashing below. I watch birds and a small plane flying between two tiny white clouds. We've pulled our boots and socks off, securing the socks into the laces so they don't blow away. My sponges are once again dry. Dry-footed walking is now a cherished pleasure.

We meet many day walkers with their dogs today. Like at home, some bag their dog's poo and leave the bags in odd places. There are dog-poo-collection bins along the trails and near carparks, but we've seen weathered poo-filled bags sitting by the trail or hanging on fences and in trees. Today we see one placed in the centre of a picnic table, a seagull taking interest.

Despite poo bags and the long, ugly fence of another military area, the day and the coast offer enjoyable walking through glorious countryside, no rain showers or tides chasing us along. Tiny Portreath Arms Hotel welcomes us with friendly hospitality, offers two cozy rooms and provides an excellent dinner.

14 May. To Hayle.
Sleeping Seals and a Quest for Deeper Meaning.
Our walk starts with yet more upping and downing. This path is as tough – maybe tougher – than some treks I've undertaken in Nepal. Pat and Marianne agree that we've underestimated the ruggedness of this terrain. Despite warnings from friends, we'd expected a more refined trail.

Marianne relishes the scenery, and that's enough to provide all the satisfaction she needs from the route. But Pat and I have been discussing our ambivalence. This is the longest path in Britain, so shouldn't we feel our usual sense of excitement, inspiration and accomplishment? It brings us past Iron Age forts, 19th-century mines, sites of terrible shipwrecks, smugglers' coves, through quaint villages and stunning coastal scenery. So, what's missing?

Although not a historic route, as with almost everywhere in England, parts of the path have ties to an exciting past. Smuggling peaked in the 18th century. Barrels of French brandy and gin and bushels of tea and tobacco provided lucrative returns for smugglers sneaking their contraband goods into Cornwall's tiny hidden bays. Villagers who turned a blind eye or helped in the trade also earned some relief from grinding poverty.

A popular myth has it that some enterprising Cornishmen – tin miners and fishermen are given much credit – lit beacons on dangerous headlands to lure ships onto reefs to flounder, break up and spill their cargo into the sea to be washed ashore. The law held that salvage was only a right if all souls on board a wrecked ship were dead. Many hapless sailors who might have made it to shore alive were rumored to have been dispatched by mobs of desperate Cornish salvagers. In her book, *Cornish Wrecking, 1700 – 1860: Reality and Popular Myth*, Cathryn Pearce argues that there is no evidence of rampant deliberate wrecking. For centuries there were shipwrecks aplenty, and Cornish communities have salvaged cargo and flotsam. They also rescued survivors.

In response to smuggling and wrecking operations, the Preventive Water Guard was founded in 1809, followed by the Coast Guard in 1822. Seeking and trying to apprehend innovative Cornish smugglers and salvagers, Coast Guards patrolling between newly established lighthouses created sections of what is now the Cornish Coastal Path. As law enforcers and government men out to persecute the local heroes, they were distrusted, despised outsiders. How many generations does it take to change attitudes?

The Coast Guard patrols came to an end in the early 20th century, and their well-tramped route was incorporated into the Coastal Path, the last section created and opened in 1978 after much negotiation with landowners. Today this long-distance route ranks as one of the world's finest recreational walks. For those who complete it, boasting rights are well-earned. But path-side fences and No Trespassing signs remind walkers that we are unwelcome interlopers for at least some of the local population.

When we talk with a barkeep or fisherman or farmer, we understand that they could have a not-so-distant ancestor who was a hard-working tin miner or fisher and also a smuggler. That person would have distrusted strangers, especially those prowling around on the headlands, peering down into smugglers' coves and sticking their noses into village business.

Although unlikely to run afoul of smugglers, today's walkers face an ever-present danger. These cliffs are unstable and in a constant and active state of erosion. In 2011, a massive chunk of cliff along which the trail had led – before being re-routed just days before – broke away and plunged into the sea. With that near disaster in mind, walkers are confronted with black and yellow warning signs reminding us to beware of unstable cliffs. The signs don't say what to keep an eye out for, but subsidence or cracks in the ground come to mind.

As we walk past a tiny bay called Hell's Mouth because it lies beneath a 300-metre-high cliff, we also see signs asking people to please whisper, to not let their children shout or their dogs bark.

"Christ," I mutter. "That's pretty unstable if we can't make a noise."

"Doesn't make sense," says Pat. "Look, the path is paved here and there's a carpark."

"What are all those people doing looking down over that railing?" wonders Marianne.

"I guess they didn't get the 'mind the edge' memo," I add.

Curious, we tiptoe to the railing, and look over. At the bottom, two Atlantic grey seals bask in a patch of sun. We look at each other and shrug. Carrying on through crowds of whispering people, we come to the carpark where we pause to read a more detailed sign. All this church hush has nothing to do with cliff instability but is to ensure we didn't disturb the seals.

Three touring motorcycles rumble into the carpark, surely creating too much seal-disturbing racket, and I wonder about cliff-destabilizing vibrations running through the rock beneath our feet.

For a while the path holds level around a few more cliffs and bays until we come to the longest, widest beach I've ever seen. We climb down to the golden sands, remove our boots and wade knee-deep across a swift stream flowing towards the sea.

While enjoying our barefoot walk, we stop to watch a school group of ten- and eleven-year-olds have a surf lesson, then later we stop for lunch on a grassy dune. Noticing the beach narrowing with the incoming tide, we wipe the crumbs off our faces. With waves closing in, we dust sand from our feet, pull on our socks and boots and return to the path to walk the short distance into Hayle and our quaint The Mad Hatter B&B.

We're welcomed with a complimentary tea in an Alice in Wonderland-themed tea garden. While the tea includes treacle tarts, there are neither Mad Hatter visitations nor Dormouse tales. Our host shows us into a bright family room with three beds where Alice and her friends continue to hold sway in the patterned sheets and on most surfaces. Pat looks concerned. She's not one for clutter and whimsy.

15 May. To St Ives.
An Urban Interlude.
A cloudy day greets us, but there's no wind and it's warm and dry. In a more urban environment, we detour around the head of Hayle's estuary, which seems to take forever because sharing a paved road with cars for the first time in several days is unpleasant. Then we walk in and out of suburbs and along a railway track. In places, the trail is squeezed into a narrow strip of land between the track and the cliff edge. I hope no train comes roaring by.

The development and placement of this section of the trail seems to have met with even more than the usual resistance from local landowners. At one point, we creep along the edge of a subsiding bank just above the water level. There are signs warning that the path floods during high tide, but there is no inland option suggested by the guidebook, nor does our map offer one. In another area, the path detours through a fenced hotel property. The hotel is in the process of expanding its grounds with apparent disregard for the path's route. Even though our dress isn't as clean and refined as the guests, we stop for morning refreshments.

When we arrive in St Ives at noon, just nine and a half

kilometres after leaving Hayle, the receptionist at Cohort Hostel has no issues with checking us in. After we wash laundry, Marianne goes to visit a sculpture gallery while Pat and I head out on errands and then for a town lunch.

Across a busy street from a pharmacy, a gaggle of elderly tourists disgorges from a bus. They assemble themselves – clinging one to the other in a mass of large flailing handbags and walking sticks – blocking the sidewalk and spilling into the street. Other pedestrians and motorists take evasive action.

Pat and I watch, worried that if one gets nudged, they will all fall over. People do nudge them as they squeeze by. Pandemonium and wobbles ensue. Dodging between moving cars, we run across the road and dash into the pharmacy to update our dwindling supplies of ibuprofen. Horrors. Half the Wobbles follow us in. They fill the narrow aisles with their glacial and ponderous manoeuvring. Purchases made, we ease through the mob in retreat.

A pub next door offers sanctuary.

The young barkeep has been watching the scene outside and welcomes us to the pre-season madness of St Ives.

"Keep your elbows out and be glad you're not here when it's really busy," she says.

Fortified with lunch, we go in search of postcards and stamps – an easily accomplished task in this town – then find a table by the port to write the cards and people-watch while sipping wine. Across the street, a sign by the harbour warns diners to shield their food and to be aware of gulls. The bold birds hop between occupied tables and onto empty tables, squawking and scavenging. They seem uninterested in our wine.

St Ives is famous for its art galleries, so we pop in and out of a couple but see nothing that impresses.

"This place is a reputed centre for artists. Turner came here because he liked the light," I tell Pat.

"Well, they've got the good stuff well-hidden," she figures.

St. Ives – tourist mecca or purgatory? We're not sure what all the fuss is about.

I later discover – my editor told me – that when Emily Carr came to St Ives to study, her painting teacher wanted her to capture beach scenes, but she preferred the nearby woodlands. A sentiment I understand.

Back at the hostel, we meet up with Marianne and go back out to find another pub for dinner. Eating at pubs in the UK is different from most North American dining experiences. Here, upon arrival, we go up to the bar, pick up a menu, order and pay for our beer – or sometimes wine – find a table and sip while perusing the menu. Daily specials are sometimes printed in the menus, sometimes on boards above the bar. Some pubs offer table service for food ordering, but at most, we take note of our table number if there is one, then return to the bar to order the meal and perhaps another drink. The food is delivered to the table. When finished, we return to the bar, pay and leave. Tipping is optional and not expected. One advantage to this system is being able to check out all the beer and cider on tap, and taste test unknowns before choosing. I enjoy the friendly banter with the barkeeps who always offer interesting insights into the place we are visiting.

Tonight, Pat and I share a room with a bunk bed. Once again, it's my turn on top. Unlike the musty beds in the peacock chalet, these have been built to withstand hard adult use, and the bottom bunk has as much headroom as the top. I climb the ladder to my lofty bed where a shelf and outlet accommodate my iPad and a skookum railing ensures I won't tumble out should the hostel suddenly go to sea and experience rough weather.

16 May. To Zeenor.
Ancient Stone Circles, Port and Pretzels.

Young revellers making their way home from a night out on the town, parade past our window at two in the morning. Neither Pat nor I sleep well after the rousting. Marianne has enjoyed an undisturbed slumber because her room – more like a closet – has no window.

This is a self-catering hostel, so we haul our breakfast from the communal fridge. The sliced mango we bought yesterday is too unripe to be edible, and our individual pots of yoghurt don't match the caloric intake of the robust English fare we've become used to, so we shoulder our packs and head out. Hopes of finding an open café at this early hour are met with disappointment, but not surprise.

The sky broods today, a forbidding grey sea sends angry waves beating against the black cliffs and a mean-spirited wind breathes damp chill down our necks. The rock-tumbled bays exude an undercurrent of hostility.

We make good time for the first kilometre or so, but today's section is described in the guidebook as: *pretty hard going, ... the most stunning ... the toughest section of the whole path*. The book goes on to tell us to beware of mud, bog and great difficulty to be encountered climbing through boulders. When I'd related this to Pat and Marianne at breakfast, they'd scooped yoghurt and joined me with a sigh.

"Didn't we already have the toughest section a few days ago?" asked Marianne.

We are now confronted with some muddy trail, but nothing as muddy as we previously encountered. There are also boggy bits, but boardwalk has been built across the worst of them. In the bays, there are a couple of boulder beaches that need to be scrambled through, but these stretches are not long and the three of us have no trouble negotiating sure-footed passage. It all lends interest to the walk. There are, of course, the continuous uppings and downings, but they don't seem as difficult as those we confronted out of Bude and Crackington Haven.

While negotiating a longer – and challenging – section of huge boulders, we meet a couple coming in the opposite direction. The man passes first with nimble, long-legged leaps and the assurance of youth. About 300 metres behind him comes a struggling woman. She's inept at navigating through the boulders, trying to lean on her poles that skitter on the rounded smooth surfaces. She creeps and crouches, climbing up and down every boulder, flailing her poles from straps around her wrists, her smooth-soled shoes offering no purchase.

I smile at her. "Best collapse your poles," I suggest.

She looks at me.

"They aren't helping you. Use both hands to hold the rock."

She responds by flailing down into a narrow space between two boulders and assuring us that we have a long difficult way to go. "It's simply dreadful," she finishes, brushing at the seat of her butt-hugging designer pants.

Pat adds her suggestion to mine, that she put away her poles and steady herself with her hands.

"I don't like touching the rocks," she says, fluttering her manicured fingers.

"You might be better turning around," suggests Pat. "You're not wearing the best shoes for this path. It gets muddy, and there's lots more of these boulders."

The woman looks like she's going to cry. The man has disappeared.

Marianne arrives. "Your boyfriend's waiting for you just around the bend," she says.

"He's not my boyfriend for much longer," she huffs, as she fumbles with her poles and clambers up and over another boulder.

We wish her good luck and continue on our way, hoping that the evening news doesn't report a hapless woman with a clueless ex-boyfriend being rescued from the path.

The guidebook has indicated that we will pass an ancient stone circle today. As we draw near the spot marked on the map, we keep an eye out and make a short foray off the path to investigate a couple of potential stones. An archeologist might get "circle" out of the scene, but we just see a couple of age-worn stones.

A little further, we round a corner and there is the stone circle. Pat's guidebook reads: *a recently constructed ancient circle.*

"What does that mean?" asks Marianne.

There are numerous ancient sites around here, but this isn't one of them. To confirm our suspicions, we enter and stand within the circle. I sometimes get a buzz at an ancient site. No buzz. No time travel either. Further on we cross a stone slab bridge, but it, too, is new, so no trolls hide beneath.

Upon arrival in Zennor, we visit St Senara's Church to see a 600-year-old mermaid's chair. Legend has it that a mysterious woman sometimes attended services here and sat in this chair. The church warden's son fell in love with her, followed her home and they were never seen again. Sometime later, a mermaid is said to have asked the captain of a ship anchored in the nearby cove to move his ship's anchor as it was barring entry into her home. The villagers then realized that the mysterious visitor was none other than a mermaid and that the young lovers were living together beneath the sea. I find the marriage between mermaid myth and Christian ideology a fascinating blend and wonder if this is meant as a cautionary or a happy-ever-after tale.

The church visited and mermaid chair admired, we enjoy a late fish and chips lunch at the Tinners Arms. A sign tells us it has been a pub since 1271. Oh, what tales these walls could tell. We then walk another one and a half kilometres inland and check into the 250-year-old Tregeraint House B&B. Our host, Sue, offers to drive us back to the pub for dinner, but with the fish and chips so recently consumed, we settle in our room, sipping complimentary port and eating pretzels. Being cozy and safe from the potential of prowling mermen has much appeal.

17 May. To YHA Land's End.
The Industrial Revolution and Cornish Bogs.

The sun, a calm blue sea, and seemingly endless rocky headlands accompany today's walk. The scenery changes a little, gentle slopes now strewn with fantastical white or grey granite outcrops. Even though the sun provides a sense of friendly terrain, there are a few boggy bits to negotiate.

English bogs have figured in both fiction and history. Emily Brontë imbues the boglands surrounding Wuthering Heights with character as strong as Heathcliff and Cathy. Had Culloden Moor been less boggy, perhaps the tide of the Scottish rebellion would have changed.

The bogs we encounter today have been well visited by cows. Besides eating grass, cows wander around and poo. When they poo in bogs, they create stinky quagmires. Trail crews have done a great deal of work to arrange steppingstones through some of the mire, but there remains plenty of opportunity for a slip and plunge. We cross several sections of treacherous bog, our trekking poles sinking deep and deeper into bottomless slime.

Pat tests a grassy hillock. It feels like *terra firma* so she puts her weight on it. Down goes her foot into the muck. Although that is the only part of Pat that disappears, considerable leg, sock and boot clean-up is required before we carry on.

We enjoy a lunch break at the re-naturalized site of an old tin mine, then come up over a rise to encounter a startling wasteland. No heath. No meadows. Just rough rock, ruined chimneys and mine buildings. This is Geevor Tin Mine which only closed in 1990. In 1992 it was purchased by Cornwall County Council as a heritage museum.

As we pick our way through the desolate landscape of ruins, we realize that not so long ago, many other areas of this beautiful coast would have been industrial wastelands just like this. I contemplate the lives of tin miners and their families.

Life expectancy for tin miners was at best forty years. Their families would not have fared much better. Girls and women – known as *bal* maidens – laboured at the surface smashing large ore chunks into smaller pieces. Young boys worked with their sisters and mothers until they were twelve when they joined their older brothers and fathers underground. Low oxygen, intense heat, toxic dust, dangerous ladders, collapsing tunnels, and seawater drownings when pumps failed were constant dangers.

The discovery that copper and tin could be melted and blended to produce bronze marked the end of the Stone Age. Archaeologists have found evidence that tin has been extracted in this area since before 2000 BCE its use and export contributing significantly to Bronze

Age developments. At first, tin was extracted from alluvial deposits, then from shallow open-pit cuttings, but by the 16th century, it was being mined from underground shafts, some of which extended deep under the sea. Even as the Iron Age progressed, bronze remained a preferred metal for many non-weaponry purposes, thus tin mining continued as a profitable enterprise. Some historians postulate that it was tin that encouraged Rome to invade Britain.

Tin mining became so important to the mediaeval economy that in 1201, King John signed a Stannary Charter – the Latin word for tin being *stannum* – creating laws to protect miners' rights and activities. These laws pre-dated Britain's other legal codes. One Stannary law entitled a tin miner to search for tin on anyone's property, another exempted tin miners from taxation. When I consider the harsh conditions of a tin miner's life, I expect these laws were more about increasing the economic benefits of tin mining than about protecting the miners themselves.

Researcher and poet James Crowden captures the life and pride of Cornish tin miners:

> *Hard rock breeds hard men*
> *Who slip between earth's cracks for a living,*
> *The dark chasm which closes around you,*
> *Tight like a fist, draws you down*
> *Into the mine's gullet, the belly of the beast*
> *Hewn out of granite, the ledger of tin,*
> *The ingot of tradition, a labyrinth of strong voices*
> *That still chisel the dark, the rich seam,*
> *A stream that runs through each generation,*
> *A lode that anchors a man's life.*

James Crowden , The Wheal of Hope: South Crofty and Cornish Tin Mining, *2000*

The tin mines of Cornwall provided much of the tin required during the Industrial Revolution of the late 18th and early 19th centuries and, by extension, to the colonial expansion of the British Empire. For many years, the deepest mine in the world was Cornwall's Dolcoath tin mine, but by the mid-19th century, Cornish mining declined. In 1875 alone, 10,000 Cornish miners emigrated. Even so, the last working tin mine in Europe – South Crofty – didn't close until 1998. The *Poldark* TV series, of course, comes to mind as we tread through a land that once rang with the din of ore extraction.

I imagine a bone-weary family trudging along the path we now walk. They are returning to their small home after long hours of brutal labour. The woman stokes a fire and begins cooking a meagre meal. An older daughter digs a turnip or two from a small garden plot. The man repairs a leak in the roof, then slips out to the pub where he and his mates discuss the previous night's wrecking operation. Later, the children asleep, the man and woman will fall into bed beneath a thin blanket, holding each other against cold and despair. And under that bed hides a barrel of fine French brandy.

Seventeen kilometres after leaving Zennor Head, we trudge into YHA Land's End. We are, however, near to Cape Cornwall, not Land's End, and have no idea why the hostel has this confusing name.

We do know that we like our private room with ensuite, deep bathtub and ample hot water. The hostel sits on a hill commanding a view along a wooded valley to the shoreline. The setting sun shines golden across a wide green lawn on which we sit at one of the bright blue picnic benches to enjoy the welcome ambience.

As there is no nearby pub, we have arranged for full board, so the charming young man who checks us in changes into barkeep role and sells us wine and beer, then slips into his chef's garb to cook us wholesome bangers and mash with peas – not traditional mushy peas, thank goodness. While mushy peas are popular here, they are a dish we find unappealing. Apple pie and ice cream follow for dessert. And then it's time to leave our blue bench and climb into comfortable beds in a room with a view to the sea.

18 May. To Sennen.
Travesty and Revenge.

After a sound night's sleep and a filling breakfast, we receive our lunch bags and set off on an easy day. The trail rises and falls over rocky promontories, but none are high, and nothing is challenging except for a little clambering to negotiate a few rocky crags. Soon we're climbing down onto the sandy beach of Sennen Cove where we eat lunch and take advantage of the warm day by wading into the chilly ocean.

We've seen several military choppers patrolling just off the coast over the past couple of days. Each time there's been a low fly-by, we wave and smile at the soldiers sitting in the open side doors of the chopper. We are a distinct threesome, so if anyone's paying attention, they will realize we don't walk too far each day. We aren't sure if these patrols have to do with refugees crossing the Channel or if they are part of ramped-up security for Harry and Megan's upcoming wedding.

Leaving the coast, we cut inland to Sennen village where there is a church dating from 520 CE. Of more interest is the First and the Last Inn – built in 1620 – that was once a smugglers' hangout. A hole in the pub floor leads to underground passageways to the sea.

At our pleasant Sea View House B&B, we receive a warm welcome and have the entire upper floor to ourselves. With an afternoon of leisure ahead, we dump our packs, wash and hang our smalls, then step back into the sunshine. I have read about what a tacky tourist trap Land's End has become. Marianne is a keen sightseer and is hopeful that the place will live up to her expectations. With more realistic expectations, Pat heads to the smugglers' pub for a beer, commenting about resting her legs. I join Marianne to see what Land's End has to offer.

As advertised, extensive development scars the approach to the rugged point. The once-beautiful headland that marks England's most western point is now home to a plethora of gift shops, cafés, amusement venues, an imitation stone circle, miniature replicas of Cornish buildings, an expensive hotel and restaurant and a massive tour bus-filled carpark. The smell of popcorn and cotton candy fills the air. The sound of over-sugared grumpy children tearing around in a playground drowns the cry of gulls overhead. Bits of candy wrapper and cigarette butts litter the ground. Why couldn't the buildings have been placed further from the shoreline, leaving the cliffs to their once-natural glory? Why do people travelling to Land's End want to occupy themselves at an overpriced arcade? I've no answer to either mystery.

A trail leads past the "attractions" towards a rocky point of land beyond, but the mood is spoiled.

"Sorry, Marianne, this isn't for me," I say, turning my back on the travesty.

Later, we enjoy a delicious meal at the First and Last, look down the smugglers' hole – known as Annie's Well, and are regaled with a gruesome story of revenge. Back in the 1800s, a couple – Joseph and Annie George – managed the inn for Dionysius Williams. Joseph was William's smuggling agent, and he and Annie blackmailed Williams for free rent. When Williams put an end to the blackmailing by evicting the couple, Annie gave evidence against Williams in court, and he was sentenced to prison. Most of the village was involved in the smuggling operations, and Annie's evidence resulted in several more arrests and convictions. Angered, the villagers captured Annie and staked her out on the beach where she drowned in the incoming tide. Before burial in an unmarked grave, her body was laid out in one of the inn's bedrooms, and her ghost – Annie's Shadow – now haunts the room and the dreams of any who dare to sleep there.

19 May. To Treen.
A Chance Meeting and a Royal Wedding.

After passing the still-closed Land's End arcade, our footsteps soon return us to green pastures, rocky outcrops and cliffs kissed by an aquamarine, calm sea. No wind, no earthshaking waves, no steep ups or downs.

As we take our first morning break, a young woman comes

jogging along the trail. She stops to say hello, then carries on, springing up a slope with apparent ease, becoming a speck in the distance. We are walking again when she comes upon us a second time. She slows to walk with us, and we start chatting. Emily is a medical logistics army captain, currently posted to an instructor's position at a nearby base. So much common ground: Pat's experiences as a Médecins sans Frontières (MSF) outreach nurse, my days as a logistics army captain. We walk together with Emily for the rest of the morning and part ways after cappuccinos at a tiny café along the route.

We see another *Poldark* filming location today, and the nearby Coastal Watch capitalizes on the series' popularity with postcards and stories about the filming and hobnobbing with the actors. A display of photos provides interesting comparisons between today's scenes and the same spots in period dressing.

Since beginning this path, we've looked north and west over the Celtic Sea and the Atlantic Ocean, and the morning sun has warmed our backs. Today, the English Channel is to our south, and we walk with the morning sun in our faces. The vegetation has changed too, with more woodlands and larger trees.

Arriving in the tiny village of Treen in the early afternoon, we settle in at the local pub as our B&B host doesn't want to see us until four thirty. These late check-ins are inconvenient as we have limited options of where to wait around, and we don't have time to get smalls washed and dried during daylight hours.

Beginning to feel chilled in our sweaty clothes, we leave the pub, walk the one hundred metres to Treen House B&B and ring the bell three minutes early. No reply. Peering in a window, we see a woman sitting at a kitchen table. She looks at her watch. Perhaps she's resting after rushing around all day getting the room ready and shopping for tomorrow's breakfast. She might really need this moment of peace. We look at our watches and wait. She opens the door at four thirty.

"Check-in is at four thirty," she greets us, then adds, "You may leave your boots outside the door if you like."

"No, thank you," says Pat, as we unlace our boots that we'll carry upstairs.

"Did you allow my pack in early?" asks Marianne.

"It's in your room," she says, then adds, "What time would you like breakfast?"

"At seven," I say.

"Eight thirty is better," she counters.

"That's too late," I say. "We'll eat at seven and be out of your hair bright and early."

"How about seven thirty?"

We agree, and she brings tea up to our room. Peace.

Harry and Megan tied the knot today. When we return to the pub for dinner, the TV is on, the barkeeps and patrons glued to the exciting news. That is the only item being aired on this channel. Wars? Famines? Diseases? Refugees? Today these things are of no consequence. The Brits do love their Royal family. So, a privileged young couple got married? Pat suggests that had they taken the money spent on their wedding and contributed it towards stamping out a disease like malaria, there would soon be no more malaria. Not wanting to rain on anyone's happy nuptials, we shelve our comments and join in the watching, but the continued media babbling and analysis is worse than reality TV. Ahh, but this is reality TV.

20 May. To Penzance.
What Does the Place Make of Us?

As we enter the breakfast room, our host hurries into the house. She's struggling with a bag of groceries.

"So sorry. I slept late," she says.

"You don't live here?" I ask.

"No. The owner is away and I'm running it for her. Just give me a moment and I'll get breakfast on for you."

We make a quick decision to forego the usual cooked breakfast. Getting on the trail at a reasonable time is more important.

"No need to cook for us," says Pat. "We're happy with something quick."

It takes a bit of convincing, but we settle on fruit, cereal and yoghurt. Out the door not much later than we'd hoped, we leave the bemused woman to figure out what to do with the extra eggs and bacon now on inventory.

Long stretches of today's trail are overgrown with stinging nettles and brambles. Our bare legs burn with stings and bleed with gouges. Bits of grass fall into our boots, and brambles catch at our clothes. Other areas offer mud pits. Some spots are so steep that we need to scramble up and over and through rocky headlands. At one point, we balance and hop from boulder to boulder along the shore.

At the tiny cove of Penberth, we hike down to the hamlet where a small fishing boat is being hauled up onto the shore. The winch man and the fisherman are a friendly pair who answer our questions and explain the modern and ancient workings of the winches used to haul the boats – called Coves – up out of the sea.

Leaving the men to their work, I adjust my pack's waist band. I'm carrying an extra half litre of water because one litre hasn't been quite enough on these warm days. Today's Cornish pastie is also enormous. I momentarily envy Marianne her lighter day pack, then think better. I'm not day-hiking. I'm through-walking. We are, however, all becoming quite tired.

Barefoot during one of our rests, our socks drying in the sun, we lie back in the bracken, and listen to bees murmuring around us. I consider Robert Macfarlane's *The Old Ways – A Journey on Foot*. He doesn't mention this path. He does, however, contend that: *people understand themselves using landscape and that we are adept ... at saying what we make of places – but we are far less good at saying what places make of us.*

What does the Coastal Path make of we three? I sense its lack of interest, perhaps even a simmering hostility, as it teeters between land and sea. It feels my feet pounding against it, but there is no deeper connection. The path and I have not established a relationship. It remains separate from me. I am at odds with it.

In *Wanderlust – A History of Walking*, Rebecca Solnit writes: *Walking has created paths, ... senses of place, ... a vast library of walking stories and poems ...* She continues: *Walking, ideally, is a state in which the mind, the body, and the world are aligned, as though they were characters finally in conversation together, three notes suddenly making a chord.* Solnit discusses a symbiosis between the rhythms of walking and of thinking.

This is a symbiosis I am usually aware of, and it has become an essential aspect to my walking journeys. But here my stride and thoughts do not fall into a comfortable rhythm. My brain is too occupied with minding my steps and with keen awareness that, as a tourist, I am, at times, unwelcome.

In 2021, when I read *The Salt Path* by British writer Raynor Winn, I note her several references to being unwelcomed as she and her husband Moth walked this path. In one scene, Raynor has just been pushed by an angry dog: *The woman with the white dog prodded me with her foot.* In another passage Raynor writes about a person telling them: *You can't pitch a tent without paying first – can't you read the signs?* Many times, this English couple was met with lack of tolerance and overt unkindness. With more funds available, we have not been as vulnerable as the Winns, but we too have experienced unkindness from folks in the Cornish hospitality industry.

As I give the Coastal Path more thought, I realize that other than *The Salt Path*, I have found no literary references to the route as an entity. While the area is rich in stories – Winston Graham's *Poldark* and Jamaica Inn by Daphne du Maurier come to mind – there's a dearth of storytelling involving the path itself. Perhaps when the path matures to the point of fabled status, it will fulfil a destiny, gain a soul, and become a place where people tramp in the company of others who have come to understand its landscape through the soles of their boots. But for now, it exhibits the arrogance and impatience of an over-indulged youth.

We pull on dried socks and aired boots, then get to our feet to set off into another patch of stinging nettles. According to the guidebook, by the time we reach the postcard-perfect village of Mousehole – pronounced Maw-zul, we've only walked seven kilometres. According to our legs, the distance has been twice that.

"I don't think they measure the ups and downs as part of the distance," says Pat.

While eating lunch, we decide we've had enough. The guidebook informs us that the last six kilometres into Penzance are all on tarmac road.

"No ups and downs," I say.

"Not doing cars and road," says Pat.

"Me neither," from Marianne.

We check for local buses. One will be along in a few minutes. It comes. On we hop. The driver drops us on the corner of the road near our hostel and right outside a pub. The passengers wave as they drive away. They are used to Coastal Path walkers avoiding the road by riding their bus into town.

As we relax in the pub because we can't check in at YHA Penzance until five, we review the guidebook and discuss our route for the next three days. None of us has much enthusiasm to continue, so a new plan – that doesn't involve three days of walking – hatches over a second beer. We stay at the pub for an early dinner, then walk a further kilometre to our hostel where we kick off our boots and attend to our usual evening activities of washing clothes and selves and putting our feet up. Tired, and disenchanted with the nature of this route, we're in bed even earlier than usual.

21 May. To Marazion.
St Michael's Mount.

After breakfast, Marianne and I walk into town to pick up a few supplies. I'd left my English plug adapter behind in Treen. The thing is so massive, I'm not sure how I managed to leave it in the wall socket without noticing, but Penzance hosts enough foreign tourists to have electronics shops that might carry North America-to-UK adaptors.

The first store I enter has them – bulky and heavy, but what I need. Next door at Boots – a major English pharmacy chain – Marianne picks up more ibuprofen. We then set off along an uninspiring shore-side path towards Marazion. Pat is taking a break from walking in the hope that a day off will ease the considerable pain that has been developing in her Achilles.

Our walk begins between the railway track and the harbour, but eventually it leads us down to the beach. We stop at a café where the young man who owns the enterprise serves coffees and teas in an eclectic mix of china cups that had belonged to his grandmother. He also rents surf boards and invites people to partake in yoga and gymnastics. Marianne and I sit at one of his little tables along the sea wall and enjoy an excellent view of St Michael's Mount as I sip a coffee and she a tea, our pinky fingers extended in the Victorian manner encouraged by the delicate cup handles.

Six kilometres after leaving Penzance we're at our hotel in Marazion. It's just after eleven, and we're hours too early to check in. Leaving our packs with the receptionist, we head over to St Michael's Mount by one of the little passenger ferries. A rich cream tea – much better than the one at Tintagel – serves as lunch, but again, I don't get through it all.

After exploring the Mount's church, castle and gardens, we kick back on a sunny grassy meadow to watch the tide fall and the causeway emerge above the water line. St Michael's Mount has an interesting and long history. As a tidal island, it has always been a good defensive and trade position. In the 1st century BCE, Cornish tin was exported from here for onward shipping to the Mediterranean. From the 12th century, it was a Priory until Henry VIII's dissolution of the monasteries in 1548. Over time, the priory had been fortified. It was a Royalist stronghold until surrender to Cromwell in 1645 after a lengthy siege during the Civil War. It is now inhabited by the St Aubyn family and is open for public exploration.

We walk back to Marazion across the now dry causeway and find Pat has arrived with positive news. Before catching the bus from Penzance, she noticed a Chinese medical clinic. Acupuncture being one of the treatments advertised, she went in. She's been well stuck with needles, had some other mysterious treatment and will return tomorrow for another session.

"I'm hopeful that this and a couple of rest days will see me able to continue on the Ridgway," she says.

22 May. To Porthleven.
And That's a Wrap.

Marianne and I walk out of Marazion under a cloudy sky and into a cold wind. Pat, meanwhile, catches the bus back to Penzance for her appointment with the Chinese medicine woman.

We haven't walked far when the sun appears, the wind dies and the day warms. Off comes a layer of clothes. Today's walk offers all the best of coastal walking. There are ups and downs but none too strenuous. There are cliff edge paths but none too close to the edge. There are no boggy bits and no crazy boulder fields. It's a gentle walk around coves, past wildflowers, over headlands.

We watch a family embarking on a coasteering expedition. We'd never heard of coasteering until a couple of days ago but have learned that it is a combination of climbing, scrambling, swimming and caving along a coast. The participants have donned wetsuits, life jackets, helmets, booties and gloves and are clambering and swimming around a cliff. This is a gentle day with no smashing waves, but we've seen some video of a wilder version of the sport.

Later, we watch skilled climbers scaling a cliff that rises above the ocean lapping at its foot. This is another popular sport in the area, and we've seen many climbers lugging their gear to and from climbing locations.

Arriving in our room at the Harbour Inn, we find Pat and a bottle of celebratory wine. While sipping, we check bus and train schedules for our onward journey, then go downstairs to enjoy our last Coastal dinner. Our time here is over.

Upping and Downing on the Cornish Coastal Path

With every climb, there was anticipation for a breathtaking view from the top – the bay below, the headlands beyond – and always the pounding sea.

Chapter Five

Revisiting the Ridgeway

... to understand many of the sacred landscapes of Neolithic Britain we need first to understand the importance of the ancient paths that both link and bypass them.

Robert Macfarlane , The Old Ways – A Journey on Foot, *2012*

The Ridgeway's enchantment is most evident in the magic of nature's seasonal tapestry. In spring, chartreuse leaves of the hawthorn unfurl, followed by prolific white blossoms. Queen Anne's lace blooms and rain shadows sweep across the Vale, driven by breezes blowing showers of white petals across the white chalk path.

26 May 2018.
In the Vale of the White Horse, Wiltshire and Oxfordshire.
Near the Neolithic burial mound known as Wayland's Smithy, the air thrums. Listen. Open your mind.

We are the ancients, still inhabiting this place where time is nonlinear. Migrating along this chalk ridge as northern icesheets receded and the climate warmed, we were the first humans to live here, fabricating our flint tools and hunting the mammoth. Over the millennia, now referred to as the Stone Age, we built our great stone circles and long barrow burial chambers. In time we began melting tin and copper, pouring them together to create the bronze we used for our tools and weapons. It was during this time – now known as the Bronze Age – that we carved the White Horse and further developed our great henges. Once we learned to smelt iron ore, our forges rang with the sound of smiths pounding and shaping better weapons and tools. We built the hill forts to protect ourselves from well-armed foe and made ploughs that furrowed deep into the soil.

"Kim, you think you walk alone, but as your mind fills with memories of skipping along this track years ago, you see your child self on the path ahead, face turned up to your mother's. Smiling, you relive your first awareness of us.

"Your mother takes your hand. 'Do you feel it?' she says.

"Child You nods, joyous in your shared recognition of the magic. 'What is it?' you ask of a deep hum vibrating into your being.

"She points towards our burial chamber. 'It's the ancients.'

"Child You looks. Adult You looks too. Ah – you sense us again, don't you? We feel you opening your mind once more to our possibility. You know us. You are of us and again your footsteps fall where ours once trod. Our existence thrums through your being with each beat of your heart.

"You see the signs of our labours, our life, our beliefs all around you. You hear the clamour of our battles and the laughter of our children. You smell wood smoke from our village fires and see shadows of our ceremonies.

"This is where you and we recognize our innate knowledge of each other. This is where our shared humanity is the connection that binds us. Here, you understand that you are both finite and infinite.

"As your adult stride takes you past Child You and Young Mother, you rejoice in ancestorial echoes while looking forward to what is to come. Still aching for Mike and missing your mother, you treasure life and are finding your way as we have found ours – our quests never ending."

23 May. To Avebury, Wiltshire.

Leaving the Cornish Coastal Path, we depart Porthleven on the 8 AM bus, then take another bus, a train, another train, a third train and then third bus to arrive in Avebury by four thirty, feeling as tired as we are after trudging up and down cliffs all day.

For £195.00 per night, we stay at Avebury Lodge. Pat, Marianne and I had shared the task of finding accommodations before leaving home. Avebury was on Marianne's list. Explaining our need for three beds, she had asked the host about the dimensions of the advertised king-size bed – English king beds being several centimetres narrower than their North American counterparts. The host had assured Marianne that the bed met North American standards and was ample for two of us to share. Upon arrival, we are confronted with an ancient queen bed occupying most of the space in a small room.

Our unrepentant host agrees to place two mats on the floor instead of the one already negotiated. Knowing she has a captive audience, she refuses to apply a discount and assures us that she is most displeased about our refusal to cuddle together in her lumpy old bed.

The thatched-roof Red Lion next door has been a pub since the

1600s, and it offers up great beer and good pub grub. After dinner, Marianne goes out to stroll among the stones with the last of the tourists and the setting sun. Pat and I indulge in a second glass of wine in preparation for our night on the floor.

24 May. In Avebury.
We spend a cool, rainy day wandering through the world's largest stone circle – henge. Built over time by Neolithic people between 2850 to 2200 BCE, the henge grew to include one hundred megalith stones. Having been left alone by the Romans, they also survived numerous English wars. Then in the 12th and 13th centuries, several of the stones were buried in pits. Some historians postulate the Christians were hiding evidence of pre-Christian belief systems. But, as the stones were buried, not destroyed, it's also feasible that they were being hidden to protect them from damage.

Even so, over the centuries, local people smashed many of the unburied stones to build houses and barns. The entire henge may have been destroyed, but in the 1720s, antiquarian William Stukeley realized the henge had historic significance and that the remaining twenty-seven stones should be preserved. As with other Neolithic henges – such as the newer and smaller Stonehenge, thirty kilometres to the south – that significance remains a mystery.

In the early 1900s, archaeologist Alexander Keillor took interest in the henge. To assure its preservation, he bought some of the henge land in Avebury, began excavations and had some of the stones re-erected. In 1943, he sold the land to the National Trust.

Continuing Keillor's work, today's archaeologists are now sure Neolithic people did not live within the henge. It would have been an important gathering place, perhaps for trade, worship, or other ceremonies. There is certainty that the henge was not built for defence but was designed to impress with controlled entry and exit points. The ancient builders were intelligent, organized, wealthy, creative and interested in the metaphysical.

During the Middle Ages, the village of Avebury grew around and within the circle. With the village came a road that was once the domain of foot traffic and animal-drawn carts. Today, high-speed drivers with apparent disregard for inhabitants, visitors and the ancient henge itself threaten the safety of pedestrians trying to cross that road where it bisects both village and henge.

Once safe within the wide grassy areas surrounding the stones, sheep and tourists are free to wander at will. Unlike at Stonehenge, where the stones now stand behind a fence, here, people may still touch and lean against them, while pondering their mystery. Today, there are few other tourists, so we enjoy peaceful contemplation. Pat and I test a theory popularized by Diana Gabaldon's *Outlander* series that perhaps we can pass through a stone into another time. Marianne stands by to record the event; however, as we have no precious gems with us, our attempt at time travel is thwarted.

Avebury is also home to a manor house, the modern addition having been built by the Tudors in the 1500s. The house is open to the public, and the BBC has decorated the rooms in keeping with the furnishings of various owners from the 1500s to the early 1930s. Visitors are invited to sit on the chairs, read the books, touch the bedding, clothing and kitchen implements. In each room, a knowledgeable person chats with us about the house and items of interest. After exploring an extensive walled kitchen garden in full operation as well as the ornamental gardens and an orchard, we enjoy a traditional Victorian lunch and tea served on delicate period china in the library.

Later, sitting on my mat on the floor, I accept that Marianne and I will walk the Ridgeway without Pat because her heel is not recovered enough for her to continue. Sitting on her mat, Pat seeks accommodation. She tries Chester, from where one of her ancestors immigrated to Canada, but this being a long weekend, nothing is available. Neither is there anything affordable in Oxford, Wells, or even in Edinburgh. Reading seems to be the only town in the UK with room availability.

"Where's Reading?" asks Marianne from her lofty position on the lumpy bed.

On a direct trainline from Swindon and in the same general

direction as we are headed, Reading is a viable place for Pat to rest and wait until we reconvene at Princes Risborough for our last night before flying home to Canada. She is disappointed to be missing this walk. Like me, Pat has a passion for walking historic routes, and the Ridgeway is one of the world's oldest surviving footways.

25 May. To Ogbourne St George.

As Marianne and I set off into a drizzly morning, my legs find their stride and my spirit lifts to a familiar state of quiet euphoria. I am at home on this path.

Since the end of the last ice age, the Ridgeway has supported human migrations, trading, herding, invasions and settlements. History oozing from the chalk under our feet, we walk where our Stone, Bronze and Iron Age ancestors once trod. Tramping and riding along this elevated ridge, safe from swamps, with a clear line of sight, their passage is scored into a wide white path in the chalk.

The route leads us through the atmospheric remains of Iron Age Barbary Castle. When the Romans came, they occupied the fort as either a settlement or military garrison. The Britons were defeated here by the invading Saxons in 556 CE. Anti-aircraft guns were installed on these ramparts during WWII. Archaeologists have found layer upon layer of artifacts, including traces of Iron Age round houses, within the ring of defensive earthworks.

Past inhabitants left behind many traces of their passage, now curated and treasured in museums. Today, we ramblers mostly drop traces of our visits in periodic litter bins. A string of orange peel offends. I scoop it up, carry it to the next carpark, add it to the crisp wrappers and pop tins bursting from the top of a bin, and wonder what future inhabitants of the planet will think about the people of this time.

Offering wide vistas of open farmland interspersed with copses and white blooming hawthorn trees, the broad path follows an undulating, sweeping ridge across the downs. Downs – from the Old English word *dūn* meaning hill. The countryside rolls away into a purple distance, the fields glow green with new growth or yellow under the bloom of rape – Canadian canola – blossom.

Drizzle continuing, we see few other walkers, the easy kilometres melt under our boots and we're in Ogbourne St George just after lunch. The pub is closed. We are two hours earlier than I'd anticipated, but there is no place to shelter.

Early arrivals at B&Bs often cause scowls or unopened doors. Here, the door is opened with a warm welcome and gentle chastising. After we apologize that we found the local pub closed and for not sitting outside in the rain, our host offers tea.

"The pub opens at four o'clock on weekdays," she says, as she sets the steaming pot and two cups on a table. "That's posted on my website," she adds, implying that we should have planned accordingly.

Gracious, she allows us to spend the afternoon reading and sipping tea in her bright conservatory. Our room is spacious, the bathtub is deep, the water hot, the two beds are as advertised, and we are "only" paying £120.00.

The pub, when it opens, offers warm hospitality and good fare.

26 May. To Court Hill Centre, Oxfordshire.

Our host provides a wholesome breakfast and generous picnic lunch, then sends us on our way four hours earlier than required check-out time. I wonder if an early departure excuses yesterday's early arrival.

"I'm done with B&Bs," I say to Marianne.

"Why? That place was lovely," she counters.

"It was. But B&Bs aren't suitable when travellers show up before check-in time. I respect that hosts desire down time. But they charge too much to be so inflexible."

"Well, the hostels are just as rigid. Worse," Marianne protests.

"They are. But much less expensive. Even so, inns are the best value. Flexible. Friendly. I like the ambience. They'll be my first choice *if* I visit the UK again."

"If? You love it here."

"Agreed. But accommodation is priced beyond my budget," I insist.

We walk on, each absorbed in our own thoughts.

The day starts cool and misty, but the sun burns through, and we strip down to our short sleeves to walk under a blue sky.

Wayland's Smithy, where the ancients still hold sway.

White Queen Anne's Lace, white blossoming hawthorn trees and a white chalk pathway contrast with the greens of new spring growth. Captivated by the beauty, we pause again and again to take pictures, but Marianne's pauses are longer than mine and I continue, invisible fingers pulling me forward, a familiar vibrating hum filling my being. Mum used to tell me that the veil between past and present is thin in these parts. As I approach Wayland's Smithy, a Neolithic long barrow, I see a child walking with a woman on the path ahead.

"Do you feel it?" I hear the woman ask. I know she's my mother.

The child – who is me – nods. I remember the joy of knowing Mum also recognized the magic.

"What is it?" Child Me asks of the deep humming.

"It's the ancients," Mum says, pointing towards the long barrow. Child Me looks. Adult Me looks too, and I sense the ancients swirling around me. I know them, as again my footsteps fall where theirs once trod. Their existence thrums through my body with each heartbeat, and I recognize our innate knowledge of each other. This is where our shared humanity is the connection that binds us. Here, I understand that I am both finite and infinite.

As my swift stride takes me past Child Me and Young Mum – they do not see me pass – I rejoice in ancestral echoes and look forward to what is to come. Still aching for Mike and missing Mum, I embrace life while finding my way – always questing.

As I continue along the white path, bordered on both sides by burgeoning spring flowers, the breeze loosens hawthorn blossoms to fall like confetti all around me. Soon, I approach Uffington Castle where I climb the earthworks and sit for a few moments. Overhead a red kite stills its wings and glides on a thermal. Small white clouds scud across the sky, their shadows chasing each over the vale below.

Leaving the castle and taking a short detour from the Ridgeway path, I walk over to the top of White Horse hill. The view of the horse is poor from where I now stand near one of its ears. Etched into the escarpment, the 110-metre-long stylized horse is best seen from a distance or from the air. Created sometime between 1380 and 550 BCE by deep trenches cut into the ground, then filled with pounded chalk, the horse needs regular upkeep to keep the chalk white and the grass from covering it over. Every seven years, volunteers come to do the work, celebrating their labours with a festival. No one knows for certain the purpose of this glorious artistic expression, but the enigmatic animal is the oldest such horse in Britain.

When I was a child, we camped near here, and I woke in the night to the sound of the horse galloping on the downs above our campsite. The thunder of hoof beats still reverberates through this magical and ancient land, and I am aware again of a thrumming underpinned by whispered voices reverberating across time.

From the ear of the White Horse, I look down to the flat round top of Dragon Hill. Legend suggests that St George may have encountered a dragon here. I used to imagine the dragon and the horse uniting to send St George packing and remember Mum agreeing that this was a fine idea to add to local lore.

Three hours later, Marianne has rejoined me as we arrive at Court Hill Centre Hostel. Here we enjoy beer in the garden. When we report to the dining room at the appointed time, the avid historian who runs the place and cooks the set meals entertains us with anecdotes about King Alfred the Great.

"He only became king because all his older brothers died," he tells us. "They and his father spent years fighting and mostly losing to the Vikings. Of course, you know the Vikings had a winter camp near here in Reading. They were all around these parts."

I hadn't known, but nod.

"Alfred fought the Vikings too," he says. "But he was a statesman so made several truces with them. That reduced the number of battles. He was a learnèd man, initiated social reforms and had Latin books translated into Old English. As a child, he went to Rome – twice. Imagine that."

Leaving us to consider the rigors of Alfred's childhood journeys to Rome, our historian disappears into the kitchen, and we hear the sound of chopping then a sizzle of frying. Back at our table to deliver our meal, he leaves Alfred and jumps forward a few centuries.

"You know Tolkien and Lewis lived nearby in Oxford?"

We nod.

"They came here many times. You'll recognize features of Wayland's Smithy in both authors' books."

I have never considered this, but now conjure the lion Aslan at the stone table in Narnia. Maybe. Tolkien's Middle Earth could have been inspired by the burial site, but our historian cook has returned to the kitchen, so I don't have an opportunity to quiz him.

While we eat, Marianne and I recall the day on the Coastal Path when we took eight hours to cover seventeen kilometres. Today, we walked over thirty-three in less than eight.

"How is that possible? asks Marianne.

I propose an answer. "This is an ancient route – wise and mature – developed over millennia to enable swift, safe travel from one place to another. The Coastal Path – frivolous and youthful – a scenic route, no question – has no regard for the practicalities of efficient travel. The Ridgeway has served many functions – for drovers, traders, armies. People with herds, carts, armies, horses. Places to go. Things to do. Not so the Coastal Path."

"I liked the Coastal Path," says Marianne.

I shrug. "The Coastal Path, like a glamorous young person, does cause heads to turn in awe as each hilltop and cliff offers a dramatic view. The Ridgeway, on the other hand, presents the refined enchantment of someone who has weathered a long life with grace, seducing the walker into gentle discovery of her subtle beauty. It's the mysteries of the Ridgeway that captivate me."

27 May. To Streatley-on-Thames, Berkshire.

With just twenty kilometres to walk, we take our time as the hostel in Streatley doesn't receive guests until five o'clock.

Passing a monument honouring Baron Wantage who served in the Crimean War and was a founding member of the British Red Cross, I am disturbed that his cross-topped memorial is set on a Bronze Age burial mound. Wantage deserves his memorial, but I'm sure he wouldn't appreciate it denigrating an ancient site.

A mountain bike event with 700 registrants is taking place along our route, and at one of the checkpoints, we're offered slices of delicious homemade banana bread. The wide trail provides ample room for both walkers and hurried peddlers. Many cheerful good mornings are called as cyclists race by.

One cyclist pauses and talks to us during the first hour of our walk. Later he shows up again while I'm walking alone. Starting up our conversation again, he asks if I'm a rich American widow.

"Not American, nor rich, but yes, I'm a widow."

"Oh, too bad. I'm looking for a good looking, active, rich American widow to marry," he says.

Never have I been so pleased to not quite fit the bill. "Better luck next time," I call out as he cycles away.

Later in the day, Marianne catches up as I pause with an unhappy trio of cyclists. One is injured. Bringing my ski patrol experience into play, I discover he has a fractured arm. The cyclists don't know their exact location so can't tell medical assistance where to come. Pocket Earth comes to the rescue, and I'm able to give the attending race doctor an accurate location. Assuring the patient and his friends, that help is just minutes away, we continue our journey.

Upon arrival at the hostel, happy to relax in the sun at a picnic table in the front garden until five o'clock rolls around, we don't bother trying the door.

This hostel doesn't serve meals but a nearby pub – The Bull – is recommended and we are soon enjoying another meal washed down with the inevitable beer.

28 May. To Watlington, Oxfordshire.

As we leave Streatley in a thick mist to follow the River Thames, *Wind in the Willows* comes to mind. I find myself looking for Mole and his riverbank friends messing about in boats. Across a meadow of long damp grass, between high fences and hedges, through a quiet residential area with immaculate gardens surrounding grand mansions, we walk. Slender row boats rush up and down the river, the rowers all in perfect rhythm, each with a coxswain providing direction and encouragement.

We walk through a stretch of narrow woodland along an Iron Age earthwork called Grim's Ditch. This may have been a boundary demarcating one lord's land from another's. Perhaps at one time there was conflict here, but today, it provides pleasant walking as the day becomes warm and muggy. I ponder what dramas this place could tell me about if I understood the language of the rocks and trees.

We stop at a couple of village churches. At one, we're offered tea and cakes, as the local pub is closed. Another has mediaeval wall frescos. Both have benches on which to rest.

The route has become narrower with more hills, and the ups are hot in the afternoon. We pause to watch a pair of hawks circle overhead, then hang motionless in the warm air as they search for small creatures in the grass.

"Hide, Mr Mole. Hide."

Arriving at the Fat Fox Inn in Watlington, we are greeted by an exuberant host and shown to a cozy room. The ensuite has a bathtub, of which I make use. Having walked twenty-five kilometres, we're feeling weary, but having been on the road for forty-one days, my body is telling me it would like a longer rest. A change of pace. While soaking in the bath, I daydream about my garden and look forward to mucking about in a month's worth of weeds.

29 May. To Princes Risborough, Buckinghamshire.

A misty day ensures our attention focuses on the near. Dripping leaves, smooth tree bark, nodding grasses, bird song, smell of damp sheep, dimness under the canopy of a massive spreading oak. Distant sounds muted and unimportant. Mind attuned to the power and mystery of this route.

Through undulating woods and meadows, we tramp. A change in the tone marks this part of the trail as distinct from previous sections. Here I feel the squeeze of modernity pressing in on the ancient route. The Ridgeway holds sway but is under siege.

Yesterday we walked straight across three fairways of a golf course – without getting hit by zooming golf balls – the right of way of the Ridgeway taking precedence over an upstart golf course. Today we cross a busy rail line at a special pedestrian crossing guarded by gates. Even as we deal with unclasping a stiff latch, a train howls by with an air-sucking swoosh. An extensive – and unattractive – tunnel takes Ridgeway walkers safely under a roaring six-lane motorway.

As we arrive at our final destination, Ridgeway Lodge, heavy rain starts and continues unabated. Walking up the driveway, I notice a Canadian flag flying from the flagstaff. John and Miv are kind hosts who welcome us into their comfortable B&B with flag, smiles and tea. Miv picks Pat up at the train station and takes her grocery shopping for dinner supplies as we have a kitchen in our spacious suite, and there is no nearby pub.

Over dinner and wine, we catch up on each other's recent

activities. Pat's heel is no better, and she will return home to discover she has a stress fracture. Nearly ten years older than us, Marianne declares that her days of independent walking are behind her. In future, she'll walk with the support of a luggage transfer service. Undeterred by her injury, Pat and I promise each other another walk – soon.

From the megalith stones of Avebury henge to the earthworks of Barbary Castle, this is an area where the ancients still walk among us.

"What about the Via Francigena?" Pat asks the next day as our plane loses altitude and prepares to land in Comox.

"All the way? Canterbury to Rome?"

"Yes," she says.

"Done. I'll order us some guidebooks tomorrow."

"I like Paul Chinn's Lightfoot guides," Pat says.

Chapter Six

Walking the Via Francigena

mīlle viae dūcunt hominēs per saecula Rōmam
a thousand roads lead men forever to Rome

Alain de Lille, Liber Parabolarum, 591, *1175*

A pilgrimage from the sheltered cloisters of Canterbury Cathedral
to the towering dome of St Peter's in Rome.

Day sixty-two. 24 October 2022.
From Altopascio to San Miniato, Tuscany, Italy.

Sitting at an outside table, back to the sun, sweaty blouse drying, I lean back, close my eyes, and take a moment to silence intrusive, hyper-vigilant mind chatter. Shoes off, my throbbing feet cool in the patch of shade cast by a chair.

In sixty-two days, this is just the second café to be open when I've passed by. Humming voices from within serve as a barometer informing me that unlike many, this village – Ponte a Cappiano – remains a vibrant community.

As I take a last bite of *pain aux raisins*, scoop the remnants of cappuccino foam and shove still-aching feet back into worn sweat-damp shoes, I hear British voices. Two men, shirts darkened with salt-rimmed damp, shrug off their backpacks and settle at a nearby table. One of the men wears a broad-brimmed pilgrim's hat.

Rising and swinging my pack onto my shoulders, I approach. "Are you walking the Via Francigena?" I ask, hope blooming.

They respond with smiles and affirmation. Having started in Lucca, this is their second day on the route. Their names are Stuart and David, and they will walk for the week.

"And you?" Stuart of the Hat asks.

"I started two months ago in Canterbury. Aiming for Rome. But…"

A couple walk into the square by the café. They wave to David and Stuart and call out, "Hey, how are you doing?"

The men wave back. "That's Raoul and Andrea," David tells me. "They met a few years ago on a Camino pilgrimage and fell in love."

Raoul and Andrea continue by. She's limping and wearing sandals, her boots hanging off the back of her pack.

"Canterbury to Rome," says Stuart turning his attention back to me. "That's an undertaking. On your own?"

I shrug. "My friend Pat and I started together, but she hurt her knee and had to fly home. It's not as much fun now that I'm a solo act." At a sudden pricking behind my eyes, I realize I'm near tears.

"Anyway, the trail won't walk itself, so I best get back at it." I spin away. These guys will think I'm unhinged if I start blubbering.

"I'm sure we'll see you later," David says as I leave the momentary warmth of their company.

I set off hoping that they'll walk fast enough to catch up.

A group of eight strides into the square, heads onto a small, covered bridge and mills around. We stayed at the same hotel last night, but as I thread past them while crossing the bridge, they don't acknowledge my nods and smiles. Cold shoulders are uncommon on the route. Pilgrims greet each other. But this group is travelling with large, wheeled suitcases that are being transported by vehicle. They carry small day packs. Maybe they aren't pilgrims.

At the café, while sipping my cappuccino, I'd studied the map so anticipating a left turn on the far side of the bridge, I look for the way marker. There is none, but I swing left anyway onto a grass track along a riverside dyke. The standard practice is to keep walking straight ahead unless a Via Francigena way marker indicates otherwise. That was the case through England, France and Switzerland, but inconsistent way-marking in Italy has become frustrating and constant vigilance is necessary.

Roadside garbage, abandoned buildings with windows broken and roofs caving, crumbling roads with chunks of tarmac missing, and fatigued bridge infrastructure with bits of rebar protruding, attest to current despair, even aggression. In some cases, I see where the Via Francigena signs have been deliberately obliterated or removed. The numerous *private* and similar signs along the route also contribute to my growing unease.

The softer, cooler surface of the grassy track provides instant relief to my aching feet. Yesterday, between Lucca and Altopascio, the entire route had followed foot-bruising paved roadways. The miserable walking conditions had left me physically and mentally exhausted. Now I hear chirping birds instead of rumbling traffic. I smell fresh tilled soil and cut grass instead of vehicle exhaust. I feel my shoulders and stride relax. My solitary plod reverts to a springing step.

Looking over my shoulder, I see the group of eight strung out along the dyke about a kilometre behind me. Behind them walk the tall lean shapes of Raoul and Andrea. Of David and Stuart, there is no sign. I sigh.

Rome? Do I have what it takes? Doubt whittles away at my usual confidence. Walking is the easy part. Navigating, finding accommodation, hungry waiting until restaurants open at seven or seven thirty in the evening, eating alone – those are the most difficult aspects of this journey. My resolve is fragile.

For all my repeated looking back, the distance between me and the others grows. After two months, my body is used to walking. My legs pump at a steady pace. I lose sight of potential companions as I enter and walk through Fucecchio.

Later, while I gulp a cold beer at a bar in San Miniato's main square, none of the other walkers appear. I guess that they stayed back in Fucecchio. Once again, I'm exhausted after a walk that feels like it was too far. I remind myself that these distances aren't sustainable and that an injury like Pat's will be the probable result.

My B&B host bounds across the square and greets me at the bar. "Welcome, Kim," she says, reaching out her hand for a firm shake.

We walk to the B&B where, without the usual identification formalities, she shows me my room, then suggests we enjoy the late afternoon sun with a beer on the terrace. She pours, and while we admire the view over misty Tuscan hills, tells me her family emigrated from Albania in the early 90s. Her name is Aida because her parents loved Verdi operas. She explains that people suffered here during COVID. The economic and political situation isn't hopeful. Even so she relishes the freedoms of living in Italy.

Two sweaty German men stumble in. While Aida checks them in, they tell us they started in Lucca. This is their second day, and they are exhausted. I wonder what the attraction is to start from Lucca, but keep the thought to myself.

While I shower and change into warmer clothes, I puzzle over a despondent mood that has crept up. Why today? Nothing went wrong today. There were other people on the route, the route itself was pleasant, this B&B is lovely and the recent conversation with my host has been enlightening and enjoyable. All reasons for me to feel buoyed. Again, I sigh. Probably just hungry, I reason. I'm that person who gets hangry. This must be that.

At seven thirty, I'm the first customer through the door of a nearby restaurant where I gaze at the menu. The words make more sense now than they did two weeks ago, but I'm still stumped by most options. The waiter returns to take my order. I solve the dilemma of what to eat by falling back on what has become my standard fare.

"*Pasta al pomodoro e vino bianco, per favore*," I manage in stumbling Italian.

"You'd like spaghetti with tomato sauce and a white wine?" he confirms in perfect English.

I grin at him, "*Si*," and wish I'd requested his assistance in reading the menu, but so few waiters have spoken English, I've given up asking.

The two Germans arrive. "May we join you?"

I'm delighted and we enjoy animated dinner conversation. On a week's holiday they're unimpressed by the Via Francigena route.

"Too much road," they grumble. "We didn't expect Italy to be so dirty and neglected."

Disillusioned, they've reviewed their options and tomorrow will walk a different trail to an off-route location where they will stay in a luxurious agritourism resort. They show me photos. I feel a tug of envy.

As we talk, I have a sense that I'm performing. My carefree character is strong, confident and enjoys this journey as a solitary pilgrim. When I can no longer stand the pretence, I leave the men to their after-dinner drinks and walk back to the B&B – my headlamp lighting the way along dark cobbled streets. I climb the three flights of stairs to my room, fall into bed, take an ibuprofen and contemplate my physical and mental state.

"How are you really doing?" asks a derisive voice in my head.

"OK," I respond. Defensive and trying to believe the dinner performance.

"I'm not convinced," taunts the critic.

"No? Well, I'm grumpy. Lonely. Pat and I were supposed to be doing this together. After not seeing other walkers for ages, so many people today, but I'm still solo."

"Oh, you *are* feeling sorry for yourself. Too bad those German guys aren't committed to following the route."

"Maybe they're the smart ones. But I *do* want to walk into Rome. I'm just so fed up with crappy signage, crappy drivers, crappy garbage. I want to share walk experiences with other people – pilgrims. I want to talk about more than what type of pasta to order for dinner. I'd like to tell someone how damn isolated I feel." Tears I've held at bay most of the day leak, then flood onto the pillow.

"Well, this is pathetic. Like crying is going to help. You don't have what it takes, do you? You going to quit? Give up? Let the crap get the best of you? Seriously?"

Angry now, I scrub at my wet face, wipe my snotty nose, roll over, punch the pillow, kick at the blanket, and start counting myself to sleep.

I dream of walking – triumphant and strong – into Rome, marching up to the Vatican and accusing the pope of being complicit in murdering children. He doesn't understand English, so I end up ordering *pasta al pomodoro e vino bianco* and wake up to the gold band of dawn breaking.

Day one. 24 August.
Arrival in Canterbury, Kent, England.

As Britain and Europe continue to bake in a summer-long heatwave and drought, Pat and I land in Gatwick on time, which we feel bodes well for our upcoming journey. Our English friend Liz picks us up, and as she drives us to Canterbury, we reminisce about our last visit in 2018 with Marianne and Sally.

Pat and I had returned home from that trip already talking about the Via Francigena. But first, in 2019, we realized another dream and adventured along the Silk Road from Mongolia to Istanbul. Then COVID arrived. This is our first time outside Canada since, and we're thrilled to be embarking on another walk.

Joining mobs of tourists, we pop into the cathedral to verify our pilgrim status. Without comment, a busy woman at the ticket counter applies the required stamps to our credential documents and shoves them back at us. Thus, identified as *bona fide* pilgrims, we're permitted entry without paying the usual £15.50 entry fee.

Despite the hundreds of visitors thronging through the gate, the cathedral acoustics and grounds hush the racket of excited chatter. Within the nave, the air is cool with light streaming from stained glass windows to illuminate dust motes. Footsteps echo. An organ plays. I look up into the vaulted ceiling and allow the magic of a sacred space to wrap me in its spell.

Founded in 597, this is one of the oldest cathedrals in England. After Thomas Becket's murder here in 1170, the cathedral was expanded to accommodate an influx of pilgrims who came to his shrine in search of miracle cures. Later additions contributed the Gothic architecture we see today. Although Henry VIII ordered the destruction of Becket's shrine, the cathedral survived his Dissolution of the Monasteries by closing its Benedictine monastery. It also survived targeted bombing during WWII due to determined fire wardens fighting night after night to quench fires on the roof. Today, the soaring structure stands as a World Heritage Site, a testament to over 1400 years of turbulent history. This is the starting point of the Via Francigena pilgrimage to Rome.

The Via Francigena. Two thousand kilometres. Developed over hundreds of years from a blend of road networks connecting Canterbury and Rome. Used for troop movement, trade and pilgrimage since Rome's initial conquest of England in 43 CE, the route originated as the Lombard Way, the term Via Francigena first appearing in 876.

In 990, the new Archbishop of Canterbury – Sigeric the

Serious – travelled to Rome to receive his *pallium* from the pope. His journal of the seventy-nine-stage return journey is the template from which the modern Via Francigena has been revived. Now Pat and I will add our footsteps to the millions who have gone before. Like many who travel this route, we walk as pilgrims.

Pilgrim? Pilgrimage? Historical references smother both terms under cloaks attributed to religious beliefs, but current thought provides space for broader interpretations. Today's pilgrim might be following a religious pursuit, but just as legitimate is the secular undertaking of a physical journey to a significant place with potentially transformative intent.

> *The membrane between the sacred and the secular is porous. ... In the final analysis only the pilgrim knows whether he or she is on a pilgrimage ... For every pilgrim making a physical journey, the sore feet, enforced detours, and anxieties, as well as the companionship and acts of generous hospitality, represent in microcosm the woes and weals of life.*
>
> *James Harpur, The Pilgrim Journey –*
> *A History of Pilgrimage in the Western World, 2016*

For Pat and me, our identity as pilgrims stems from our desire to explore this historic route with expectations of discovering more about ourselves and the people and cultures we'll encounter. I'm fascinated by how current attitudes connect with historic events, and Pat is an avid student of human nature.

We've dedicated our walk to raising funds for Médecins Sans Frontières, (MSF) – Doctors without Borders – with a goal of one million dollars. When we first had the idea, that goal seemed achievable, but by the time we depart Canada, reality has set in. Pat and I are not marketeers. We've tried to spread the word through feeble attempts on social media, but our Two Women Walking fundraiser is not going to be successful beyond our immediate group of friends. Now that we are on the journey, we won't have the time or energy to devote to promoting the project. Perhaps this will be our first transformative lesson as pilgrims. Accept failure and move on.

Day two. 25 August. To Whitfield.
Despite our excitement to be on the cusp of our long walk, we sleep well and are downstairs for a proper English breakfast by seven. Swinging packs onto our backs, we feel the extra weight of snacks and full water bottles.

It's not long before the city is behind us and we're enjoying quiet trails through rural Kent. Surveying a moody sky, we anticipate a promised thunderstorm that will relieve the sweltering humidity. Our desire unfulfilled, the parched fields remain shimmering and wilted. Twenty-five kilometres out of Canterbury, we stay the night in Whitfield.

Day three. 26 August.
To Dover then Calais, the Hauts-de-France region, France.
By mid-morning, we arrive in Dover with time to climb one of the white cliffs, relax in the sun, enjoy a picnic lunch, and watch ferries come and go. Descending to, and entering the port, we follow a painted walkway across the shimmering tarmac to a building where we check in for our Channel crossing.

Since Brexit, travellers from the UK must clear immigration before entering the EU. With no border control facilities to process them, P&O Ferries stopped accepting foot passengers. Responding to pressure from interest groups such as the Confraternity of Pilgrims to Rome, the company reinstated foot-passenger service just weeks before our crossing. However, we discover an inept process with inadequate infrastructure. All forty of us ticketed foot passengers come within moments of missing the sailing. We would have done so had the ferry left on time.

Upon docking in Calais, we wait for all vehicles to be offloaded, then proceed to the vehicle deck where a bus arrives and drives us through the huge, fortified port to a stop outside the fencing. We're dropped at a bus stop where a minibus awaits. In moments it fills with suitcase-laden passengers for the five-kilometre trip into Calais. Rather than wait an indefinite period for another bus, Pat and I brave the fierce heat and tarmac to walk into town. Formidable fencing around the port facilities attests to the efforts to keep migrants out.

The city presents a rough façade. Small groups of men hover around the entries of grim-faced boarding houses and grungy hotels. Graffiti mars the walls and padlocked shutters of tired buildings. We follow streets that we would not feel comfortable walking along in the dark, and I worry that I may have booked us a hotel in an undesirable part of town.

As is often the case, one block can make a difference, and our charming Hôtel Particulier Richelieu is just around the corner from a vibrant street with restaurant awnings and seating spilling out onto the pavement. After a late but fabulous multi-course French meal, we fall into bed as realization dawns that after years of anticipation and preparation, we really have begun our journey as Via Francigena pilgrims. As excited as children at Christmas, we seek sleep.

Day four. 27 August. To Guînes.

Departing Calais through a worn industrial area, we follow a canal into the sleepy countryside and on to Guînes. Upon arrival at one thirty, we quench our thirst at a café/bar, but no food is available because it is closing for the day. Next, we discover a restaurant where the waitress serves us a quick meal because they close at two thirty. The grocery store looks like it hasn't been open for months, so we spend the rest of the hot afternoon snoozing in the shade of a tree in a small park.

"Welcome to Saturday afternoon in rural France," grins Pat.

Our young accommodation hosts grant us permission to enter just before six o'clock.

Day five. 28 August. To Tournehem-sur-la-Hem.

Sundays in this part of rural France are even quieter than Saturdays. We discover that even *pâtisseries* or *boulangeries* aren't always open. Anticipating this, we're carrying the extra baguettes we'd bought in Calais. Fresh French bread is beyond compare, but stale, it's hard to chew, so when we come across a small tavern in Clerques serving after-church beer and French fries, we indulge with enthusiasm.

The last nine kilometres into Tournehem-sur-la-Hem feel longer, and we're weary by the time we arrive at Madam Lysensoone's home. This generous woman hosts credentialled pilgrims in comfortable rooms and cooks wholesome dinners using vegetables she harvests from her own garden. We share that meal with three other pilgrims.

Gabby from Germany speaks German and English. Pascal from Switzerland speaks French and German. His wife Gilliane and our host speak French. Pat's French is adequate. I'm soon blending my reasonable command of German with my minimal French into an incomprehensible jumble. Language, however, is no deterrent to lively conversation, and we all become more fluent as wine flows.

Pat and I are the secular pilgrims of the group, and this leads the others to debate the merits of non-Christian pilgrimage. They aren't convinced that we are real pilgrims. I'd like to mention the pilgrimages Muslims make to Mecca, Jews to Jerusalem, Buddhists to Lumbini, and Hindus to numerous sites, but we don't have enough shared language for such a nuanced discussion. The others are only walking for two weeks. But, while they discuss our lack of pilgrim merit, we refrain from asking if a two-week walk deserves pilgrimage status. Later Pat and I review the discussion and decide to be more circumspect about our lack of Christian identity if queried again.

Day six. 29 August. To Wisques.

That opportunity arises the following evening when we stay with the nuns at Abbey Notre Dame in Wisques. It's not our gregarious host, Sister Lucy, who asks, but a guest who used to teach theology at Oxford in England.

To her persistent questioning about the validity of our pilgrimage, Pat simply says, "Our reasons are complex."

This response silences the inquisition, and later we accept Sister Lucy's invitation to attend Vespers to receive a blessing – a generous gift that we accept in the spirit with which it is given.

Day seven. 30 August. To Auchy-au-Bois.

To date, we've walked no more that twenty-five kilometres each day. This suits us, and in the heat, it's ample distance. The thirty kilometres from Wisques to Auchy-au-Bois, however, test our endurance. There is no restaurant at our destination, so as we pass through Thérouanne just before the shops close for the afternoon, we rush to buy dinner supplies. In our hurry and hunger, we over shop, so our packs feel too heavy when we set off again after a robust restaurant lunch.

During the hot afternoon, we drink the last of our water. Thirsty, as we walk through Liettres, I see a sign pointing to a gift shop at a beer and wine-making plant.

"Pat, a gift shop. Let's go."

"You want to buy a gift?"

"Huh? No. Can't make beer and wine without water." I point and veer down the driveway towards the plant.

Pat follows. Dubious.

At the plant, I wag one of my empty water bottles at the woman behind the gift shop counter. "*Excusé. Possible* …umm… *nos* bottles *d'eau s'il vous plait?*" I blather.

She smiles, takes my bottles, and reaches for Pat's.

Pat's laughing now. "I couldn't figure out why you wanted to buy a gift." She says as we're handed back bottles of cold water.

We give thanks, guzzle and continue on our way, greeting and passing Pascal and Gilliane where they lie in a patch of shade.

"*Buen Camino*," they call out.

Weary and sweat-soaked, we arrive at La Ferme de la Vallée. A young farmer, rubber boots bearing clods of manure, crosses the courtyard from a barn. Kicking his boots off at the door, he shows us through the massive house, up into the rafters to a large slant-ceilinged room tastefully arranged with delicate antique furniture. He will leave two cold beer on the dining table downstairs. We are to make ourselves comfortable. Will a seven o'clock breakfast suit our needs? We nod to all, and he runs back to the barn where we hear milk pails clang.

Day eight. 31 August. To Bruay-la-Buissière.

After Grandma serves us a hearty breakfast, we begin another blistering day. A tramp through a cool forest is followed by a slog along a busy road where motorists signal, slow and swerve into the other lane as they pass us by. This is something we've noticed with most drivers here – they treat pedestrians with courtesy, often waving as they go by. Although road walking isn't enjoyable, we never feel unsafe.

Our approach to Bruay-la-Buissière is through an odd landscape of small cone-shaped hills which we discover are slag heaps from ancient and more recent coal mining. Although we walk less than twenty-five kilometres, the rundown semi-industrial hinterland, the paved roads, and the day's heat leave us tired and foot sore.

Day nine. 1 September. To Arras.

As we continue south through drought-scarred farmland and silent villages, realization dawns that our dreams of pleasant morning coffee breaks at atmospheric village cafés are not going to materialize. There are no cafés. Signs request drivers to slow down for children playing, but there are no children. Nor are there many grocery shops or bars. Every village has a church – at least one – and out of curiosity, we've tried a few doors – they are locked. Every village also has a smart *Mairie* – town hall – always with flags flying and usually with bright containers and window boxes of flowers outside. Having yet to pass an open *Mairie*, we wonder how township business is conducted. Walking kilometre after kilometre through a land that feels post-apocalyptic creates a surreal sense of isolation.

Today as we trudge through more open farmland, I begin experiencing vivid flashes of unease. The air shatters and groans. I stagger under a visceral sense of carnage and the stink of death. This has happened to me before. I was four when Mum took me on a tour of Culloden Moor in Scotland. She recorded in her journal that, distraught, I had asked, "Mummy, why is the air screaming?"

Sixty-four years later, I have the answer. These quiet French fields once seethed with the slaughter of a WWI battle. Scanning the horizon, I see a tower rising in the distance. The Vimy Memorial. A little further on, we come to one of the many Commonwealth gravesites in the area. We stop and I walk between the rows of gravestones, reading the names and ages of the boys who were killed. As I read, the air calms. As tears mingle with sweat on my face, I calm. I doubt the spirits of the fallen will ever calm. I recite a few lines from John McCrae's "In Flanders Fields:"

> *In Flanders fields the poppies blow*
> *Between the crosses, row on row,*
> *That mark our place; and in the sky*
> *The larks, still bravely singing, fly*
> *Scarce heard amid the guns below.*

Coming over a low rise, we notice an arcing jet of water spraying from a powerful rotating irrigation nozzle. As we get closer, we see that part of the cycle includes blasting the road we are walking along. We watch, counting seconds. If we hurry, we should be able to pass between spray cycles. The water pressure looks like it will sweep us off our feet should we get caught. At the edge of the wetness, where just a hint of mist reaches us, we pause and gage our timing.

"Now!" commands Pat.

We scurry into the wet area as the jet sweeps away on its outer arc, but then the pattern changes, switching direction, and jetting back towards us.

"Run!" I shout.

We run, screaming in anticipation of the deluge, bursts of water hard on our fleeing heels. The mist becomes a soft rain and then heavier until we're past the danger zone and still reasonably dry. We howl and dance, take pictures of the rainbows thrown up by the water and catch our breath.

Soon after, we arrive hot and sweating at the train stop at the village of Frévin-Capelle. The posted schedule scrolling on an electronic sign indicates that the hourly train will be along soon. Because of Schengen rules, we're pressed for time, so will take the train for the last ten kilometres into Arras.

Under the European Union's Schengen Agreement, non-EU citizens, are only permitted to stay in the EU for ninety days. Pat and I tried applying for a visa that would allow us a longer visit, but our reason – to walk the Via Francigena in a recommended 104 stages – was not accepted. Disappointed, I'd written to Paul Chinn – author of our guidebooks – requesting suggestions. He'd written back with several ideas for the best places to fast-forward by public transport, and a reminder that Sigeric had ridden a horse.

The countdown started with our arrival in Calais, and to avoid a fine or deportation, we must fly from Rome by the ninetieth day. Left with just eighty-eight days to complete the walk, we sit in a strip of shade and wait for our proverbial horse. It does not arrive. The electronic board now indicates the train is due in another hour. We wait for two anxious hours and become disheartened. Having already walked twenty-four kilometres, we don't feel up to walking the last ten, especially in the energy-sucking heat. Pat calls out to a woman bringing in her laundry who tells us there is no train at this time of year but that a bus will be along soon. She points to where we should stand to catch it. Five minutes later, breathing sighs of relief, we climb aboard, each paying €1.00 for the ride into downtown Arras.

Once there, a short walk brings us to our hotel by the town's central square. We dump our packs, shower, hand-wash smalls and head out to find a good dinner. In the square, thousands of people sit under colourful restaurant awnings in the evening sun. Amplified by the surrounding buildings, the roar of happy conversation fills the space. Having not seen this many people gathered in one place to socialize since before COVID, we feel momentary confusion. As crowds flow around us, we join the throngs looking for an available table.

"*Deux?*" asks a greeter as we scan the sidewalk-posted menu at a place with chequered tablecloths.

"*Oui.*"

"*Bienvenue. Asseyez-vous ici,*" he says showing us a table squeezed between two others.

While ordering a French chardonnay and an expensive meal – avoiding the horse meat options – we people and dog watch. Europeans have more gracious attitudes about dogs coming to restaurants than we do in North America. The canines settle under tables, heads on paws while their humans dine. A waiter steps over several wagging tails, but frowns at a couple of misbehaving children. Pat and I agree with the implied sentiment.

After dinner, as lights come on, we take a few minutes to admire the surrounding Flemish-Baroque-styled buildings. Each façade and scrolled gable is unique, but they harmonize – an architectural orchestra playing under the baton of a master of design – to create a fairy-tale scene. Like most of Arras, the original 17th- and 18th-century buildings were destroyed during WWI, but the town has been restored so that today it is difficult to imagine the extent of the damage.

I consider cities being pummelled into piles of rubble in current conflict zones around the world and wonder when they will rise again. It's not surprising that the souls of those who die in battles don't rest – nothing seems to have been learned from their sacrifice.

Day ten. 2 September. Arras to Bapaume.

Due to traffic congestion, crowded sidewalks and busy intersections, we don't enjoy walking into and out of major urban centres, so we depart Arras by bus to Mercatel, a village ten kilometres to the south. From there we'll walk twenty-three kilometres to Bapaume.

After we alight from the bus, one of Pat's new and expensive Black Diamond folding trekking poles won't lock into its extended position. She fiddles with the mechanism to no avail. We're standing outside a farm machinery repair garage, and through the open side door of a mechanic's van, I notice duct tape.

"Maybe we can get help in there," I suggest.

Entering the compound, Pat calls out to an overalled mechanic, "*Bonjour. Aidez moi s'il vous plaît.*"

He comes over and Pat shows him the problem. Without a word or smile, he takes the offending pole and disappears into the dark cavern of the garage. While we wait, we study the massive John Deere machines towering around us. The man re-emerges and returns Pat's pole. An adjustable clamp just under the handle has solved the problem. Pat will be able to remove the clamp whenever she needs to collapse the pole. She offers to pay, but with a gruff wave the mechanic sends us on our way. He's got bigger repairs to get on with. Thanking him, we set off into an already-hot day.

Our route takes us past several more Commonwealth grave sites. At each one we pause. I read some of the names, and we spend a few moments contemplating the horrors and futility of that "war to end all wars."

Throughout the day, humidity grows and the sky becomes gun-metal black. Within moments of our arrival at Hôtel Restaurant le Gourmet in Bapaume, thunder rumbles and a deluge begins. Rain hisses and steams against the hot pavement and pools on ground too dry to absorb the sudden onslaught. Opening our windows, we watch and listen to the raging storm.

Day eleven. 3 September. To Peronne.

A cooler cloudy day is much more pleasant for walking. The forecast predicts more rain so our ponchos ride near the top of our packs. As we walk through the village of Sapignies, the first drops land with forceful plops. Seeking shelter, we try the door of a church. It's locked, but the portal offers just enough protection from what becomes a barrage of sheeting rain. Crouching on our packs, ponchos over our knees, we huddle, watch the street transform into a rushing river, munch snacks and laugh at ourselves. After the worst of the storm passes, we continue to Peronne without getting soaked, although we do have to leap over and skirt around many large puddles.

Day twelve. 4 September. To Seraucourt-le-Grand.

We again want to shorten a thirty-six-kilometre walk by taking a bus for the first ten. However, as it is Sunday, there are no buses. Our hostel receptionist arranges for a taxi, but the driver is not available until after church. Taking advantage of the late start, we find an open *pâtisserie* where we buy our daily bread.

What would have taken two and a half hours on foot, takes the taxi fifteen minutes.

"It's a nice walk from here," our driver says, pulling over in Trefcon. "This is where I bring all the pilgrims."

"All the pilgrims?" Pat queries.

"*Oui*. Almost every day. I drive to this spot. In the summer I bring many pilgrims."

As Pat and I walk on to Seraucourt-le-Grand, we discuss what seems to be a dark secret. We've been following a couple of Via Francigena Facebook groups, and no one mentions taking trains, buses or taxis. Is this a shameful act? Having seen enough posts with competitive underpinnings, we decide to be just as circumspect. We want to avoid critiques from folk who don't whinge at multiple thirty-plus-kilometre days, Europeans with no time restrictions, or those who walk the route in short segments.

Despite claims of the supportive environment offered by these Facebook groups, both Pat and I feel a need to protect ourselves from lurking toxicity. Were it not for nurturing an on-line presence in support of our fundraising efforts, we would, at best, be silent observers. However, there is one woman whose intriguing posts we like following. Lea's daily image of her journal wherein she records thoughtful insights and useful trail notes will, over the next several weeks, offer inspiration.

Upon arrival in Seraucourt, we find our accommodation, Gîte Rural, next to a crowded bar from which the beat of "She's got the rhythm (And I got the blues)" pulses.

First stop: the bar to rehydrate and to listen to familiar toe-tapping, sing-along R&B tunes.

Second stop: the *gîte* where I ring the bell, crack open the door and call out. At fierce dog barking and frantic paw scrabbling, I close it again and we stay outside. When no one comes Pat knocks. The dogs create more din, then a sleepy man opens the door. Pat tells him we have a reservation. He tells us his friend is coming and shuts the door again. Puzzled, we wait and after a few more minutes, another man arrives by car, welcomes us, and shows us around the corner of the building to a small garage. Our accommodation.

The humble space has everything we need: two sinks, a one burner stove, a toilet, shower, plastic table and two lawn chairs. Two mattresses lean up against the wall. The man shows us that there is just enough space to put the mattresses on the floor at night. There is no fee for this perfect sanctuary. In the morning, we are to tuck the key on a ledge above the door. The man leaves. We drop our packs, lock the door, and set off to the grocery store a kilometre further down the road.

Noticing a woman dressed in walking clothes, we say hello. From Montana, her name is Laura and she's a pilgrim too. Until a couple of days ago, she was walking with her son who has flown home. Her husband will be arriving soon to continue the walk with her. She's staying at a nearby campsite. We have dinner together, Pat and I cooking pasta and Laura providing the wine. A friendship made; we anticipate meeting on the trail again.

Day thirteen. 5 September. To Laon.

It's still dark when Pat tucks the key above the door and we set off, headlamps illuminating our way. As we walk, the sun rises in a glorious display, sweeping bold brush strokes of reds and oranges across the broad horizon. Today, the route brings us to Tergnier, but unable to locate any accommodation in this rough industrial town, we head to the train station. There are no restrooms. We wait – me with urgent impatience – for an hour. Once on the train – with relief – I use the ultra-modern toilet, then enjoy the ride to Laon.

Clustered around its cathedral, the old town of Laon hugs the top of a steep hill. The train stops at the bottom, and in humid late afternoon heat, we climb 365 steps to discover our apartment tucked down an alley next to the cathedral.

Having gained a spare day by fast-forwarding the thirty-nine kilometres from Tergnier to Laon, we'll give our bodies a break and spend two nights here. The apartment has a washing machine, but after popping in a load of laundry, we're unable to read the French instructions so manage to set a super cycle. Five anxious hours later, the machine door clicks open to release very clean, well-spun clothes.

Day fourteen. 6 September. In Laon.

With a goal of resting, we explore little, but wander through the cathedral. Consecrated in 1235, it reflects a blend of Romanesque and Gothic styles. Unlike their heavy, often fortified, barrel-vaulted Romanesque predecessors, Gothic cathedrals include pointed arches supported by thinner walls and elegant flying buttresses. The light from their larger stained glass windows and the tremendous heights of their naves and spires testify to the skilled architects and stonemasons who designed and built these buildings of such magnitude and grace. In this cathedral, I imagine the architects experimenting with new Gothic arches while retaining faith in the old style and so employing both.

As Pat and I treat ourselves to a delicious meal at a restaurant in the cathedral's cobble-stoned square, we study the ornate façade, and I recall a quote from Ken Follett's *The Pillars of the Earth*: *When things are simple, fewer mistakes are made. The most expensive part of a building is the mistakes*. I wonder what mistakes were made with this construction because it presents an undecided edifice, Romanesque features in a perpetual struggle with Gothic.

Two tables over from us, a couple from New Zealand struggle

with the French menu and with great excitement tell the waiter they are walking the Via Francigena. Pat and I eavesdrop until we hear that they are starting here and walking to Reims.

"Three days," Pat whispers.

And there it is. That competitive, judgmental edginess. We have it too.

When presented with the bill, we are left in no doubt that eating under the gaze of the cathedral's gargoyles doubles the expense of a meal.

Day fifteen. 7 September. To Corbeny.

There is no early morning bus, but wanting to avoid a tedious six-kilometre urban walk down from Laon's hilltop, we'd asked the tourist office to arrange for a taxi to pick us up outside the cathedral.

"The driver will not wait. Be ready at 7 AM," we have been instructed.

At the taxi stand in the dawn chill, I scratch at an itchy spot, and then another. A string of red welts swells on my calf.

"We must have had mosquitoes inside last night," I mutter.

"I didn't notice any," says Pat.

"I've got bites. Super itchy." I rub at my elbow where three more red lumps emerge. "They had a feast."

I don't normally react to mosquito bites, but these itch with fierce intensity.

After the taxi drops us in Bruyeres-et-Monterault, we climb into a forest and up to a ridge from where we look back to see Loan's cathedral towering above the city. Along the ridge, we march, enjoying the cool morning air until descending back into sweeping farmland interspersed with tidy under-populated villages.

While eating our picnic by the extensive ruins of Abbaye de Vauclair, I scratch at more bites. My pack straps have rubbed two on my shoulder into oozing welts. Digging out anti-itch cream from my first aid kit, I dob and smear.

Pat looks at me. "Let's see."

I show her, again complaining about the severity of the itch.

"Oh. Those are bedbug bites," says Pat. "A Benadryl will help."

That evening, she sends an e-mail to our Laon host but receives no response. Over the coming week, the bites will swell. Those under my socks and pack straps will fester. The itch will continue, persistent and fierce. I will feel ill with the torment they inflict and am woozy from taking Benadryl morning and night.

Lunch remnants packed away, we explore the Abbey's monastic garden and learn about the healing properties of many plants that now adorn our modern gardens. Chickweed to relieve itch; coriander to reduce fever; comfrey to cure breathing problems; mint to ease stomach pains; rose, lavender and sage to deal with headaches and aching joints; and foxglove to treat "feeble hearts."

I figure we can munch on rosehips and sniff lavender if we run out of ibuprofen, but of immediate concern are the bedbug bites. The Benadryl has me craving an afternoon snooze, but the itch persists. Pressing a chickweed leaf between my sock and hot skin doesn't help either. No doubt the leaves need to be steamed or crushed into a paste. Perhaps an incantation is required as well.

After a long afternoon's walk, we're met at Hôtel du Chemin des Dames in Corbeny by a cheerful woman wielding a vacuum cleaner hose. Turning off the machine, she scoops our room key from a table and whisks us up to a large room, confirms it's to our liking – it is – then hurries downstairs again where the roar of the vacuum tells us she's back at work. Later we discover that as well as cleaning and greeting, she also tends bar, serves dinner and washes dishes. The only other employee working is the chef. Lack of staff does not detract from the quality of the dinner, although this one is simple fare – steak and home cut French fries.

When we return to our room after that meal, we hear another violent thunderstorm raging and driving rain against the windows. Perhaps Europe's drought has ended.

Day sixteen. 8 September.
To Hermonville, the Grand-Est Region.
Before leaving Corbeny, we stop at the village *pâtisserie* where we buy what has become our usual *pain aux raisins* and baguette.

The first is for our mid-morning break, the second – with the addition of Babybel – is lunch.

Today our route leads us into a forest where we find the storm has brought down large branches and toppled a few trees. Clambering over some, and stepping around others we note the crisp-edged leaves of drought-stressed trees. We also take the opportunity to examine how metre-wide clumps of mistletoe have burrowed their roots into branches to suck sap and eventually kill their hosts.

After exiting the forest and crossing more open farmland, we climb a hill to a small copse of trees where a memorial plaque informs us that this is the site of a 17th-century windmill. It was destroyed by German soldiers during WWI so the villagers couldn't grind grain to make bread. As we ponder civilian suffering during periods of conflict, a sudden shift in wind direction, darkening sky and rumbling thunder alert us to the approach of another storm.

"This would be a bad place to be in lightning," Pat comments as we watch a large tractor make a last dust-billowing sweep before lifting its harrow and heading down the hill and into nearby Cormicy.

Hurrying in pursuit, we march through the village where on 21 July 1429, Joan of Arc spent the night on her way to Reims to support the coronation of Charles VII. A determined commander, she led her troops to several victories, then upon capture during the siege of Compiègne, she was ransomed to the enemy English. After imprisonment and a series of sham ecclesiastical trials, she was declared a heretic and burnt at the stake. Although only nineteen, her leadership turned the tide of the Hundred Years War, and twenty-two years after her execution, the war ended with France the victor.

As we exit Cormicy, we stop to stare in amazement. The open farmland has become hillier, every slope covered in vineyards. Champagne country – once in the Champagne-Ardenne region.

On 1 January 2016, the three historic regions of Champagne-Ardenne, Alsace and Lorraine were incorporated into the new Grand-Est region as a way of reducing bureaucracy and costs. I wonder about the local sentiments surrounding this decision and find myself considering how British Columbians might respond if we were lumped together with Alberta.

The champagne grape harvest is underway. Walking between the vineyards, we catch the heady smell of fermentation. Dozens of pickers snip purple grape clusters into blue and green plastic bins, then carry the filled bins to waiting trucks and vans where they are stacked in towers to be driven away to the champagne houses.

Thousands of grape clusters lie on the ground, and we're later told that these are the over-quota crop that will be left to rot or to be scavenged as no champagne house is permitted to bottle more than their quota. While this system keeps the price high and the market stable, I think that in these times of global food insecurity, the excess should be used. Raisins? Juice? Compost?

In Hermonville, we receive warm hospitality at a 17th-century farm. Built with security in mind, like many of this era, the grand house occupies one side of a courtyard. Barns make up the other three sides with a single entry through an arched gateway. Since this is an active farm, machinery occupies the courtyard along with a giftshop and tearoom where beer is also available. Pat and I relax there in late afternoon before going out for dinner at a tiny restaurant around the corner.

This is where we hear the news: "The Queen is Dead. Long Live the King." The restaurant goes silent. Even the French liked the British queen. I feel profound loss. She was an admirable woman. I held her commission; she held my great respect.

"This may be the death knell for the British monarchy," I say as we walk back to the farm.

"Who wants Charles to be king?" Pat wonders.

Day seventeen. 9 September. To Reims.

At breakfast, we discover that the New Zealand couple are also guests. When they hear us speaking English, they gravitate to our table. The man is distraught over the Queen's death, and the woman is distressed because her pack is too heavy. Explaining that she's carrying three frocks to be prepared for all dress requirements, she wants to know how we manage with so little. We don't have the heart to tell her that dress requirements aren't really a thing for us. They're still enjoying the sumptuous breakfast offerings when we slip away. We don't see them again.

This cloudy day is cool with wind and a few moments of light drizzle. Our walk begins through more vineyards but then we enter open farmland again. Eating our lunch within a massive farm machinery barn, we wave to the farmer when he drives by on a harvester. He waves back, unconcerned that we've taken shelter among what we determine to be his seed and slurry spreaders, plough, harrower, harvester and baler.

Arriving in Reims, we remember everything we don't like about city walking, but after dropping our packs at our hotel in the heart of the city, head out again to shop for needed groceries. I also buy replacement insoles because, over the past couple of days, the originals have been disintegrating into small dusty bits and causing annoying blisters that won't be so easy to get rid of.

Day eighteen. 10 September. To Condé-sur-Marne.

Before leaving town, we admire a bronze statue of Joan of Arc outside the cathedral, then enter to see where all but two French kings were crowned over a 1000-year monarchy. Despite the long and grand history, the cathedral presents a gloomy interior – no one has turned on the lights – so we head instead to the train station.

We had expected to walk from Reims to Verzy but due to the ongoing Champagne harvest, accommodation is fully booked by pickers. Now, departing Reims by a train that arrives twenty minutes late, we ride to Sept-Saulx. From there, twenty-two kilometres along a paved canal path takes us to Condé-sur-Marne where we have been able to find beds at a *chambre d'hôte* – a French B&B.

Upon our arrival, the host, Denis, asks where we are from. We tell him Canada. He tells us he has a nephew who lives in Canada.

We ask him where. He tells us the Comox Valley.

"Us too," we declare in astonishment.

His nephew works on Mount Washington where Pat and I met while ski patrolling. Denis is so excited, he video calls his nephew so we can all chat.

Day nineteen. 11 September. To Châlons-en-Champagne.

Denis sends us on our way with a baguette, reminding us that we won't find an open *pâtisserie* on a Sunday. While Pat and I admire the French commitment to a healthier work/life balance than we seem to have in Canada, the weekend and afternoon closures create a need for vigilance.

The day remains foggy and cool. Pleasant for walking, this isn't so comfortable when we take breaks because the trail-side grass remains wet and not conducive to lounging. Instead of lying back with our bare feet up on our packs, we now perch on our packs with our feet on our pack covers. Although we know we should rest for longer periods, in the damp we soon feel the chill of inactivity so pack up and carry on.

Like yesterday, we tramp along a canal-side path and the constant pounding on pavement without adequate rest periods takes a toll on our feet and legs. Keeping an eye and ear out for the many spandex-clad Sunday runners and cyclists is also fatiguing. These weekend athletes take their outings seriously and do not appreciate slow-moving, pack-laden pilgrims blocking their hurried progress. In the fog, we trudge along, single file, feeling the tedium of uninspiring scenery settling heavy on our shoulders.

We've settled into a comfortable apartment by early afternoon. Having fast-forwarded when leaving Reims, we will take another rest day. My initial optimism about making it to Rome in eighty-eight days is fading. Despite being pushed for time, this will be our third day off in less than three weeks. While we'd spent months training for distance, we hadn't considered how much paved surface we'd walk along, and we now need to allow our aching feet and legs recovery time. The forced inactivity is more difficult than walking, and I feel an inner conflict raging.

Day twenty. 12 September. In Châlons-en-Champagne.

Châlons-en-Champagne is a charming town of cobbled streets and restaurant-rimmed squares. It also boasts a cathedral. Curious to see how it compares to the last two, we enter and are astounded by a peculiar Playmobil display depicting the stations of the cross. The incongruity of plastic Roman soldiers whipping a cute plastic Jesus and other toy soldiers nailing a bloodied Jesus to a cross seem inappropriate. Disturbed, we leave the cathedral without further exploration and return to the square for beer and French fries.

Having since discovered that Playmobil creates theme sets depicting various historic events including a French Revolution guillotine with figures, I resist imagining gleeful children playing at crucifixion and decapitation. To my chagrin, the company doesn't market sets of sore-footed pilgrims, but perhaps those little figures would be too boring.

Lying in bed that second night in Châlons-en-Champagne, I review my reasons for undertaking this journey, recognizing that the need to fast-forward by public transit or taxi detracts from my joy of slow travel by foot. Now this miserable plague of bites and blisters undermines my usual enthusiasm and resilience.

"This defeatist attitude will not do," I chide myself, acknowledging the need to accept – and stop railing against – the challenges.

Smiling up at the ceiling, I conclude that this little pilgrim has achieved another transformative moment. Having also decided there is nothing boring about a pilgrim's journey, I sleep.

Day twenty-one. 13 September. To Coole.

We begin our day by catching a bus for the first five kilometres to Coolus. This sets us up for what will be three days tracing the path of an original Roman road. Romans built their roads to maximize speed of troop movement. Straight.

Following a route laid down by Roman legionnaires, we march along a straight chalk road that stretches to the horizon and beyond.

"Well, this is daunting," says Pat as we pause on the first rise and gaze down that road.

The same chalk bedrock that characterizes much of southern England's landscape also underlies the thin layer of topsoil in this region of France. The road, an exposed white ribbon of that chalk, reaches to the far horizon, testament to a vast geologic structure laid down between sixty-five and one hundred million years ago. A geologist with the British Geological Survey, Dr Andrew Farrant, states: *The English Channel is really a minor thing. It's the same deposit basically, so there's no Brexit with the chalk.*

"I hope we have enough water and snacks," I say as we begin, each step kicking up a puff of fine white dust that settles onto our socks and sticks to our lower legs.

The weather has reverted to hot and hazy. We sweat, tiny rivers trickling down through leg-clinging dust. With very few trees, there is no shade. We squint into the sun. We march, then plod, while the scenery seems to stand still.

For hours, we pass through an enormous wind turbine farm, the turbines whispering as they rotate their arms in a gentle ballet. One turbine isn't turning. A door at its base is open, a van parked nearby. From within the turbine comes the echoing sound of a vigorously employed hammer.

Despite the sameness, the vast sweep of land bisected by the long white road speaks to the essence of this journey. Surely, the towering Alps, then the Apennines and at the end St Peter's hide just out of sight beyond that horizon. The vibrations of marching Roman legions, and Sigeric too, brushing by on his horse, send thrill-prickles rushing along my spine. On this road, the past swirls around and mingles with the now. There is no one else – other than the turbine technician – yet we walk in the company of thousands, our shoes slapping against the chalk in a steady kilometre-devouring cadence.

Arriving in Coole, more tired than expected after a twenty-five-kilometre walk, we find 17 rue de Châlons where a smiling woman rushes out to greet us. Monique and Jean-Pierre Songy host credentialled pilgrims in their home, and we're immersed in their warm welcome. After drinks and a visit on the patio, I walk with Monique to the *pâtisserie*, meeting half the village on the way. The five-minute walk takes close to an hour with all the socializing.

On the way back, we stop at the village distribution centre which functions like a massive vending machine. Farmers rent space, place products such as a dozen eggs, a pot of honey, a head of cabbage, a bag of potatoes, a bouquet of flowers, a cucumber, a kilo of chicken or pork into glass-fronted, numbered cubicles with the prices posted. At the central control panel, shoppers drop in coins or swipe bank cards and punch in the cubicle number. The individual door unlocks, and the items are released to be carted away in shopping bags. This co-operative, centralized approach to farmgate shopping reduces theft and enables the few people still living in these small communities to shop for local products without driving into the larger towns.

Back at the house, Pat helps with dinner preparation while I fight Benadryl-induced lethargy. With the dark, Jean-Pierre returns from picking apples, and at nine o'clock we all start eating a delicious meal with local red wine. Pat and I are usually asleep at this hour, but the conversation is enlightening.

Many people are giving up the farm life and moving away. The schools, shops, cafés and bars that help a community stay alive have closed. Some farms have been bought by large corporations, so farmers now just rent the land and don't always live in the villages. The Songys have been farmers for generations and still own their land. Their son now farms it, but each year he makes less money than the last. It is not sustainable. Personal financial and national food security are at risk.

All food for thought as we collapse, exhausted, into our beds.

Day twenty-two. 14 September. To Corbeil.
We are sent on our way after a hearty breakfast with the sense that a friendship has been made and with a deeper empathy for a farmer's life. On to Corbeil we march. Same road. Same sun and heat. Same scenery. Same curious blend of boredom and elation. No trees. Lots of wind turbines. Ghosts of others who travelled this straight white road.

Several enormous mower/harvesters roam around cutting and baling clover from vast fields. Clover, we find out later, is a valuable cash crop that is processed and shipped to areas of food scarcity around the world as a source of protein.

The whooshing turbines and grumbling machines in the otherwise empty land begin to work on our imaginations, and we're soon entertaining ourselves with creepy *War of the Worlds* scenarios. The turbines become marauders and the machines giant bug transformers. Banding together, they terrorize the land.

Once in Corbeil – having not been attacked by turbines or transformer bugs – we are met by Béatrice who, with her husband Michel, hosts pilgrims in the town hall. They provide two camp cots, microwave dinners and breakfast supplies. There's no shower, but there is a plastic basin and a cold water tap in the public rest room. We have all we need and are grateful for it. Were it not for the kindness of Béatrice and Michel Mirofle, there would be no place to stay in this area.

Noticing the evening sun painting the sky and surroundings in a brilliant orange glow, I go out to take a few pictures. Moments later, I dash back inside as a violent thunder and rainstorm tears leaves from trees and shreds petals from flowers in a municipal garden across the street. Not sleeping well on the little cots, we listen to the rain pounding for most of the night.

Day twenty-three. 15 September.
To Hôtel Air Lane, near Brienne-le-Château.

By morning, the sky is blue again. We munch day-old bread with homemade jam and drink Nescafé for breakfast. Our lunch will be a tough two-day-old baguette we've brought from Coole as there is no café or *pâtisserie* in Corbeil.

We set out for our third day along the straight white road. While we rest under a lone tree by a clover field, a security van creeps by. We'd seen these vans patrolling the vineyards and figured security is necessary around the valuable champagne grapes. But clover? Apparently, the "clover police," as we nickname them, don't find us a threat and they carry on by.

Although mystified as to how a clover theft would be conducted, we've passed many fields from which potatoes have been machine harvested. Machines speed up the process, but they leave a lot of potatoes behind. With permission, people arrive at the fields by foot, bike or car to collect the leftovers, filling bags or car trunks. We wonder if the security patrols help ensure that legal scavenging – gleaning – doesn't overflow into theft of unharvested crops.

Paul Chinn offers further enlightenment about gleaning – a legal right in France since 1554 – by introducing me an emotive 1857 painting by Jean-François Millet. "Les Glaneuses" depicts three peasant women hand-picking grain from a stubbled field. Behind them, a bountiful harvest has been piled high on carts and a man on horseback watches their labours.

In Canada, the practice – which mitigates millions of kilograms of farm produce waste every year – has become more structured with organizations established to liaise with farmers. Groups of volunteers gather to glean on specific days at participating farms. Many of these organizations provide donations to foodbanks, with some requiring a membership fee. While this indicates a more affluent demographic than the original peasant gleaners, it also speaks to an urban/rural disconnect in this country. With few public transit options outside major centres, an impoverished city dweller in Canada is unlikely to have access to a farm from which to glean.

Our destination is Hôtel Air Lane. At day's end, as expected, the route takes us around the outer rim of an airport. It's derelict. That is not expected. As we near where the hotel is marked on the map, we pass several abandoned and decaying buildings. Alarmed, I envision camping out with rats. Then we come upon tidy Hôtel Air Lane with a sign on the locked door informing us that reception will open 5 PM. Three hours! We make ourselves comfortable on the grass beside the parking lot, but while waiting, continue to worry. Will the restaurant be open? Will someone really show up at the appointed time? What will we do if they don't?

Our concerns are unnecessary. The reception opens early, the lounge is modern and comfortable, as is our room. The beer is cold, the restaurant starts serving at seven o'clock. Every aspect of this busy truck-stop hotel is operated by the owners, Murielle and Bruno, as they've been unable to find staff since COVID.

We ask Bruno about a bus into nearby Brienne-le-Château in the morning. There is no bus, he tells us. We ask about a taxi. No taxis either. Somehow, we aren't surprised, so explain our conundrum that the thirty-five kilometres between here and our next stop in Bar-Sur-Aube is more than we want to tackle in one day.

"No problem. I will drive you to Brienne-le-Château," he promises.

Day twenty-four. 16 September. To Bar-sur-Aube.
After breakfast, Bruno closes the reception desk, calls up to Murielle who is stripping beds, grabs his keys, and we hop into his car. On the way, he tells us that the airport closed at the end of the Cold War when Canadians left. The derelict buildings and his hotel were once the barracks. He goes on to say that although he now works as an architect and helps his wife run her hotel, he is a retired paratrooper. I tell him that I served in the Canadian military, and we share that moment of connection.

As he drops us outside a *pâtisserie*, Bruno also tells us that this town is where Napoleon Bonaparte went to a military school reserved for French aristocrats. Born in Corsica within months of the island's purchase by France from Genoa, Napoleon was teased by the noble boys for his small stature and for being a low-born foreigner. No doubt those bullies kept their heads down when the little Corsican boy became their Emperor.

Today, our route meanders up and down hills, through woodlands and past vineyards. We're grateful for the change of scene. Row upon tidy row of now-harvested champagne grape vines spread across rolling slopes. The thin topsoil covering porous chalk bedrock provides the perfect growing medium because the capillary action of the chalk matches that of the grape vines. The two work in concert to produce the right amount of moisture for the grapes to mature. Usually. This year, with the water-preserving chalk drying out, the grapes have been harvested a month early.

We pass several large champagne-house complexes where flags, signs and fancy entries invite people to come for tastings. Glass-fronted showrooms display expensive bottles of champagne. Huge vats tower in warehouses where the processing, double fermentation and bottling takes place. Neither Pat nor I like champagne, so we aren't tempted. My drink of choice is pilsner and Pat enjoys chardonnay. As we walk through Bar-Sur-Aube, we pass numerous champagne shops where we see bottles ranging in price from €20.00 to €300.00. We're pleased to have more modest tastes.

Our quaint Hôtel de la Pomme D'Or occupies a corner near the far end of town. The receptionist is also the barkeep, so we wait for a couple of elderly men to receive their drinks and have a prolonged chat before we're shown up a narrow staircase and down a slanted hallway into a tiny room with faded, frayed bed coverings. The room is clean. The shower delivers hot water. The bar staff and clientele friendly. We are content.

Day twenty-five. 17 September. To Orges.

Pat, who seems tired this morning, enjoys good coffee, and the coffee here is to her liking. So, she has a second cup while I go in search of an open *pâtisserie* where I buy our usual supplies. Back at the hotel, the taxi we'd ordered yesterday arrives to drive us the first five kilometres to Baroville because once again there is no bus service. From there we continue walking through vineyards until the route takes us into a wooded valley. The heavy rain of a couple of days ago has created a lot of mud. Grumbling, we pick our way around a few deep mires until we come to an intersection where route markers point in both directions.

One trail slopes down into more mud. The other leads up. We consult our Pocket Earth apps. Pat has an older, but still reliable, "Traildino" route marked. I have Paul Chinn's newer route. Usually, they agree. Today the new route indicates straight into the mud. The older route is shorter and leads left up the hill. Liking the shorter, drier option, we turn left.

We walk up and up and after a couple of kilometres realize we should have seen another trail heading right. Retracing our steps, we search the dense woods and discover the faint remnants of an overgrown path. Consulting our maps again indicates that unless we head all the way back down the hill to the muddy route, we'll need to bushwhack.

Progress is slow. I hold my iPad so that I can keep an eye on the arrow marking our position. We clamber up a steep slope through tangled vegetation until we come out on a grassy track. Where we need to be. During a short rest, we calculate how much farther to Orges. Farther than we'd like.

Having anticipated a twenty-three-kilometre day, we arrive in Orges after walking more than thirty. It's five o'clock, and the temperature has dropped to 12°C. Even so, our host wants to sit outside and chat. Shivering, we tell him we'd like to go inside to get warm, yet still he chatters away. His English is minimal, and our French isn't up to much conversation, especially when we're tired. We stand, pick up our packs and point at the door. He gets the hint and shows us in, insisting that our shoes come off and stay at the door. We pad up the stairs in sock feet, leaving damp tracks. He shows us to our room, shows us around the room, shows us the bathroom. Then leaves. He'll order us a pizza for dinner because there is no place to eat in Orges.

We've just started unpacking when, without knocking, he bursts back into our room, sits on the couch and carries on with his monologue.

"We are cold and tired. We need to have showers," says Pat. "Now," she adds.

He leaves. I bolt the door. The guy is a creep.

Later we hear knocking on the house door. The knocking goes on, and I wonder if our pizzas have arrived. Running downstairs, I see our host sleeping in his office chair, mouth open and drooling. I open the door to the pizza delivery boy. He has five pizzas.

"We ordered one pizza," I say, too tired to hide my frustration.

He doesn't speak English and shows me the €53.00 bill.

"*Un pour moi*," I manage, holding up one finger.

This results in a stream of excited French.

"*Un moment*." I stomp to the office where our host snores. "Wake up!" I bellow. "The pizzas are here."

He opens bleary eyes. "Huh?"

"Pizzas. Five of them. We ordered one."

"*Deux,*" he says. "*Je en ai commandé deux.*"

"OK. I will pay for two. You pay for the rest."

I go back to the door, present €20.00 to the boy and select two boxes off the top of his pile. Our host arrives and much debate ensures. Retreating to the kitchen, I put the pizzas down and run upstairs to tell Pat dinner has arrived. She's sitting on her bed looking exhausted.

"You OK?"

"Just tired. That walk was too far today."

Back in the kitchen, we open the boxes. Black-rimmed pizzas look up at us. We eat burnt pizza because there's nothing else and we're hungry. Our host shoves the other three boxes into his fridge. The kitchen is a mess, dirty dishes cluster a filthy counter, pots teeter on the stove. While we eat, he babbles. We keep shrugging and saying that we don't understand but that doesn't stop his monologue. Desperate for peace, we add half-eaten pizzas to the counter mayhem, haul our weary bodies upstairs and lock our door. I shove a table in front for added security before we fall on our beds smothering peals of laughter in our pillows.

Day twenty-six. 18 September. To Mormant.

When we come downstairs, a woman and child greet us in a tidy kitchen – our host's daughter and granddaughter. We enjoy the best breakfast of our journey – fresh yoghurt, fruit and crêpes, then step out into an uncomfortable -3°C day. Marching along at a brisk pace, we soon warm up and begin peeling off layers of clothes.

"I liked wearing the extra clothes," I say while stuffing a fleece into my pack. "They weigh less on my body then they do in my pack."

We spend the next kilometre trying – without success – to figure out the physics of that truth.

Once in the mediaeval village of Châteauvillain, we find the gate into a vast deer park. The park, created in 1655 as a hunting reserve for the son of the Duke of Vitry, was once the private domain of the town's aristocratic rulers. Today, deer continue to roam within the confines of high stone walls, and the public are welcomed to enjoy the network of trails through the forest. We're looking forward to a quiet walk that will reduce our distance for the day by several kilometres.

As we walk through the dappled shade – hugging the sunny bits to stay warm – we contemplate the life of serfs labouring on strips of land outside these walls, subsisting on meagre grain and vegetable gruel while paying steep tithes to pampered masters who romped around in these woods killing deer and indulging on a diet heavy with meat.

"Oh no. What's this?"

We stare at a locked gate in a high fence. Like serfs of old, we're forbidden entry. With no option, we retrace our steps, then walk around the outside of the walls along a road. Later, discovering that the locked section of the park is off limits while the deer are in rut, we grumble and wonder why no one thought to post a sign to that effect.

We do, however, see warning signs about *la chasse* and soon after hear shotguns firing in the nearby woods. It's not long before we spy the hunters themselves. Despite our concern about walking in such proximity to armed men, they look silly. Dressed in head-to-toe camouflage, they've topped their ensembles with bright orange safety vests. The safety vests we get, but over camouflage? Their manhood reduced to boyhood, we hope the man-boys know where they're aiming and that they recognize the difference between two pilgrims and a partridge, deer, boar or whatever it is they are intent on killing.

Thirty kilometres after leaving Orges, we trudge up to our accommodation at l'Abbaye de Mormant. There are only two other guests, so Pat and I have a four-bed dorm to ourselves. Later, we join two cyclists for a delicious venison and potato stew. While ladling generous portions, our host tells us that her husband shot the deer and that the potatoes were grown on their farm. She also explains that in the village of Mormant half the homes are now empty, farmers having given up and walked away from family farms.

That night, Pat says her knee is painful. "Nothing to worry about," she assures me. "But a shorter day tomorrow would be good."

Recalling that a few days ago she had mentioned that her pack was bothering her hip, I suspect this isn't the first day Pat's been in discomfort. She's also been more tired than usual at the end of the past few days. Of the two of us, Pat is the stronger walker, slowing to accommodate my modest pace, but still often walking a little ahead. Recently, I've been walking at the fore and now feel a stab of guilt that I haven't paid attention.

Day twenty-seven. 19 September. To Langres.

Having walked two long days in a row, and because Pat's knee continues to ache, we ask our host about catching a bus for the first few kilometres. She assures us that no buses come by the village anymore, but as she needs to shop in nearby Beauchemin, she'll drive us that far. I look at our map and see this will leave us with a short twelve-kilometre day to Langres. We accept with gratitude.

Today's walk takes us up and down numerous hills. At the top of one, while crossing an open plateau, we hear a fighter jet and are startled when it appears low over the near horizon to screech overhead with a deafening roar. Perhaps it's my imagination, but I'm sure the field grasses bend in the wind of its passing. Standing erect again – we had ducked – we postulate that the pilot must be seeking the two women who loll about beside the clover fields. Although I had worried that we'd be swept off our feet by the blast, and we'd squealed in excited amazement, we try to comprehend the terror such a fly-by would instil in a population expecting death to follow. I'm incapable of conjuring the horror.

Perching on a hill's natural rampart, Langres was well chosen as a defensive position. As we get closer, the town tricks us into thinking there is just one more hill to climb, but first we need to descend from the plateau into a steep-sided valley and climb up the other side.

Pat powers up hills with a long stride and always leaves me far behind. Today is no exception, and she's leaning against a stone battlement of Langres' outer fortifications when I catch up. Given the speed she just walked, I figure her knee must be feeling fine again and expect her to set off upon my arrival, but she just stands there. I pause and take a picture. It's nice to have a moment to catch my breath.

"How much further?" asks Pat.

"We're close – less than two kilometres." I start walking.

She follows, but her pace is slow. I check my stride. When her pace drops again, I feel a prick of worry.

"You good?"

"Just tired," she says. "But, yeah, my knee is getting quite painful."

That afternoon Pat stays at the hotel while I go to buy our groceries and takeout for dinner.

There's a TV in our room, so while eating, we watch the Queen's funeral. Twice. Nothing else is being broadcast. We decide to give Pat's knee a day's rest. As my left foot has started giving me intermittent stabbing pain, a day off will do me good too. Attempts to find a bus that will take us on to our next stop are unsuccessful. There is no bus.

"*Quelle surprise,*" Pat grumbles.

I go downstairs to get help ordering a taxi. This isn't straightforward either because drivers don't like leaving town, but after several phone calls, the hotel receptionist finds one who will take us at ten thirty tomorrow morning.

Day twenty-eight. 20 September. To Grandchamp

Our priority is finding an open pharmacy where Pat can purchase a knee brace. A sign on the door of the orthopedic pharmacy across the road from our hotel proclaims an 8:30 AM opening. We try the door at eight thirty-one. It's locked, the lights not on. Impatient in the morning's chill, we wait. At eight forty-five, a woman hurries to the door, messes around with keys, unlocks, enters, relocks. Just before nine, the lights come on. We're at the door as she flips open the inside deadlock.

Pat explains her needs while I explore French pharmaceutical mysteries. Lots of baby wipes and diapers. Shampoos, bodywashes and smelly soaps. Vitamins. Canes. Braces. A foot-care section invites closer inspection, and there it is – the solution to my tender foot. A set of two cushioned elasticized wraps. I've never seen anything like them but understand how they will support and pad my forefoot and can feel the comfort just by looking. We both leave the pharmacy positive that our aches and pains will soon be resolved.

I've contacted our La Vallée Verte host in Grandchamp, so he's expecting our early arrival. After the taxi drops us in the village square, it's not long before Stéphane has welcomed us to bask in the sun on the flagstone terrace of his 16th-century home.

Later he and his wife, Nathalie, prepare a delicious multi-course gourmet meal. We sit with the four other guests, a couple from England and another from the Netherlands, and once again engage in animated conversation.

The Brits, on their way to a second home in Switzerland, and the Dutch, on a driving tour of France, are interested in what motivates us to want to walk such a huge distance. We keep our responses light and say we enjoy slow travel. But, as our hosts have already explained that there are no buses and seem reluctant to offer a ride, Pat asks the Brits which way they are going. They agree to drive her the twenty kilometres to our next stop.

Day twenty-nine. 21 September.
To Champlitte, the Bourgogne-Franche-Comté Region.
Breakfast, just as tasty as dinner, is not to be rushed. I leave, my left foot comfortable with its support, just a few minutes before Pat climbs into Jeremy and Bethany's car.

The walk is pleasant, up and down gentle hills, through quaint villages, farm fields and woods, but it's peculiar not to have Pat to kibitz with. I rest from time to time but never for as long as when we're together. Daydreaming, I listen to birds and breeze and watch light play in overhead tree leaves as I saunter along the trails.

Saunter. Thought to be derived from the Middle English word *saunteren* meaning to wonder or muse or to be in a state of reverie. Over time, it came to mean physical wandering. John Muir provides another interpretation, suggesting that when villagers asked early pilgrims where they were going, pilgrims going to the Holy Land would respond: *A la sainte terre* and so came to be known as sainte-terre-ers – saunterers.

My reverie is interrupted by a string of French swearing. I don't understand the words, but the tone leaves no doubt. A muddy farmer emerges from under an enormous multi-row tiller. The spaces between the blades are clogged with mud, and he's using a crowbar and foul language in a futile attempt to clear the mess.

Seeing me watching, he straightens. "*Bonjour. Je m'excuse,*" he calls with a smile and shrug, waving his muddy crowbar at the tiller.

I wave back. "*Pas de problem. Je ne comprends pas. Bonne chance.*"

Belly laughing, he calls, "*Je pense que tu as très bien compris.*

Bon voyage," then returns to busy farm work.

He's right. I did understand, and walk on, celebrating a whole conversation in French.

I arrive at Hôtel du Donjon as Pat returns from picking up a few groceries before the shops close for the afternoon.

"Oh, I'm so glad to see you," she says. "You need a phone. I was getting worried."

Had Pat and I been walking together, we would, no doubt, have arrived earlier, but while I've sauntered through the French countryside, Pat has endured hours of boredom. I'm sure I don't need a phone; her knee will be fine after a couple more days of rest, and I don't want to be burdened with more weight.

The next stop on the Via Francigena route – Seveux – is a small village, and there is no bus or train that will enable Pat to get there. The stop after that is the city of Besançon and we can get there by bus, so I decide to skip two days walking and to ride with her.

"I'm ruining your walk," Pat worries.

"I'm good," I say. "This will give us more leeway further on. We don't have time to walk the whole distance anyway, so this makes sense."

Day thirty. 22 September. To Besançon.

We step off the early bus from Champlitte to Gray before nine, but the scheduled departure for the connecting bus to Besançon is not until 1:30 PM. After café hopping, we sit shivering at a park picnic bench and watch tour boats plying the Saône, manoeuvre in and out of a set of locks.

"Thank you," says Pat. "This would have been a really long day on my own."

Once in Besançon, we catch a tram to our hotel. After hopping on, we discover that we were supposed to buy tickets at a kiosk before boarding. Two rotund women about our age, swollen feet bulging from sequined slippers a few sizes too small, frown and make derisive comments. In excellent English, a young man tells us not to worry and punches his multi-ride card two extra times to cover our illegal ride. We each give him the €1.50 fare, but the two women continue to give us the stink eye from under their hijabs.

**Day thirty-one and thirty-two. 23 & 24 September.
In Besançon.**
Although dry, the weather has turned single-digit chilly. Feeling the need for warmer clothes, we take a city bus out to a mall with a huge Decathlon Sports store. Pat gets an extra fleece, and I find jogging tights and calf sleeves.

After lunch at the mall, Pat drags me into an electronics store so I can get a phone.

"The simplest one you have," she instructs the young clerk. "She doesn't use a cell phone," she adds, making sure he understands.

He looks at me, askance.

"There's no cell coverage where I live," I explain.

He now looks horrified. Pat and the clerk discuss the merits of the Kim-appropriate phone, and he sets it up so it's ready for use. I'm impressed with his patience as the process takes some time, so ask to speak with his manager. The clerk is new to the job, and both he and the manager are pleased with the positive feedback. I, on the other hand, am not so delighted to now be carting around an extra 284 grams but agree with Pat that while walking solo, I should have a phone.

The next day we mail home a few items we don't need, and in so doing are introduced to the French postal system. Customers are required to use automated machines. The machine asks for, "*Votre adresse.*" We each type in our addresses, but it refuses to accept letters in the postal code. Trying to explain that Canadian postal codes have letters, we ask for help, but the staff keep serving other customers and ignore us. After two hours of frustration, and with the help of another customer, Marie, we're no closer to success. The staff then tell us they're closing for the day and that we must leave. Marie tells them we aren't leaving until they help, so one of them comes grumping over to show the idiot foreigners how easy it is.

"*Votre adresse,*" she hisses through clenched teeth.

I tell her my address.

"*Votre adresse française!*" She raises her voice and rolls her eyes.

"I don't have a French address," I say, rolling my eyes in turn. "I'm a tourist."

In response to a tirade by the annoyed woman, Marie suggests we use her address. "It will be the only way around this machine," she says.

We punch in Marie's address, and the machine allows us to move to the next step, "*adresse du destinataire.*"

Insurance and customs declarations come next. Then the machine demands hefty payment. That accomplished through credit card swiping, it spits out forms to be kept, and other forms to be stuck on the parcels. We hand our well-insured parcels over to the impatient woman who has now worked ten minutes overtime, with an assumption that we'll be filing claims. We're wrong. Our parcels arrive home within the week.

We take Marie out to lunch. She takes us to her favourite spot – a local restaurant we'd never have found on our own. With a Master's in agriculture, Marie is involved in a research project about how the lack of crop biodiversity and rural depopulation threaten food security. We waste no time in telling her what we've noticed and what farmers have told us. She nods in agreement. The situation in rural France is serious.

Day thirty-three. 25 September. To Foucherans.

Having not walked for four days, Pat reports that her knee is less painful. But still not up to continuing, she will stay in Besançon one more day. This is where she began her Via Francigena walk in 2014. Her face betraying disappointment that she won't be retracing those well-remembered steps, she assures me – and herself – that when we meet in two days in Ornans, she'll be ready to walk again.

I set off into a foggy morning and head south once again, feeling refreshed after three days of easy living. The bedbug bites no longer itch although a couple have left scars. The foot support has eased the pain in my foot and my blisters have healed. I mailed enough that – even with the damn phone and new clothes – my pack feels no heavier. My stride is firm, and before long, I'm climbing up a steep hillside leading away from the river and am soon level with Besançon's citadel.

Movement in the mist alerts me to two animals. Looking closer, I see they look like ibex. Well, that's not possible – ibex live in high mountains.

Two spandex-clad men jog by. "Ibex," one says pointing.

At the top of the hill, I sit on a bench to catch my breath. The city lurks within the mist, but I can just make out the citadel ramparts below. As I devour the *pain aux raisins* I'd picked up from a stall on my way out of town, two backpack-laden men appear out of the murk below.

"*Bonjour*, Kim," says one.

"*Bonjour*," I say. "How do you know my name?"

"Oh, we met your friend Pat. She was watching some kayakers from the bridge in town. She said we might see you."

Victor, the talkative younger man, is from Geneva and Alain, the quiet older man – who walks in sandals – is from Paris. They met a few days ago and are walking the Via Francigena for a couple of weeks. I pack up and we carry on together. They don't saunter, so after a couple of kilometres, I claim need for a longer break and encourage them to continue at their speed without feeling they should slow their pace for me.

The day remains chilly and I'm glad for the added warmth of the new jogging tights under my skirt. I wear a Merino long-sleeved base layer all day too. The country becomes wilder, and I pick my way along a forested path atop a ridge with views down either side. Despite not being in a hurry, I'm too cold to spend more than a few minutes resting. Although it's not raining, I pull on my poncho and tuck my knees under it while eating a hasty lunch. The mist rises but grey clouds darken and lower.

Within ten minutes of my arrival at Gîte d'étape du Musée, earnest rain falls. Jacques, who manages the gîte, tells me two other pilgrims will also be staying, so he turns on the heat in the kitchen. I'm delighted because the place is bone-chilling cold. He explains that there are shortages due to the Russian invasion of Ukraine, and everyone is asked to conserve where they can. I pull my chair close to the radiator and put my hands out in anticipation of eventual warmth, then call Pat to let her know I've arrived. She's had a long day at the hotel and will be catching the bus to Ornans in the morning.

A couple of hours later, Victor and Alain arrive. It turns out they took a circuitous route and they're both soaked. While the kitchen is now warm, the rest of the gîte is uncomfortably cold, so they're blue-lipped by the time they re-enter the kitchen in dry clothes.

Jacques returns and opens his little grocery shop. The three of us agree on supplies for a simple pasta meal for which we each pay €2.00. I cook. Alain asks Jacques if he can find us some wine, and Jacques returns with a fine 2014 Bordeaux from his own cellar. We three pilgrims have a jolly evening, Victor translating for Alain and me because he's the only bilingual one of the three of us. The men wash dishes, then I turn off the heat as promised, scurry into my cold room, and without undressing, plunge into an icy sleeping bag. Outside the rain continues.

Day thirty-four. 26 September. To Ornans.

Under-equipped, Victor and Alain endure a cold night and pull on still-wet clothes in the morning. After we share bread and jam with instant coffee, they're away into the rain with a longer day ahead of them than I face. Ornans is only twelve kilometres away. Not wanting to be there too long before Pat's arrival, I dawdle, hoping the rain will stop before I leave. Just before ten, my wish is granted.

Again, the temperature remains cool for walking and too cool for comfortable resting, so with such a short walk, I don't stop. As there is no *pâtisserie* in Foucherons, I don't have my daily *pain aux raisins* anyway.

The rain has flooded a section of the paved bike trail I'm following today. While wading through water that threatens to slop into my shoes, I pass several workmen leaning on their rakes and shovels. Another, heaves heaps of debris off a storm drain with his hands. The water starts flowing and with it my fear of a soaker subsides.

The bike trail has been built on a disused railbed. At one point, it crosses over a high sweeping viaduct. Leaning against the stone balustrade, I pause to admire the misty Gainsborough-painting view across a valley of verdant meadows interspersed with wide-limbed oak and maple trees. The yellowing leaves glow bright against the greyness of the sky. Sheep and cattle graze, bells around their necks ringing in a harmony that echoes of childhood memories – happy alpine wanderings with my parents.

Accompanied by those memories, I continue to Ornans where I meet Pat off the bus, and we spend a comfortable night in a cozy apartment by the rain-swollen Loue River raging through the village.

Day thirty-five. 27 September. To Mouthier-Haute-Pierre.
The morning arrives, a misty 12°C. In the dampness, it feels colder. Pat's knee demands she take the bus again. I sense how difficult this is for her, but we remain optimistic that she'll soon be back on the trail.

Walking along the river on my way out of town, I pass a Gustave Courbet gallery and museum and try the door, but even though the hours posted indicate it should be open, it's closed. Born in Ornans in 1819, Courbet painted many of his compositions here. Peering through the window at some reproductions, I recognize the ridge above town and a couple of the buildings too. Paris Salon critics were uncomfortable with his images of peasant subjects. From the little I see, his attention to realism portrays humble rural living conditions, which may well have upset upper-class sensitivities of the day. Further on, I pause at a viewpoint that was one of his favourite places to paint. Even on this damp cloudy day, it's easy to imagine Gustave standing at his easel illuminating life in his village. I take a picture, an image captured in the blink of an eye.

The route marker points up a steep hill where I follow a broad forested trail far above the river. Ahead, a man and woman wearing enormous backpacks walk with a stroller and dog. When I catch up, we introduce ourselves. Iris and Dave and their dog Blaze from Quebec are camping their way along the Via Francigena. We walk together for a few kilometres, as the trail meanders back down to the river. But when the route leads up into the hills again, this time on a narrow trail, they need to divert to the road because of the stroller – which is for Blaze.

Following the markers and the track I've plotted on Pocket Earth, I enter a cow patty-laden pasture through a difficult-to-open and harder-to-close gate. Climbing up through the steep pasture, I avoid the deepest cow-poo mud but see no sign of the beasts themselves until I come to the gate on the far side. Here, the cows crowd, hock-deep in goo, mud-encrusted rears pressed together. I hear ominous ticking from the electric fence on both sides of the gate. With no other choice, I tap the cow rears with my trekking poles and start squeezing between their warm bodies. One hard push and I'll be in trouble. The cows are ten deep. By tapping and shoving, I ease between them to arrive at the gate. Live electric wire curves across the gate and barbed wire wraps the latch.

Beside the gate, a narrow, arched metal grid offers escape. Barbed wire and electric fencing hug both sides of the grid, so there are no safe handholds. My mud-covered shoes slip on the metal surface. The cows regard me with curious long-lashed eyes and nudge me with soft damp noses. Tossing my trekking poles to the other side, I drop to my knees and crawl up and across the grate, spinning at the halfway point to slide feet first down the far side.

"Sorry girls," I say to the cows. "You can't come with me."

I see the turreted old mansion where Pat and I are staying on the far side of the valley long before I get there. The route takes me down and down into the valley, across a bridge under which the river roils, bits of debris swirling and racing in the flooding current, then up and up to the house where no one answers the door.

I phone Pat. "I'm at the door," I say.

She comes to let me in. It's not much warmer inside than out, but the afternoon's drizzle has turned to rain, so at least it's dry. Later, we brave driving rain to scurry into the town where, for an extortionate €36.00 each, we eat local river trout at the only open restaurant.

Back at the house, our aristocratic hosts have lit a fire in their opulent living room. I ask if we can leave our wet shoes on the hearth. They nod then go back to the quiet of reading their books and sipping something amber from crystal glasses. In that moment, I sense their discomfort. They will accommodate our shoes but paying guests are socially awkward – perhaps an undesirable necessity so they can pay the bills.

Outside the cozy living room, the lighting is so dim we use our headlamps to negotiate creaking stairs and hallways to our sparse room on the third floor at the top of the house. Up here, under the roof, down a draughty hall, a cavernous bathroom with protesting plumbing encourages hurried teeth brushing.

"We're in the servants' quarters," I comment.

Perhaps it's the weather, maybe the cold house, the too-expensive dinner, Pat's knee – a combination of all, but we feel an uncharacteristic gloom as we wrap ourselves in cold sheets and thin blankets that night. We both pull out our sleeping bags for added warmth.

Day thirty-six. 28 September. To Pontarlier.

The deluge continues with the dawn. Our breath plumes as we hurry in the bathroom and pack with chilled fingers.

"I'm going to catch the bus with you," I say as we drink coffee in a high-ceilinged, wood-paneled dining room.

Pat smiles. "Good idea. It's foul out there."

The bus pulls up at nine thirty, and by ten we're walking into the warm reception area of a large hostel in Pontarlier.

"I need to take the train on to Lausanne," Pat tells me. "This hopping forward day by day is just too hard, and my knee's still not ready to walk."

It's a sensible decision, so we splash through rain and puddles to the train station for Pat to buy a ticket. The office is closed for the next three days, and the automated machine is being repaired by a frustrated employee who's having no success. He stops his troubleshooting long enough to find the schedule on his phone.

"If the machine still isn't working in the morning, just get on and ask to buy a ticket before sitting. Just don't sit without a ticket," he advises Pat.

Back at the hostel, we find Victor waiting out the foul weather in the common room. He tells us that there may be a French rail strike the next day. "But your train will be Swiss," he assures Pat, "so it will run."

I go out again and buy us take-out and a bottle of wine for dinner. Later, we fall asleep hoping that Pat won't end up standing all the way to Lausanne. Unticketed riding is illegal and carries a hefty fine.

Day thirty-seven. 29 September. To Jougne.

Heavy rain continues and I'm tempted to join Pat on the train, but a stronger motivation compels me to walk this next section so I can cross into Switzerland on foot. Supplied with *tartes au fromage* from the *pâtisserie* – they've run out of *pain aux raisins* – I set off, clad in flapping poncho, determined to make the best of the next three days.

Tramping along a bike path running beside the rain-swollen Doubs, I hope the river doesn't overflow its banks. Fifteen minutes later, wading through water swirling at the base of benches set between the path and river, I wonder what I'll do if it gets much deeper.

Having reviewed the route, I had expected way markers to lead me across a bridge before leaving town, then away from the river, but red and white route tags painted on tree trunks and stone walls convince me that, despite still being on the "wrong" side of the river, I'm on the correct path. Although a nagging doubt percolates, not wanting to open my pouch in the deluge to confer with Pocket Earth or Paul Chinn's guidebook instructions,

I keep going. The route has been well posted in France. There's no reason to worry.

Head down, hood up, glasses rain-splattered and fogged, I'm soon plodding along an overgrown path running parallel to a rail track that runs parallel to the river. In places, leg-soaking weeds grow taller than me. Smashing at spider web-festooned vegetation with my poles, I add wishing for a machete to growing internal grumbles.

"Not too many pilgrims walking this stretch," I mutter as water trickles into my shoes.

"Oh fuck," my shout bursts out with a rush of despair.

The trail drops down to join a road where a faded route marker points across the river. Hard-hatted workers swarm around on a cement slab where the road ends in a tangle of protruding girders and rebar. There is no bridge.

"You should have trusted your instincts," taunts a voice in my head.

"Shut up. Not helpful," responds my other self.

I consider options. Return to Pontarlier? Not ideal. A few metres back, the railway line swings away from the path and crosses the river. Seeing that bridge through the trees, I investigate and discover I'm not the only person to have been confronted with this dilemma. A narrow path traces along the slippery bank above the river then up to the rail embankment. Gripping tree branches, I pick my way along. If I slip, I'll be swimming. In this water, drowning is the more likely scenario. On hands and knees, I crawl onto the rail bed.

"Yes!"

Just one line crosses a bridge that's wide enough for two. Even if a train comes thundering along, there will be room for me and it. Heart thumping, I scurry across. On the other side, there's a two-metre vertical drop to the road that ends in chunks of broken concrete at the river edge. I drop my poles down and lower myself by clinging to spindly shrubs.

Once on the road, I turn away from the river and squeeze through a small gap in the industrial fencing that blocks traffic from plunging into the river and find myself at an intersection. Traffic whizzes by. As much as I don't enjoy walking along roads – and this one is busy and narrow – I'm delighted.

In the distance, crouching in low cloud, Château de Joux sits atop a bluff, and it's not long before I'm climbing a leg-burning path to visit this fortress that for centuries has guarded the frontier. Looking forward to a dry interlude in the castle museum – imagining a hot lunch at a pleasant restaurant – I round the last corner and walk towards the entrance. A sign informs me that for today – just today – the castle is closed.

Swearing, I march up to the shelter of the entry tunnel, hunker down and open a squished cheese pie. While eating, I pull out my route notes: *Lightfoot reports bridge out on direct route out of Pontarlier. Use official route.* I can only laugh.

Later, as I trudge, shivering, beside a disused rail line, past old train cars and machinery, the rain falling with ever-greater intensity, I realize I haven't seen any route makers for a while.

"This is just not your day, is it?" says that annoying inner voice.

When an old-style open-air train station with picnic benches materializes out of the fog, I take shelter. I pull off my poncho, hang it on a convenient nail, sit at one of the benches, eat some chocolate and call Pat to let her know all is well. I figure if I tell someone all is well, it will be.

A small train huffs into the station. Brakes squeal and it stops. No one gets off, but dry people stare out. I stare back. Waiters pass back and forth, serving plates of steaming food. The curious eyes turn from me to their hot meal, and I watch the business of eating until enough condensation accumulates on the windows to block my view.

On the railbed again, I hurry. The train has no choice but to return on this track. I want to beat it. I don't want those dry people to stare at this little, wet, lonesome pilgrim. The walking is unpleasant along the now-used rail line, the loose fill uneven under my stumbling feet. After several kilometres, I win the race and drip away from the track without further train encounters.

When I arrive at charming Hôtel la Couronne, the receptionist hands me a laundry basket. "Put your wet things in here," he says. "I will hang them in the laundry room. They will be dry for you in the morning."

The hotel's restaurant opens at seven. I make a reservation and am grateful for a tasty meal for which I am not overcharged and for which I don't have to go out in the rain.

Our pilgrimage through France has provided a myriad of sensory experiences. Deep sorrow at the war graves, delicious flavours of baked goods, heady aroma of grape fermentation and momentary despair at finding a bridge is out, to name a few.

Day thirty-eight. 30 September.
To Lignerolle, Vaud, Switzerland.

Wearing still-sdamp shoes, but with raingear stowed in my pack, I head for the border. A dirt track between rows of stacked firewood covered in blue tarps brings me to a sign: *Douane, Zoll, Dogana*. It informs me – in French – that I may not cross with a motorized vehicle and that my goods must be customs-cleared personal effects. The Swiss firewood piles are more uniform than the French, and while French tarps had flapped in the wind, the Swiss tarps are arranged and secured with precision.

Entering a forest, I walk along a stretch of original Roman road that has been excavated from beneath centuries of soil accumulation. Sitting on that ancient road, nibbling on undeclared French chocolate, I marvel at the expanse of time this chariot-grooved pavement represents and contemplate living in a place where I could sense personal attachment to such a depth of history.

My ancestors only began arriving in what is now Canada a little over 250 years ago. As a descendant of those settlers from Scotland, Wales and England, I have no claim on Canada's ancient past. Yet were I to return to my ancestral homelands, I'd be a foreigner.

Feeling the chill of the stone road, I get to my feet and continue walking while wrestling with my quandary. With a Celtic indigenous identity, how do I discover my place in my birth country? My home. How many centuries will pass before the DNA of my descendants will respond with a knowing of belonging?

Leaving the Roman road, I descend into a wide valley and walk beneath an A9 highway viaduct. Its so high that the sound of vehicles rushing overhead is muted by the distance. Built to ease transportation between France and Italy, the viaduct enables rushing vehicles to seemingly fly over with no connection to the landscape below. Today the surroundings – tidy farmhouses and pastures – appear undisturbed, but the building of this massive road must have meant years of disruption. I would not want this monstrosity, supported by its massive concrete legs, marauding across the otherwise beautiful place I called home. But the smaller roads and villages are, no doubt, safer and quieter without all the through traffic.

As it descends from the valley and deeper into a gorge, the trail gets steeper and narrower and appears seldom used. I dig out my iPad and review the route. Yes, this is the Via Francigena. Route markers on trees also assure me that I am where I should be. So where are all the other pilgrims? I'd like to know. I'd like to walk into this claustrophobic gorge with a companion.

At the bottom, a river roars beneath a rotted-looking bridge. I study that bridge and debate. How slippery is it? Very. I can see the slime. How sturdy is it? Not very. I can see it vibrating. Options? None. I unclip the waistbelt of my pack – if the bridge collapses, I don't want to be burdened by a pack I can't get off. The bridge wobbles as I cross. On the other side, pleased to have met today's challenge, I re-buckle and carry on.

Then, the next obstacle presents itself. I figure I've arrived in a *Temple of Doom* movie and hope Harrison Ford pops out of the bushes to rescue me, but I'm no Kate Capshaw. So, on my own, I creep along a three-metre-high, less-than-half-metre-wide concrete catwalk above the raging river. Even though the catwalk has a skinny wiggly railing on both sides, my vertigo gets the upper hand before I'm halfway along. I'm too afraid to go back. I'm too afraid to go forward. I'm going to fall.

"Focus on the end. Stop looking at your feet. Keep moving."

"Where did you come from?" I ask.

"You know I'm always with you," says Mike.

Walking behind me, his hand steady on my shoulder, Mike pours comfort into my ear and gives me courage.

On the other side, I turn. "I love you," I say into dense spray kicked up by the water as it smashes against the concrete base of the catwalk. I reach to my shoulder where I'd felt his hand, the pressure of my own fingers no more substantial than his touch had been. "I still miss you."

The gorge trail continues wending along the river, sometimes through little tunnels cut into the cliffs, sometimes on cantilevered structures clinging to the rock, but always in gorge-bottom gloom. The river's roar drowns all other sound. I now walk with a sense of being in Middle Earth. Is that Gollum? No, just a stump.

Emerging into the fading light of late afternoon, I walk into the village of Les Clées, then climb farm roads up and up, under another towering A9 viaduct to Lignerolle. Although the village is not on the Via Francigena, a few days ago, Pat and I had arranged to stay here because it's on a bus route. When she decided to continue to Lausanne, I hadn't bothered to cancel. As I huff up the hill, I begin to regret that decision because tomorrow I will be retracing my steps back down to Les Clées to rejoin the Via Francigena.

Today's walk along a Roman road, through a deep gorge and under a modern viaduct.

My hosts, Audrey and Phillipe, invite me to join them at a dinner party they're hosting for several of their friends. Their home fills with laughter and chatter, the language flowing around and through me. As is often the case, wine improves everyone's level of bilingualism to the point that I forget that I can't speak French because I'm understanding, and the others seem to understand me too. When I slip upstairs to a cozy bed at ten o'clock, the party is still going strong.

Day thirty-nine. 1 October. To Lausanne.

After a chaotic breakfast, everyone in the family off in different directions, I head back down to Les Clées, my return taking less than half the time of yesterday afternoon's hike up the hill. Like yesterday, the weather remains chilly with low cloud, but it's not raining.

Back on the Via Francigena route, I'm soon tramping through woodland to the sound of shooting, so pull out my neon green pack cover and tug a neon green buff over my hat, hoping Swiss hunters won't mistake a bright-clad human for prey.

Once out of the woodland, a cold wind encourages me to pull on my jacket, fighting to get my arms into flapping sleeves. Ahead, a 4x4 forestry police vehicle sits by the track. Two forestry men wearing bright red uniform jackets emerge from nearby trees, each with a large dog straining on a leash. I call out a greeting. One of the men comes over, and while his dog sniffs my shoes and legs and buries an inquisitive nose into my hand, I ask if it's safe to walk through the forest when there's active hunting.

In a poetic blend of French and English, he assures me there have been very few accidents and that the *forêt* where I'm headed is not *ouvert pour la chasse* on Saturdays, but he also points to the sky. "*Beaucoup de vent aujourd'hui.* Big wind. Big – *pluie* – rain," he says. "*Ne restez pas longtemps dans la forêt.*"

Thanking him and his dog, I hunch into the growing onslaught of buffeting wind gusts. At first, in the shelter of the forest, the walking is easier, but soon branches sway and leaves swirl in confused air currents beneath the canopy. Small branches begin littering the trail. Then the racket of wind beating and cracking larger branches and hurling them to the ground increases. I run. The forest groans. I run faster, using my poles to launch myself into a longer stride. Out of breath, I leap and run. Full of wind, the forest sways and snaps.

Bursting out into the village of Romainmôtier, I stop to catch my breath, then rain begins driving out of the black sky. I scamper down the street and dive into a café. Peering through fogged glasses, I order a cappuccino and a slice of homemade berry pie. A seat facing the window offers a cozy place from which to watch the storm rage. An inside-out umbrella flies by followed by a small table rolling down the street. A man struggles to retract a billowing awning, another couple of men gather bouncing chairs. Blossoms shred and tear off window-box flowers. More people crowd into the café. Standing room only. Needing to give up my spot, I pull on rain gear and pack, squeeze through the crowd and head into the maelstrom.

There has been a priory here since 450 CE, and like thousands before me, I take shelter within. Sigeric, however, did not stop here, travelling instead north from Lausanne to Orbe and then on to Pontarlier. Entering the church, I'm startled by the organ leaping into a thunderous rendition of Handel's "The Arrival of the Queen of Sheba." Always one for an occasion, I grin at two women surrounded by flowers with which they are creating huge bouquets, and dance down the aisle past other women tying bows onto the aisle-side chairs.

"*Bravo, Madam*," says one of the women, and we all share in a laugh.

There will be a wedding this afternoon.

The rain lets up enough for me to continue, but the wind remains fierce, so I decide to walk to nearby Croy where there's a station. I'll catch a train the last twenty-eight kilometres into Lausanne. I'd planned on taking a train for the last ten kilometres anyway because I have no desire to walk through the urban sprawl.

Once in Croy, I negotiate the automated ticket machine and receive a ticket just as the train whisks into the station and whisks right out again. With an hour before the next train, I enter a glassed-in shelter and wait. During that hour, the wind tears apart a fence, one panel at a time, smashing each one into bits and strewing them across the ground. It then attacks the metal roof of a shed, bouncing it up and down, a little more up and a little less down each time, until the last screws give out and the roof sails away. The wind hammers and rattles my little shelter but it remains secure. Two other women arrive near train time. One shows me the remnants of her umbrella, then we blow out onto the platform and into the train.

The train station in Lausanne occupies a rough area of town where many homeless people huddle in doorways, under wet blankets and leaking tarps. Since leaving Calais, this is the first time I've been confronted with human misery of this magnitude. I think they may refugees. By the time I reach the hostel, I've given away all my change – over €20. While my purse is lighter, I feel the heaviness of sorrow and recall a few of lines from Warsan Shire's impactful poem "Home:"

> *No one leaves home unless*
> *home is the mouth of a shark ...*
> *You have to understand,*
> *that no one puts their children in a boat*
> *unless the water is safer than the land.*

At the hostel, I find Pat struggling with cabin fever, but she reports a much-improved knee. When we eat dinner that evening in the hostel, we share the large dining room with other travellers, as well as Ukrainian families, and longer-term guests representing a broad international spectrum.

Day forty. 2 October. In Lausanne.

The wind and rain continue unabated. We hunker down, eat three meals in the hostel and enjoy the hospitality of the bar, neither of us going near the outer doors. But Pat is ready to continue with the caveat that for the next couple of weeks, we keep our daily walks to under twenty kilometres. We plan our next days according to that need and hope for an improvement in the weather.

Day forty-one. 3 October. To Aigle.

Before leaving home, we'd decided to take one of the historic paddlewheel boats along the north shore of Lake Geneva to Villeneuve at the east end of the lake. We depart the hostel into a clear dawn and ride a city bus to Port d'Ouchy where we confirm our second-class tickets. As we wait, a group of boisterous school children arrives and joins the line.

"Should we upgrade?" I ask Pat.

Pat hands me her ticket. "Go for it."

I dash to the ticket window. "Do those children have second-class tickets?"

"Yes," says the ticket woman. "Sorry. Your trip will be noisy."

"Is it too late to buy first-class tickets?"

She smiles. "Not too late. But €15.00 extra for each ticket."

I push our tickets through the slot. "Two upgrades please."

I'm back in the line as it begins flooding towards the gangplank. Once on board, we flash our first-class tickets at the purser who points us towards the upper deck. Soon the wheels start turning and we settle down to watch the shore slide by. First, we pass luxurious mansions, some with private marinas, yachts bobbing. Then past vineyards climbing hills bisected by rail lines and roads. Trains zip back and forth. Sometimes we see three and four at the same time on different lines racing between the tunnels. The scene reminds me of the train set Dad built and the two of us played with when I was a child.

The A9 highway follows the lake as well, into tunnels and across viaducts, vehicles zooming along, sun glinting off their windshields in tiny glimmers and flashes. A popular tourist attraction, the boat calls in at ports along the way, more people embarking, some leaving. Most of the passengers will make the return journey this afternoon.

Disembarking in Villeneuve, we catch a bus out to a commercial area to shop for warmer clothes. There has already been a blizzard up on the Col du Grand-St-Bernard. We won't cross the pass in a storm but expect to be walking in sub-zero temperatures and maybe in snow. Over the past week, I've been wearing all my layers and have not felt warm enough. Even in this morning's sun, the temperature has remained in the single digits.

Pleased with our purchases, we exit the store into a 23°C afternoon. Laughing, we pull off layers and stuff them into already-bulging packs. An easy twelve kilometres through a broad flat valley brings us to Aigle where we stay with Bernard and Marion in their third-floor condo home.

Bernard, a retired paediatrician, spent most of his career working for NGOs in impoverished areas of Central and South America. Marion is a comedian with more interesting things on her mind than attending to the cooking of a gourmet meal. They both offer the genuine hospitality of people who have received welcome from others. Although their English is minimal, we enjoy hearing their views on the responsibilities that should be inherent with neutrality. They tell us that Switzerland has joined the EU in sanctioning Russia, but they feel their country should take a stronger stand on many global issues. Struggling to find enough common language to explore our shared apprehensions over the plight of millions of refugees trying to find safety within Europe's borders, we agree that nations must enact more tolerant immigration policies.

We sleep on mats on the floor of their grandchildren's playroom, Pat unplugging a rotating mobile to charge her iPad, me removing a pink unicorn from my pillow.

Day forty-two. 4 October. To Orsières, Valais.

We take the train to Saint Maurice which is where we would have spent the night had we walked. The train station is in an industrial area, so what we see does not appeal. Instead of exploring, we catch the next train on to Martigny. Again, not feeling that we're missing any charming villages or beautiful scenery, we continue on the train to Sembrancher where we miss a connecting train to Orsières by seconds. Walking into the village, we find a café, then head back to the station to await our next, and smaller, train. No longer on the main line, this little train climbs a steep grade into Orsières where we alight in a quintessential Swiss Alpine village.

Pat has been in contact with Laura, whom we'd first met in Seraucourt over a month ago, and she joins us on our tiny hotel balcony to sip a late afternoon glass of wine and to watch the setting sun turn the peaks rosy with alpenglow. Her husband has gone home, and she will now continue on her own until a friend arrives in a couple of weeks. We suggest walking together but Laura isn't an early riser, so we agree to keep an eye out for each other tomorrow in Bourg-Saint-Pierre.

Day forty-three. 5 October. To Bourg-Saint-Pierre

I wear my new jacket with gratitude when we set off into a sub-zero morning, but as soon as the sun clears the eastern ridgeline both Pat and I are peeling off clothes down to bare legs and arms. Up and up, we climb. Despite being breathless, I feel surges of joyous energy. Perhaps high places are where my DNA feels most at home. I revel in the space and the nearing peaks.

At one point the path has been dug up, a sewer pipe lying exposed within a trench. There is no way around, so we climb down into the trench and up the other side. Later, when we come upon an electric fence strung across the trail, Pat worries that we'll have to walk around by the road.

"No worries," I say. "Look. This is an insulated handle. We just unhook the fence. Like this. And step through without touching the wire."

"How do you know that?" asks Pat.

"I've done this several times over the past week," I say. "Was scary the first time, but sort of made sense, so I tried it."

Following a ski lift cutting up a hill, we arrive at Hôtel Bivouac Napoleon. We're enjoying an afternoon beer on the sunny terrace when Laura comes marching along and joins us. She's staying the night at a hostel further up the road in town so continues an hour later with the hope of seeing us somewhere in Italy.

Pat and I have just ordered dinner when Laura reappears. "Nothing is open in the village. May I join you?"

"Of course. We're having a cheese fondue."

It's a delicious fondue, but after Laura leaves and Pat and I waddle to our room, we're sure we'll have indigestion for days.

Day forty-four. 6 October. In Bourg-Saint-Pierre.

Another sunny day greets us; however, determined to keep Pat's knee in working order, we resist the temptation to continue to the pass. Instead, we catch up on e-mails, revise our onward itinerary to accommodate shorter days and relax at the hotel's spa. The jacuzzi is too cool, but the sauna is just right. Wrapped in fluffy housecoats, our feet in slippers, we sip tea in the solarium and gaze at the surrounding peaks. When I pull my clothes on again, they feel grubby despite yesterday's handwashing.

Day forty-five. 7 October.
To the 2469 Metre Summit of Col du Grand-St-Bernard.
"Happy birthday, Pat."

She stretches and smiles. "A good day to be seventy." Jumping up, she tests her knee. "And a good day to go to the col."

The ground is frost-covered when we set off, but as we climb, the sun climbs and soon the temperature climbs too. Up past a Heidi cottage, then along a huge reservoir, up above the treeline, ever up. Euphoria lends my legs wings and allows my mind to revel in a kaleidoscope of sensations. Seed pods pop and tap in the breeze. As the trail narrows, our legs brush berry-heavy branches to release the sharp tang of juniper. The oranges, golds and greens of sparse vegetation reach to steeper barren terrain. Grey rock faces climb to white peaks that slice the cobalt sky. I fill and overflow with wonder.

Below, a man peddles his bike, straining up the road. We wave and wish him well, our voices gliding on wind currents. Looking up, he raises an arm. We will never meet, never speak, never know each other's names, but we have connected.

Overhead, a raptor soars, wing feathers grasping subtle eddies. Pausing to admire its grace, we look up to meet the raptor's gaze. Spying prey, it plunges behind a ridge. We will never know what it hunted, but in this wild place, we feel connected.

Every once in a while, we notice the ventilation shafts that keep fresh air flowing in the St Bernard vehicle tunnel. Running deep beneath our feet, the tunnel offers a speedy weather-proof alternate to the famous but tortuous Road 21 along which the cyclist labours. Road 21 was not completed until 1905 and is still the only vehicle access up and over the pass.

Up a final steep slope, we clamber to arrive at the stark summit of Col du Grand-St-Bernard. Grey snow lies heaped in shady places. A bitter wind whips across the open pass from the Italian side.

Goose bumps rising on our sweaty bare arms and legs, we dash into the hospice that has sheltered pilgrims and other travellers since it was first opened by Saint Bernard of Menthon in 1049.

As we check in, I ask about visiting the resident St Bernards. The breed originated here 360 years ago, but we're told the dogs have been transported into the valley because of the snow.

"They don't like the snow?" I ask. "What kind of mountain-rescue dog doesn't like snow?"

"Well, maybe they like it, but the hospice and pass close tomorrow, so they will stay in the valley until the spring," explains the receptionist.

Bred at this hospice for the purpose of rescuing travellers lost in blizzards and under avalanches, the dogs have saved hundreds of lives. I'm saddened to learn that these days, their descendants' main function is posing with tourists for selfies – and only in pleasant weather.

While I'm brooding about the decline of dog chivalry, the receptionist hands Pat a package. In it are letters from her brothers and sister and drawings from her five grandchildren. At dinner the staff present her with dessert complete with a sparkler. Since we first considered this walk four years ago, it's been Pat's dream to be here on her birthday. Dreams do come true.

From valley villages in pouring rain to ascending Col du Grand-St-Bernard in the sunshine – Switzerland offers glorious scenery at every turn.

Day forty-six. 8 October.
To Etroubles, the Aosta Valley, Italy.

Yesterday's endless views across slow-clad peaks are obliterated by swirling fog.

"How's your knee?" I ask, as Pat emerges from down bed covers. "We could wait and leave tomorrow."

I've no desire to spend the day here in the chill fog, but downhill walking is hard, even on healthy knees, so I'll support Pat's decision.

"Knee's fine. And there's rain in the forecast. Up here, that could be snow. We need to go." Seeing my concern, she grins and adds, "No pain at all."

At breakfast, I review the highlighted route on my iPad. If the fog doesn't lift, we'll need to pay attention. The pass swarms with intersecting trails, some leading to the surrounding peaks. There will be no brandy-keg-carrying St Bernards coming to our rescue if we get waylaid.

When we step outside, our breath plumes. We're bundled in Merino base layers, fleece, vests, jackets, toques and gloves. For the first time since leaving home, I'm wearing rain resistant capris over my jogging tights instead of a skirt. Our packs sag, half empty and light.

Departing the hospice on a surviving stretch of Roman road, we cross into Italy. Below us, a silver sports car plies Road 21, passes an unstaffed border hut – where the road becomes the SS27 – then disappears into the fog with a tap of brakes and change of gears. We are left in silence, ghosts of the pass swirling grey, touching our faces with damp tendrils.

The Col du Grand-St-Bernard – being one of the most accessible routes through the Alps – has been in use since the Bronze Age. The first recorded invasion force marched south via this route in 390 BCE when Celtic Gauls swept across the pass, advanced south, and plundered Rome. This invasion prompted Rome to turn on their northern neighbours and conquer Gaul. Of course, because Roman legions marched to and fro several times, they built a road.

The last invasion force was led by Napoleon in May 1800 when he marched on the Cisalpine Republic. Two years later, Napoleon redefined the region as the Italian Republic, but the Italy we know today did not unite until 1870. I later discover that Italy's current border was established in 1975. Although the Roman Empire was birthed here, centuries of violent conflicts, fierce loyalties and devious treachery have led to modern Italy being a younger country than Canada.

Very soon we're heading down. Some of the trail across rock outcrops requires cautious stepping on the frosted surfaces. Always down. The SS27 zigs and zags with looping hairpin bends, taking a much longer, less precipitous route. We cross the road several times but, despite its fame, only see one car. Down and down out of the fog and back below the treeline. More ventilation shafts announce the tunnel far beneath our feet. We see where it emerges, busy with traffic streaming out into the daylight, other traffic labouring up and into the mountain. Maybe today's weather doesn't invite the longer scenic drive over the pass, but perhaps the lack of SS27 traffic is because most people appreciate the much quicker zip through the mountain.

We plan to take a shortcut but, in following the signposts and not paying attention, miss the turn and don't notice until we've walked too far down the valley to retrace our steps. The shortcut would have saved us less than two kilometres, but I see Pat's fatigue when we discover our mistake. Or is it pain?

In Saint Léonard, we stop for a break. I suggest we try to get a ride the rest of the way, but Pat insists there's no need. By the time we walk into Saint-Oyen, she's limping and no longer hiding – denying – her pain. Again, I suggest a ride and again she's adamant that she'll walk. I'm undecided. Our friendship is based on mutual respect, so I accept her decision. She offers no alternative. We've been through many challenges together, from crazy kayaking adventures to scary encounters with human smugglers. She's never before shut me out.

Back in Canada, at Christmas, Pat explains that her knee pain was intense but even worse was her realization that her walk was done. At the time, she was feeling too vulnerable and – she considers this word with care – traumatised, for rational thought. She shrugs, "I just couldn't *not* keep walking."

We do keep walking, but with rain threatening and the temperature dropping, I want to walk faster than she is able. Her pace drops to a series of tortured steps between more prolonged periods of standing to lean over her poles.

I walk ahead, then stop and wait.

"Stop waiting for me," Pat says more than once.

"I'm not leaving you," I tell her again and again.

That's all I can say. That's all I can do. Pat has erected a protective wall around herself, her pain, her misery – a wall I cannot breach. I sense that if I do invade that private space, she will lose her resolve.

I point out our hotel on the other side of the valley. Pat looks in the general direction but doesn't take it in. I know this is the end of her walk and continue alone twenty, then fifty, then seventy metres ahead. Across the street from the hotel, I stop and wait, shivering. We cross together. I hold open the door. Pat hobbles past, leaning on her poles as the rain begins in earnest. In our room, she collapses onto her bed and closes her eyes.

"You want a beer?" I ask.

She nods, "But you'll have to bring it to the room."

At reception, I ask about a bus into Aosta. Tomorrow is Sunday, so there is no bus but the hotel can provide transportation. At the bar I order two beer and take them back. Pat hasn't moved.

"Maybe you should get out of your damp clothes."

She nods and doesn't move. I warm up in a steaming shower, then drink my beer. Pat doesn't move. There's no Internet in our room, so I catch up on my journal and think. What next?

"Should I bring dinner to our room?" I ask an hour later.

"No." she says. Struggling from the bed, leaning on both poles, she makes her way down the hall and into the crowded dining room. She doesn't have her usual glass of chardonnay.

"I have to go home," she says when we get back to our room.

"I know. We'll sort it out tomorrow. We need Internet to plan."

A few minutes later, I ask, "Should I come with you?"

"No! Absolutely not. I feel terrible enough about this. Kim, you walk to Rome."

"I'm not sure you can manage on your own," I say.

"Yes, I can. I'll be fine. You're not coming home with me."

"Well, it's raining cats and dogs out there and supposed to be worse tomorrow, so I'm getting a drive with you to Aotsa."

Pat snorts. "OK. But after that – you walk."

I nod and agree. I want to continue, but if she needs me to help her home, I will. It's what friends do. Grumbling about sketchy Internet, I go back to reception and e-mail the hotel in Aosta, explain the situation, and ask if we can check in early.

Day forty-seven. 9 October. To Aosta.

One of the hotel managers drives us to Aosta through pouring rain. I might have enjoyed walking this section on a pleasant day, but as I peer from the car's rain-streaked window at wind-tossed tree branches, water rushing down hillsides and deep puddles on the road, I have no regrets.

When we arrive at our hotel before ten, our room is ready. The receptionist offers to help in any way she can. Pat gets to work on the formidable task of planning her departure from Europe. After several hours, we have a plan. I will accompany her by bus to the Malpensa airport in Milan, then return here for a second night. Pat has a flight booked from Milan to Heathrow. She will need to stay there for three days until she can get a flight to Canada.

The receptionist orders us a pizza for dinner as the restaurant isn't open. We enjoy it with a bottle of wine and try to cheer each other up.

"You'll be able to catch up with Laura," says Pat. "She's just one day ahead."

"I sent her a message this afternoon. I'm sure we'll meet up. And you'll be home to start working on your house renos."

Pat struggles to find enthusiasm.

Day forty-eight. 10 October. To Milan and return to Aosta.

Pat can't walk, so the receptionist has ordered us a taxi to the bus depot. The bus trip seems to take forever, and we arrive an hour later than scheduled. The Milan depot is a graffiti-covered, garbage-infested dump where we discover that there is no longer a connecting airport shuttle. We have to take the Metro to Milan's main train station, then catch a train to the airport.

"Pat, I won't have time to get to the airport and back before my bus departs. I'll come on the Metro, but you're going to have to take the train on your own."

"It's OK. You've already done enough," she says as she hobbles into the crowded Metro where we manage to get tickets from the machine, then squeeze onto an overcrowded train.

My arms occupied with holding onto a central pole in the lurching subway, and to Pat's pack, I don't notice the pickpocket removing my passport wallet – which includes my bank and credit cards – from my purse – which is secured on my chest – until another passenger gives the alarm and points to my passport now dropping to the ground at our feet. As I crouch to retrieve it – difficult in the press of bodies – I see my cash has also been dropped. I don't see the pickpocket.

Shaken by the near disaster, I follow Pat out onto the platform where we flow with the mob up escalators and through the labyrinth of the underground station. Pat sees a kiosk where she buys her train ticket to the airport. We continue up out of the bowels of the earth into the enormous train station. There's airport-type security, so without a ticket, I can go no further. Pat's train is due to leave in less than five minutes.

With no time to say good-bye, I hand over her pack, she heaves it onto one shoulder, then leaning on her poles, limps through security and out of my line of sight.

I feel naked. No pack. No Pat. I look in my violated purse – passport wallet still where I shoved it back, grit from the Metro floor smudged across the cover. I feel sick. Shaken.

Looking up at the huge station clock, I realize I need to get a move on. Back into the frenetic Metro maze. Buy my ticket. Find the right platform. Hop on the train. Hop off at the right exchange. Hop on the next train. Arrive back at the bus depot. Time to grab a bite to eat. The sandwich is revolting.

Needing to use the toilet, I pay €1.00 and enter. The toilet is even more revolting. Gagging from the appalling stench, I hold my clothing away from the bowl and hover over the grubby seatless rim. Emerging, I use half a mini bottle of hand sanitizer. By the time the bus arrives, my head is pounding with a fierce headache. I climb aboard and close my eyes.

Day forty-nine. 11 October. To Saint Vincent.
I have tried to find accommodation at the next town – Nus – but nothing is open, so I catch the train to Nus. Eleven minutes after boarding, I disembark in Nus and start walking to Saint Vincent, passing one of the closed hotels on my way out of town.

The trail takes me past prosecco vineyards and through small villages, one of which is derelict. Walking past the crumbling buildings offers a spooky glimpse into the hard lives led by the farmers who once called the place home.

Twenty kilometres after leaving Nus, I arrive at my hotel in Saint Vincent. Looking into the dining room as I check in, I ask about dinner.

"We are closed for dinner," the receptionist tells me. "But there are restaurants further up the road in town. They open at seven thirty."

At seven thirty I'm at the door of a restaurant recommended by the hotel receptionist.

"*Hai una prenotazione?*" asks the host as she unlocks the door.

"Um. Reservation?" I clarify.

"Do you have a reservation?" she repeats, her voice louder.

"Sorry. No reservation," I answer.

Her impatience translates into aggression as she huffs, "With no reservation, you cannot expect to eat."

Hunger has been gnawing for three hours. Vulnerable and

swallowing alarm, I persist. "You've been closed all afternoon." I point at the sign. "I walked into town a few hours ago. How could I make a reservation?" I study her face for a sign of weakening. There is none. Desperation rising, I plead, "I'll eat quickly if you would be kind enough to let a hungry pilgrim buy a meal." I smile, hoping my lips don't produce a snarl.

A voice from the kitchen issues a command. With a dramatic sigh the woman points at a table by the door.

"Eat fast." She scowls.

I sit. She thumps a menu on the table and flounces away. Scanning the Italian words until I recognize *ragù alla Bolognaise*, I call out to Mean Woman.

She returns. "What do you want?"

"I want this." I point. "And a glass of white wine."

I've had the menu for all of thirty seconds and feel satisfaction as I hand it back. She's fawning over two other guests when a rotund chef delivers a generous bowl of steaming spaghetti bolognaise with a wink and smile. I gobble, clean my plate, gulp my wine and stand at the bar to pay my bill within fifteen minutes. Eleven of twelve tables remain unoccupied.

Day fifty. 12 October. In Saint Vincent.

I spend an extra day here to sort out next steps because I'm too tired and hungry after a day's walking to put much effort into planning. Answering a message from Laura – she's in Ivrea taking a day off with a sore foot – has me looking forward to catching up with her tomorrow.

I've been following interesting posts from Lea since the beginning of the walk. Now reading her Facebook post that she's made it to Siena but isn't walking any further, I feel the loss of a fellow pilgrim I've never met.

My son – Brian – whom everyone, including me, calls Fly – has offered to join me. Because he walks much faster than I do, I suggest he come for a holiday after my walk, instead. We text back and forth. He likes the idea. I start calculating when I might get to

Rome, as I need to depart the EU by 23 November. I'm still mulling over the possibilities when I fall asleep.

Day fifty-one. 13 October. To Ivrea, Piedmont.

I check my messages. There's no answer from Laura, so I set off towards Verrés hoping we'll connect this evening. With each step, I notice the mountains receding and the expansive Po plain pressing into the widening Aosta valley. The bus trip to and from Milan provided enough of an introduction to this region for me to think I might not enjoy days of walking through such flat terrain.

Meantime, today's trail leads me up and down several steep inclines, and I'm soon warm enough to be short-sleeved and bare-legged. Stopping to take a picture of a garden overflowing with flowers and vegetables growing in haphazard profusion, I imagine Claude Monet would be delighted with this colourful tapestry. A woman walks into view and pauses. I wave and point at my camera. She ducks out of sight. After taking the picture, I walk down some stone steps to her garden gate. She stands, waiting, a harvesting basket on her hip.

"You have a beautiful garden," I say as I show her the picture.

She smiles. "*Bella.*"

"*Bella,*" I repeat.

She points out her vegetables, naming each one and encouraging me to learn the words. Having shared our love of gardening, the joy of the simple encounter and the word *pomodoro* stays with me when I continue on my way. Now I'll recognize tomato dishes on Italian menus.

Further on, a sign informs me the trail is closed, so I backtrack a few metres and follow a detour down to and along a busy road. This is where I discover that the Italian drivers on this stretch of road on this day – not wanting to generalize – are not as courteous towards walkers as the French drivers Pat and I had encountered. They do not slowdown, they do not move over; instead, some nudge closer to the edge of the road as they speed by. Maybe they get a kick out of seeing the terror spread across my face as I leap into the ditch.

By the time I'm off that stretch of road, rage bubbles, my body's fight-or-flight defence systems fully activated and in exhausting conflict.

Over the next weeks, I will begin to recognize a pattern of inhospitable behaviours exhibited by some Italians. In Italy, foreign transients – such as a person marching along carrying a pack – are not always welcome. I will meet more kind than unkind people, but never knowing which to expect will take a toll, undermine my confidence, and leave me teetering with alarming fragility. There will be plenty of opportunities to revisit those gentle moments with the woman in her garden and allow that memory to ease the misery of rejection.

Twenty kilometres after leaving Saint Vincent, I walk into Verrés where I catch the train a further thirty kilometres to Ivrea in anticipation of finding Laura. Ivrea's train station is a filthy introduction to the town, but as I walk up a hill towards my hotel, the dilapidated urban environment is replaced by a tidier tourist area where I stay near the castle walls.

At the hotel, I check my messages and there's one from Laura. Excited, I open it. My momentary joy is dashed. She's on the train to Milan, starting her journey home to Montana because of severe foot pain. I'm so disappointed that it takes a moment to feel appropriate empathy.

As the idea of having a post-walk holiday with Fly has taken hold, I've been pondering about how to make that happen without rushing through Tuscany. With no one else's desires to consider, I send Paul Chinn an e-mail requesting suggestions on which parts of the route might best be skipped.

While eating another solitary dinner – a dinner I'd imagined eating with Laura – I begin worrying about when an injury will send me home. Rome becomes an unobtainable goal. Such idiocy to think we could walk that far in such a short amount of time. Damn fools. I imagine people responding to my pronouncements that I'm walking from Canterbury to Rome with derision. They'll know me for a fake. I've taken buses and trains and even a couple of taxis. I am a fake. Right now, I'm just a silly old woman who should pack up her dreams and go home.

Day fifty-two. 14 October. To Vercelli.

Walking down to the train station, I again marvel at the grubbiness of this part of town. The roadside garbage looks like it's been accumulating for weeks. The train arrives, just a few minutes late, and a couple of hours later, I alight in Vercelli. Here the clean station extends a pleasant welcome to a charming city. The B&B host also welcomes me despite my early arrival, showing me into a palatial room with 17th- and 18th-century furnishings. With pride, he points out original tile floors, and several photos of his brother winning Olympic gold medals for fencing.

A reply from Paul informs me that many people find walking through the flat Po Valley quite monotonous. By taking the train from Ivrea to Vercelli, I've already covered two walking days of that expanse. Now I'll take it further without fear that I'll be missing much.

After visiting the duomo and basilica, I spend the rest of the afternoon on the sunny B&B terrace poring over the map, measuring distances, sending e-mails to potential accommodation for the next three nights and refining an itinerary that will enable me to walk into Rome by 9 November. This will leave me with plenty of time to enjoy a holiday with Fly.

I begin dreaming about visiting Firenze and Venice, the promise of Fly's arrival providing added motivation to finish this walk with Olympic-medalist pride. A pride that will only be mine if I set my nagging worries and fears aside, walk tall and journey well. Reminding myself that I do have what that takes, I turn in for a good night's sleep in an enormous 17th-century bed.

Day fifty-three. 15 October. To Pavia in Lombardy.

I take the train on to Pavia, covering four days of foot travel in just one and a half hours.

Pavia. Filthy train station. A first impression that defines my visit to this faded city. Lunch at a nice-looking restaurant is a microwaved seafood lasagne that's still frozen in the middle. Dinner at a neighbourhood pub is inedible because the cook is more interested in watching a football game on TV than preparing a meal in the kitchen. My expensive but tiny attic room is up four flights of narrow steps. Access to this room requires three enormous keys. One lets me in an outer gate into a small courtyard. Another opens an outer door and the last unlocks my room.

Day fifty-four. 16 October. In Pavia.

Weeks ago, Pat and I had talked about a potential rest day in Pavia. During a quick on-line search about the city, I'd noticed that one of the best things to see here is the Leonardo da Vinci Museum of Science and Technology. I'm excited to visit it, so will stay here a second night. During breakfast, I look up the address to discover that the museum isn't even in Pavia; it's in Milan.

"What?"

My failed sense of humour recovers over a second cappuccino. Serves me right for scrolling through Trip Advisor. The site is filled with erroneous nonsense. I know better.

Now, with a two-night hotel reservation, I'm stuck with an unwanted spare day so embark on a walking tour of Pavia's highlights. I soon conclude that not even the weed-infested, garbage-ridden, broken-benched, historic Piazza Leonardo da Vinci offers anything that interests me.

I go out for dinner at a tiny restaurant with outside tables where a courteous waiter takes time to explain several menu items and recommends a delicious *bistecca alla fiorentina* – a regional beef dish. My appreciation for Italian cuisine grows as does my ability to read the menus. A complimentary limoncello sends me back to my attic room in a much-improved mood and looking forward to the next leg of my journey.

Day fifty-five. 17 October. To Orio Litta.

I wake to fog so dense that I need to use Pocket Earth to find my pre-dawn way back to the station where I catch a train on to Santa Cristina. All previous trains have had digital signs and announcements informing passengers of the next stop. This train has neither, so I keep Pocket Earth open to track my progress and am soon hopping off at a tiny fog-enveloped station. The train stops for thirty seconds. No one else gets off. No one gets on.

After extending my trekking poles for the first time in three days, I set off towards Orio Litta, knowing the rest has done me good. I feel the joy of the road beneath my feet once more and realize my mojo is back. I miss Pat, but the remainder of this journey will be what I make of it. I look forward to coming adventures.

The fog swirls and creates an intimate world as I walk along a small dyke, past irrigation canal sluice gates and insubstantial farm buildings. Spider webs festooned with beads of moisture decorate trailside shrubs. Rosehips glow in the soft grey world. Church bells peel from an unseen steeple. Somewhere a dog barks an enthusiastic greeting.

My swift stride takes me between the ubiquitous Po Valley rice fields – all harvested to brown stubble – and an easy eighteen kilometres melts behind. I walk into Orio Litta at noon. The village is clean. Having seen so much filth since arriving in Italy, I find the contrast remarkable.

No one is at the locked hostel, so I walk across a weedless square to the Bar Sport where owners Elena and Luigi greet me like an old friend.

"Welcome, come in. Do you want lunch? Are you thirsty?" They show me to a shaded outside table, well away from the old men smoking inside.

I'm soon devouring an enormous bowl of pasta *pomodoro* and gulping a cold beer. A smiling man comes to say hello. He used to manage the hostel, but now someone else does and she will be here right away to let me in and show me around. The current manager arrives as I finish lunch and shows me into the spacious hostel. I will be the only guest, she tells me.

Where are all the other pilgrims? I scan the guest book and see a few names I recognize from the Via Francigena Facebook group. How can they still be ahead of me when I've done such big jumps forward by train? Unless they are walking sixty-kilometre days, they must be doing the same thing. But the subject remains taboo. I keep the secret too.

Later, after dinner at the bar, the only eatery in the village, my footsteps echo through the empty hostel as I close all the blinds for the night.

Day fifty-six. 18 October.
To Fiorenzuola d'Arda, Emilia-Romagna.

Leaving with the dawn and crossing the square, I see two grey-haired men and a stooped, kerchiefed woman sweeping leaves that have fallen during the night. The woman bends over, picks up a bit of foil wrap and drops it in a separate bin from the one they are scooping the leaves into. They pause their friendly banter to wish me a good day and journey. So, this is why the village is so clean. Orio Litta has offered a pleasant respite: the citizens friendly, the streets clean, the gardens tidy and the bar lively. I'm sure this is all connected.

I walk in dense fog. The silence, except for the crow of a rooster, the bark of a dog, the low of a cow, feels timeless. Softened lines of an aging Villa Litta Carini provide the suggestion of its past grandeur. I've walked into the 18th century.

There are two ways for pilgrims to reach Piacenza. One includes a passenger ferry across the Po. I like the idea because guidebooks and social media posts describe the ferryman as a character worth meeting. But according to my Lightfoot guide: *the long entry into Piacenza unfortunately uses the very busy via Emilia Pavese SP10.* I've developed a loathing and fear of walking along Italian roads so will take the alternative twenty-five-kilometre route and cross the Po by bridge. Soon I climb to the top of a long winding dike that keeps the Po from flooding the surrounding farmland. I will walk this dike all the way to the bridge.

When the rising sun burns through the fog and the temperature rises, I stop, strip off warm layers and shove them into my pack without squishing today's delicate breakfast pastries. Italians like coffee and sweet pastries or cake for breakfast. No protein or fruit has appeared on any breakfast table I've encountered since leaving Switzerland. Carrying breakfast to eat partway through the morning, I've consumed a few squashed-beyond-recognition tarts and cream-filled delights. They don't travel as well as pain aux raisins, so I've adapted my on-the-go packing methods to mitigate gooey mess.

The day becomes muggy and buggy. I drink most of my water well before I'd like to be confronted with a near-empty water bottle. My feet burn as I trudge along the pavement at the top of the dike. My body pours sweat. I slap at annoying tiny flies intent on crawling between my glasses and eyes, getting tangled in my damp curls and pestering my chapped lips.

Ahead, the bridge looms. An ingenious pedestrian and bicycle cloverleaf wanders along and under the vehicle approaches and then straightens to cross the bridge, a high barrier keeping the vehicles to their own lanes. The barrier cannot deaden the roar of traffic. The bridge deck shimmers with heat. The Po – the mighty Po – trickles beneath. I know there's been a drought but seeing the low water level – even after the recent rains – is shocking.

Once in Piacenza, I skip another section of the route by catching the train to Fiorenzuola d'Arda. Once aboard, I lean back to enjoy the cool relief of an air-conditioned carriage. Ten minutes is all it takes. The speed of train travel seems ludicrous when compared with my walking pace.

Given my end-of-long-hot-day fatigue, I do not appreciate the peculiar setup at this evening's hotel. I find the address but can't get in. I walk back to a bar, order a beer, and then call the hotel, once again grateful to Pat for her foresight. It would be difficult to travel here without a phone because at nearly every place I've stayed, a call has been required to encourage someone to come and unlock the door. This hotel is worse than normal. The voice on the phone seems to be telling me to go to another address, but my Italian isn't up to understanding where. The person on the other end thinks that yelling will improve my comprehension.

In desperation I hand the phone over to the bartender. She yells at the voice. The voice yells at her. She writes an address on a notepad, hangs up, smiles at me with an eye roll, then tells me the hotel reception is quite close – just a couple more blocks. She helps me find it on Pocket Earth and refuses payment for the beer.

I eventually check in, make a reservation for dinner, then walk back to a hotel annex where one key lets me into the building, and another gives access to my room. The place seems deserted. Later I walk back for dinner and then back again to my room. Having added six more kilometres to a long day, I've now walked thirty-one kilometres.

My feet and legs throb, but worse, my emotions wobble along a rollercoaster of outrage at rude drivers and dismissive restaurant staff, frustration with various check-in shenanigans, gratitude to people like the gardener and bartender, and appreciation for times when the service is excellent and the meals delicious – like this evening at the hotel restaurant. The physical fatigue and pain I can deal with. The daily dramas are wearing me down.

I take an ibuprofen before sleep overtakes my tired body and exhausted mind.

Day fifty-seven. 19 October. To Fidenza.

Still tired, I struggle all day in oppressive heat. Yesterday, I strode along, but today every step seems a stumble, my feet hurting within the first two kilometres. Much of the walk is along pavement, and that surface is the enemy of happy tramping. But today offers a rare opportunity – an open café. I've walked past before I realize the sacrilege of not stopping, so spin around and return. Sitting with a cappuccino, I raise my cup to Pat. She'd like this place. She'd be having an Americano.

After a few more kilometres, I take a rest on a bench by a cemetery and hope baring hot feet in such a place isn't taboo in Italy. Later, I slip into a church to enjoy the cool and to sneak some lunch, while hoping eating in a church pew isn't taboo. Resting another time in a bug-infested farmyard, I munch the last of my lunch and realize the house and barns are deserted. Plums lie rotting on the ground. Weeds grow tall in a nearby field. There's no one to critique my behaviour here.

I've booked a hotel next door to Fidenza's train station and wonder what surprises await. The biggest surprise is an open reception desk with a kind receptionist, just one key to access my room and a restaurant in the same building, that serves an excellent meal.

My fellow diners are an eclectic mix of industrial labourers attired in dusty work clothes, a large raucous family celebrating someone's birthday and a table of nine pleasantly inebriated old men. Here, in people-watching heaven, my joy is complete.

Day fifty-eight. 20 October. To Filetto in Tuscany.
South of Fidenza, the Via Francigena climbs up and over the Apennines for five walking days. I'd been looking forward to this mountainous part of the journey. But...

Pat told me that when she walked this section in 2014, she often felt vulnerable, isolated and anxious about the nearby hunters. I, too, am walking during hunting season and have yet to meet another pilgrim. I haven't managed to secure accommodation at two of the hostels along the route. My phone calls and e-mails unanswered, I don't even know if they're open. The weather forecast predicts heavy rains within the next forty-eight hours. This time of year, at the 1200-metre summit, that could mean snow.

Despite my disappointment, those are four sound reasons *not* to walk, so I climb aboard an early morning train that whisks me through numerous tunnels to Pontremoli. Although I've missed crossing both the Cisa and Crocetta Passes, upon exiting the station, I'm happy to see steep tree-covered hills rising above the roof tops. I haven't missed all the mountains.

Once I find my way out of town – the Via Francigena signs being few – then along a busy road – the drivers true to form – I enjoy a tranquil walk along an undulating forest trail. When I exit the trees, the day's heat assails me and saps my strength, so as I approach Filetto and see people sitting at tables in the shaded garden of a bar, I turn in.

"*Chiuso,*" one hollers. "*Chiuso,*" more shout, as I stop and stare.

I've seen enough *chiuso* signs in windows of closed shops and restaurants to know what *chiuso* means. Even so, my legs need a second to stop moving. My brain needs two seconds to process. My response is too slow for these people – all men I notice.

"*Chiuso,*" they continue to shout more loudly, arms flapping.

As I turn to leave, I can't resist a parting shot. "I wouldn't want to have a beer with a bunch of grumpy old men like you lot anyway," I toss back at them.

They shut up. Maybe they understood. I return to my solitary tramp down the road.

A block later, I see another bar, door open, an *aperto* sign hanging in the window.

I enter to the immediate growl of a woman yelling, "*Chiuso, chiuso, chiuso.*"

"Well, your sign says *aperto, aperto, aperto,*" I say, turning and flipping the sign as I exit. It falls against the window with a satisfying clatter.

Of course, being denied refreshment has accentuated my thirst, and the rudeness has undermined the joy of a pleasant day's walk. Continuing into the mediaeval part of the village, I trudge along a narrow cobbled street where I see an open door in the wall. Two tiny tables and four chairs sit on either side of the door. I peek inside to where a young man wipes the bar.

"Are you open? *Aperto?*" I ask. Tentative. Ready to run.

"*Si.*"

"Really?"

"You are surprised?"

"*Si.* But very happy. May I have a *birra bionda, per favore?*"

"*Si.* Of course. *Prego.*"

He brings me a cold blond beer, ribbons of condensation

running down the glass, and a bowl of pretzels. "Are you staying at B&B Luna and Stella?"

I nod.

"I will phone and let Sarah know you are here," he says.

My beer finished, I walk around the corner, through an arch and into a square where Sarah meets me and shows me up to a beautiful room in her 16th-century home. She phones the restaurant next door and makes a reservation. That dinner, served in a vaulted cellar, is described as a wild-meat dish. It's brought to the table by a chef who awaits my lip-smacking pronouncement of "delicious," before heading back into his kitchen.

The behaviour of the *chiuso* people has been eclipsed by the kindness of others, and I fall asleep having enjoyed the best day since Pat left and with renewed sense that all is well and will continue to be so.

Day fifty-nine. 21 October. To Valpromaro.

Sarah has ordered a taxi to whisk me eleven kilometres into Aulla because there's no bus service and I have another train to catch. When the taxi arrives, she sees me off with a hug, packed lunch and a stream of instructions for the driver.

Although the station is quite large, it's deserted. I buy my ticket at a machine and am soon roaring through tunnels and away from the last of the mountains then along the Ligurian Sea coast. At one point I notice what looks like snow stretching all the way down a steep mountainside but soon realize it's the scar of marble mining. The train stops at several towns where warehouses of stacked white marble line the tracks. Raw marble in its unpolished form is not as attractive as it is on church floors, or as pillars, statues and countertops.

One and a half hours – the equivalent of four walking days – after leaving Aulla, I alight in Pietrasanta where I begin the day's twenty-kilometre tramp. I'm in a perfect position to complete the last twenty stages to Rome in the twenty days between now and 9 November.

Pleased, I set off, first on a road out of town and soon along quiet pathways. All goes well until I ascend into the village of Monemagno where the Via Francigena signs point in one direction and the route in my guidebook indicates otherwise. My experiences in Italy have been such that I think I should follow the signs. To do otherwise invites confrontations with locked gates and various Italian equivalents of no trespassing notices.

Still, I pause, undecided. A traffic sign pointing down the road indicates: *Valpromaro 3.6 km.* Italian Via Francigena route markers have led me on detours to closed restaurants more than once. Now I don't trust where these ones might lead or for how far.

With trepidation but suspecting that this is another detour created with devious intent, I ignore the route signs and start walking down the road following the guidebook map. Much to my relief, Via Francigena markers point the way. Although these last kilometres are fraught with several ditch-leaping episodes as I engage in a battle for survival against inconsiderate drivers, I continue with confidence that I am where I should be.

I later discover that, although it would have been further, I could have – should have – followed the off-road Via Francigena signs along a newer, more scenic and much safer woodland route. It's another example of what I've named the "Italian Quandaries." I tease myself with trying to guess what quandary each day will present.

Valpromaro is small, so finding the hostel is easy. A rotund man sitting outside the door welcomes me and bellows at a woman inside that a pilgrim has arrived. She speaks no English, but I know the routine so pull out my passport and pilgrim credential. Rapid-fire Italian instructions result and when I can't answer – even when she turns up the volume – she bellows at the man to come to her aid.

"Do you have a sleeping bag?" he translates.

"Yes."

"You pay by donation," he continues at her bidding, pointing to the box by the door.

I nod and ask for the Wi-Fi code. He gives it to me, shows me where to put my shoes – on a shelf outside – then takes me upstairs to a dorm packed with sagging beds. Most are in groups of three – two side-by-side and a third across the foot of each pair. I pick a solo bed in a corner by a window. As soon as he goes downstairs, I hear the woman complaining. Something about her tone lets me know it's about me. I listen.

"*Sporchi stranieri*," I hear more than once.

Curious, I look up the translation: "filthy foreigners." Can't be.

After showering and changing – I don't take long because the hostel is freezing and the water lukewarm at best – I go back downstairs. The woman is in the kitchen with a couple of other people. The rotund man sits on a couch. I sit opposite him.

"What does *sporchi stranieri* mean?" I ask.

His intake of breath is all I need. He goes into the kitchen where there are quiet words spoken by the three men and louder ones by the woman. He returns, apologizes, explains that they are volunteers – like that should make a difference – and tries without success to light the wood stove.

"Here. Let me," I say. "I have woodstoves at home. I'll do it."

He sits back. I rearrange paper and kindling and strike a match. The wood catches and just the promise of heat improves the ambience. A young woman arrives. She's Italian, her name is Elena, and the hostel woman offers a warm welcome. A little later, a Swiss man about my age arrives. He speaks French, his name is Jean-Paul, and he receives a similar welcome to mine.

Rotund Man has continued sitting on the couch by the fire. I've continued feeding wood to the fire. The room is becoming cozy. The other three volunteers have remained in the kitchen from which sounds of chopping and smells of cooking emerge. My stomach rumbles. Elena, Rotund Man and I chat.

Elena asks me where I'll be staying for the next couple of nights.

"Lucca tomorrow, and I've just confirmed a room in Altopascio for the next night," I say.

She's staying further than Lucca tomorrow but has no place to stay in Altopascio. I realize that perhaps I should offer to share my room. When I suggest this, she jumps at the idea, asking for the name of the hotel and my contact info. I tell her I'll check if the hotel has a twin room and confirm she'll pay her share of the room. She agrees. I send an e-mail.

In silence, Jean-Paul sits on the other side of the room at the long dining table. Darkness falls. I check the time – seven o'clock – almost dinner. At seven thirty there's still no sign of a meal but the sounds and smells of cooking continue.

Jean-Paul steps to the kitchen door. "*A quelle heure est le dîner, s'il vous plaît?*"

Lots of shouted Italian emerges, but both Jean-Paul and I remain mystified, so I ask Rotund Man, "What time is dinner?"

"Just a minute." He heaves himself to his feet and waddles into the kitchen. More loud conversation. He returns with an oblique, "Soon."

"*Bientôt,*" I translate for Jean-Paul.

"*Parlez-vous français?*" he asks.

"*Un petit peu.*" I pop another piece of wood on the fire and join him at the table.

While some Italians speak English, fewer speak French. Jean-Paul speaks neither English nor Italian, so he's finding communication challenging. Considering my limited French, our conversation is simple. As eight o'clock comes and goes, we run out of words and stare at the kitchen door.

At Jean-Paul's request, I approach Rotund Man who is snoozing by the fire. "Please say that we are very hungry. It is late. We need to eat."

His query on our behalf is met by the woman's rising shrill voice. Elena's eyes widen as she looks at Jean-Paul and me.

"Don't worry, I already know she hates foreigners," I say.

"Well, I'm Italian and hungry too," says Elena. She marches into the kitchen, joins the fray, then emerges with a plate of bread.

A short time later, two more people arrive. Not pilgrims, but friends of the volunteers. The rest of the meal follows. Four courses. We finish a tasty, well-cooked meal after nine thirty. It's clear, however, that Elena, Jean-Paul and I have intruded on a private dinner party. *Sporchi stranieri*, or not, we are not welcome. Another Italian Quandary for me to mull over.

Day sixty. 22 October. To Lucca.

I wake several times in the night, wind rattling the window by my head, rain thundering on the roof and Rotund Man snoring from a nearby bed. As soon as I hear stirring, and the smell of coffee drifting upstairs, I head down. Breakfast is laid out on the table. Last night's left-over dessert. Last night's left-over bread. A fresh jar of Nutella and another of agèd jam. A jug of cold milk and a small pot of burnt coffee. I poke my head into the kitchen and ask one of the men if there is any *frutta*. There isn't.

After nibbling a bit of stale bread and taking a couple of sips of bitter, gritty coffee, I retrieve my shoes, go to the front door, and pull them on – they're cold and damp from a night outside. The deluge continues. As I rustle into my poncho, draping it over my pack, Elena appears, rubbing sleep from her eyes. Of Jean-Paul, there is no sign. Elena says it's too early for her to leave and that she'll see me in Altopascio.

An hour later, the rain stops. Soon I'm out of the woods and walking along the bank of the Serchio River. The clouds dissipate and the sun gets to work drying puddles and me. Because tall thick grasses grow between the trail and the water, I see little. But it's Saturday, so as I near Lucca, the path becomes busy with joggers, cyclists and other walkers. No one carries a pack, but I enjoy trading smiles and a cheerful "*buongiorno*" with everyone I meet.

Entering the walls of Lucca, I hear English spoken with American, British and Australian accents. I hear French, German and Italian too. As I dodge between throngs of camera-toting tourists, I keep an eye open for other pack-wearers. Not one.

Within the maze of canyon-like streets circling into the heart of the old town, the little blue Pocket Earth arrow on my iPad struggles to figure out where we are, but after several wrong turns, I find my hotel tucked into a tiny cul-de-sac next to Lucca's central square. A cul-de-sac occupied by three – maybe four – restaurants, tables, awnings and umbrellas, chatter and smells of food fill the space.

I spend an enjoyable afternoon strolling around clean streets and popping in and out of tourist-packed shops selling Tuscan pottery, dried meats, cheeses, olive oil, reproduction and original art and made-in-Italy clothing. The central square – which is an oval because it was once a 2nd-century Roman amphitheatre – teems with people enjoying the ambience of this welcoming town.

When I sit down for dinner at one of the restaurants by my hotel, the waiter places a multi-lingual menu on the table. I take the opportunity to write some translation notes in my journal. The sun sets early now, and while I eat, night falls and lights come on, casting the scene in a golden glow. The streets remain busy. The restaurants fill. A complimentary limoncello, delivered with a smile, provides a satisfying ending to a day that has produced no annoying Italian Quandaries.

Day sixty-one. 23 October. To Altopascio.

The walk between Lucca and Altopascio stands out as the most unpleasant section of the route. I spend the day trudging first through Lucca's unattractive urban sprawl, then along busy roads. The uninspiring scenery affords a glimpse into some of the county's current difficulties. At one point, the route leads through a deserted industrial area. Given that this is Sunday, I'm unable to decide if the place is still functional, but some of the structures and parking areas look so derelict, my sense is that not all the closures are Sunday related. In several places, people have used the weedy broken roadsides for illegal tipping. Mattresses, toilets, an easy chair, and heaps of garbage bags, most spilling their contents, litter the area.

I walk on, nursing flagging spirits by seeking moments of beauty along the way. A tiny vegetable garden ringed with marigolds. An old man and woman dressed in their Sunday best strolling home from church wish me a *Buen Camino*. A dog wags its tail and doesn't bark. With each pleasant moment, I seek another with keen awareness that a positive mindset is as important as a fit body.

Walking into Altopascio just after noon, I find Hotel Paola. Paola herself greets me with the news that my friend Elena has arrived, left her pack and gone into town. I follow suit, and soon spot Elena who joins me for a beer while we await the three o'clock check-in time.

After two months of staying in a different room nearly every night, I sometimes forget where I put things, so have developed a pattern to unpacking and placing specific items. As Elena and I settle into our room, I tuck my purse in its usual spot beside my pack, then continue with shaking out a change of clothes and plugging in my iPad. I sort through my food bag, tossing used napkins, wrappers and orange peels and assessing what is still edible. I've been carting the same two Babybel cheeses for at least a week – or is it two? They go back in the bag along with a dubious piece of Swiss chocolate, some energy gels Pat and I had bought in France, and a several-times-melted Kind bar I've had with me since the Vancouver airport.

After Elena is finished in the bathroom, I take my turn. Later, laundry hung, e-mails attended to, and tomorrow's route reviewed, I grab my purse off the bed, and we go out for dinner. Back at the hotel, Elena texts on her phone and I set my alarm.

"I've set the alarm for six thirty," I say. "Does that work for you?"

"Oh, I am only going to Ponte a Cappiano," she says. "I won't need to leave so early. I may stop walking there, so I guess I won't see you again."

I feel a twinge of disappointment. Having shared the room, I'd expected we'd walk together.

Day sixty-two. 24 October. To San Miniato.

In the morning, Elena doesn't stir when I get up. I go downstairs for breakfast and when I ask if I can buy some extra supplies for lunch, the cook tells me that no purchase is necessary and packs me a generous picnic.

Bumping on the stairs heralds the descent of several people struggling with enormous suitcases. Soon, eight wheeled cases are lined up by the door, and their owners invade the dining room, crowding around the coffee and buffet tables. They are dressed for walking – but the suitcases suggest something different.

My cheerful "*buongiorno*," doesn't elicit a response, and I don't recognize the language they're speaking.

Back in our room, Elena is awake but still in bed and texting. I pick up my pack and say goodbye.

She glances up from her phone, "Nice meeting you," she says.

"You, too."

At the reception desk, when confirming our €90.00 bill is settled, I receive a credit card receipt for €60.00. Elena has only paid the additional €30.00 for an extra person in the twin room. When Paola asks me for the key, I tell her Elena is still in bed.

"You don't walk together?" she asks.

"She just needed a room last night so, no, I guess not." I shrug.

"You are not friends?"

"No. Just fellow pilgrims."

She gives me a hard look and wishes me a good journey. I head out with the expectation of a pleasant day under the Tuscan sun. A day, as it turns out, where I meet David, Stuart, Raoul, and Andrea and have dinner with the two Germans. A day during which my loneliness brings me to tears. A day followed by the night of my disturbing dream about the pope.

Day sixty-three. 25 October. To Gambassi Terme.

Waking from that dream, I lie in bed for a few minutes pondering its meaning. Pat and I had discussed if we should go to the Vatican to receive certificates, and I remain conflicted. This is a pilgrimage to Rome, and the certificate will acknowledge its completion. But throughout history, the Vatican has been a violent, corrupt, abusive, thieving, repressive and delusional institution. What value would the certificate hold?

Dawn's gold band fades to reveal another cloudless day. I stretch, exploring my body for stiffness or pain. There is none.

Sleep continues to restore. My mood is much improved as well. Maybe I just needed to indulge in a full-fledged pity party, and now I will get on with the business at hand. Energized, I leap out of bed and thirty minutes later, am striding out of town, my pack bulging with the generous picnic Aida has made for me.

As I walk towards Gambassi Terme the scenery becomes more iconic Tuscany. Hills roll into a hazy distance. Mist creeps around in the valleys. Rows of slender Cyprus trees march along ridge lines. Two by two they guard long avenues leading to square stone farmhouses. Tilled fields create a patchwork interspersed with the occasional green of a winter crop. The now well-signed route follows dusty white roads into valleys and along ridges. The sun climbs and the temperature rises, Europe's drought continuing to threaten farmers' livelihoods and food security.

While I'm resting by the track, shoes and socks off, munching some of my packed lunch, the group of eight walks by, two by two, engaged in earnest conversation. In keeping with their insular manner of the previous day, they don't offer a greeting. Later, they're having a break when I come upon them.

"If we're going to keep meeting like this, we should say hello," I say, pausing for a moment to see how they respond.

Most offer a brief greeting; a couple look at me, surprise registering. I think they may have been so focused on each other that I could have walked by – invisible. During the day, we pass each other several more times and every time there is a bit more thawing. They are Danes who have known each other for twenty-eight years since they were at prenatal classes together. They are walking for a few days and having their luggage transported.

"How much does your pack weigh?" asks one of the women.

"Nine kilos when I have a full litre of water and before I eat my lunch. Usually less than seven kilos by the end of the day," I say.

"And that's all you have?"

"Everything I need," I smile.

Later, after climbing up to a ridge, I look back and see eight bright Danish specks. Then behind them two more. Even from the distance I recognize Stuart's broad-brimmed pilgrims' hat. I smile. We might yet meet up.

Upon arrival at Ostello Sigerico, I collapse onto a chair in a sunny courtyard. Surrounded by the yellow stone walls of a church hostel where Sigeric stayed when he was here, I contemplate the depth of history represented by this place and absorb a sense of peace. A young man carrying a flat of beer appears up some cellar steps.

"Welcome. I'll be with you in just a moment," he says.

"No rush. Is that beer cold?"

He nods.

"May I have one?"

He nods again and I lift a beer from the flat.

"I'll bring you a glass," he offers.

"*Grazie.*"

"When you're ready, come to the desk and I'll check you in," he says as he delivers the glass.

While enjoying cold effervescence sliding down my parched throat, I open my purse to retrieve passport and money for the night's bed, dinner, and breakfast. Low on cash, I see I'll need to break my stashed €100.00 bill. As I pull my passport wallet from its zippered pocket inside my purse, I notice the zipper is undone and chastise myself. Since the attempted pickpocketing on the Milan Metro, I've been careful about closing that zipper. I open the wallet and stare. The familiar green of the €100.00 note is not where it should be. It must have slid deeper inside. I poke my fingers into the narrow slot. No money. I search through the passport wallet. Vaccine certificate, credit cards, bank card are where they should be. Of the money there is no sign. I methodically empty my purse. Epi-pen, iPad, shopping bag, mask, hand sanitizer, pen, change wallet with €43.00 in it. Everything as expected, but no green bill.

As my heart rate speeds up, a couple of memories crystalize. Picking up my purse off the bed two evenings ago in Altopascio. Had I left it on the bed? When I paid for dinner, I'd fumbled for the exterior zippers. They were closed on the left, not on the right as I always close them. A lump forms in my throat.

Looking up I see David and Stuart round the corner and enter the courtyard.

"Hail Pilgrims!" I call out.

In the joy of greeting, I forget for a moment that I'm short €100.00, but when we all go to the desk to check in, the realization that I appear to have been robbed hits hard.

"Do you take credit cards?" I ask the young man who'd served me the beer.

"Sure," he says reaching for my card. My hand is shaking. He notices and looks up. "Everything OK?"

"No. I mean, I guess so. But ..." I take a breath. "I think I've been robbed." And I explain my discovery.

The young man asks what Elena looks like. I tell him while he scrolls around on his laptop.

"I'm reporting this," he says. "This is not the first time. It might be the same woman who's been targeting solo pilgrims."

I'll think twice about offering to share my room again. Did I offer? Or did she ask? I no longer remember. Is there another scenario? I can't think of one. There is nothing I can do. But I'll need to find an ATM sooner than anticipated. After my shower, I join David and Stuart at a picnic table in the garden.

We enjoy before-dinner beer, and later, Raoul and Andrea sit with us for the set dinner. Raoul, a Spaniard, has been learning Polish because Andrea is Polish. She also speaks English and Spanish. David speaks Spanish, so with Andrea and David's help, we enjoy animated conversation. Stuart buys a bottle of wine and that helps too. Over the evening, we decide to walk together in the morning.

Back in my chilly room, I fall asleep wrapped in both my sleeping bag and the warm comfort of being – at last – in the international company of pilgrims.

Day sixty-four. 26 October. To San Gimignano.

While David, Stuart and I buy our day's groceries at a village shop, Raoul and Andrea arrive. The shop's shelves are stocked with the sorts of supplies pilgrims need, from shoelaces to bananas, and the owner greets us with enthusiasm. An avid walker, he tells us he's walked from Vancouver to Whitehorse and offers handfuls of fresh harvested grapes with his best wishes for our *Buen Camino*. Two young German men, also pilgrims, are buying food too. We all exchange greetings as we stuff food into our packs and grapes into our mouths.

Soon we're tramping up and down the Tuscan ridges and valleys. David and Stuart set a brisk pace. Too fast for my comfort but I'm enjoying the company and our conversation, so I trot along, panting, sweating, happy and trying to ignore the worsening sharp pain in my left foot.

When I know I can go no further, I risk suggesting a break. With everyone's agreement, we stop and put our feet up in the shaded portico of a church where we relax and share our various lunch items.

Raoul presents me with a tiny medallion – Saint Christopher, patron saint of travellers. With gratitude, I tuck the charm into my talisman pouch along with a wood elephant, stone Buddha and a couple of pagan charms with the expectation that they will all get along.

While I walk with Andrea, she tells me about her philosophy that the Way provides pilgrims with what we need. She calls this, Gifts of the Way. An insightful woman, she suggests that the Way has provided me with companions when I needed them and tells me the story of how the Way brought her and Raoul together. I can't fault her logic. That kind of faith is, I think, rare and it carries with it an assured serenity.

David and Stuart also met on a Camino walk several years ago. Since then, they walk together a couple of times a year and have shared many adventures similar to those Pat and I enjoy. A financial journalist seeking different employment that will provide him with more satisfaction, Stuart is at a turning point in his professional life. David is passionate about teaching English to new migrants to the UK.

"They teach me more than I will ever be able to teach them," he says.

We talk, laugh and sweat as the dusty kilometres slip past.

A black and white dog emerges from a farm and instead of barking, joins us, trotting ahead, then waiting. He's a friendly creature with the apparent mission to guide us through his territory. Towards the top of a hill, he runs ahead to a closed gate. On the other side of the gate another dog barks. A woman comes out of a house and gives our little friend instructions to go home. She explains that "our" dog is in love with her dog, and he's a regular visitor. Romeo gives us a smirk – yes dogs do smirk – and with a lustful glance at his Juliet, trots back down the hill towards his farm.

By early afternoon we stride into San Gimignano where busloads of tourists swarm the cobbled streets and flow in and out of attractive shops displaying bright Tuscan pottery and bottles of olive oil. Finding two unoccupied tables at one of the square-side restaurants, we upset a harried waiter by pulling them together to accommodate the five of us. He forgives us when he doesn't need to deal with menus and food orders because we just order a round of beer.

The others are continuing a few more kilometres to stay in cabins at a campground on the far side of town. Tomorrow we will stay in different places as well because they will be putting in a longer thirty-two-kilometre day. I hope our ways will reconnect, but I'll need to take a bus to catch up.

When I tell them my self-imposed distance limit for each day, Stuart teases me about being a twenty-five-kilometre friend. "You won't walk further even to be with us?" he coaxes.

"Well, maybe for you two," I allow.

With promises to meet on the road to Siena, I head to my hotel, and they disappear into the throngs of tourists.

Mum and I stayed in San Gimignano in 2004 when we were on our Grand Tour, and the town holds pleasant memories. I drop my pack in my room, then head out to re-explore. At the duomo, I discover that even as a pilgrim I'm expected to pay to enter.

"Are you sure?" I ask the ticket agent. I pull out my well-stamped credential. "Look, I've walked from Canterbury. I'm going to Rome. I'm a pilgrim."

She couldn't care less. "€5.00," she repeats.

"Well, keep your duomo for the bus-tour tourists, then. I'm not paying."

I try three ATMs before I find one that works with my Canadian bank card, then walk up to the castle. Leaning against a battlement, I listen to voices exclaiming in wonder at the mediaeval towers for which San Gimignano is known. Like many towns in this part of the world, San Gimignano has a history dating back to the 3rd century BCE when the first Etruscan settlement was established. It subsequently became a Roman town and in 450 CE, was saved from destruction by Attila the Hun through the intervention of a Christian bishop. The town grew during the Middle Ages and the Renaissance as an important stopping place for Via Francigena pilgrims heading to and from Rome.

During the Middle Ages, rival families competed for status by building the tallest houses so that San Gimignano's skyline once bristled with seventy-two tower-houses up to seventy metres high. However, in 1348, the Black Death decimated half the town's population and over time many of the towers were reduced to just a couple of storeys. Today, thirteen towers remain as a reminder of mediaeval builders' ingenuity, a precursor to today's architects who strive for status by designing the world's tallest structures.

As I eavesdrop on an English-language tour group, I hear the guide telling her charges – about thirty of them – a little about the history of Tuscany.

When the guide finishes, a woman with an American twang has a question – a comment really. "I thought we were in Italy," she says.

I turn my eyes back to the tour guide. How is she going to deal with this idiocy?

"We *are* in Italy. Tuscany is in Italy. Now, over here you will see …."

As the group follows, I don't hear what else the guide says

but the woman continues to fuss in an over-loud voice about how impossible Europe is.

"How can they be so stupid to have a country inside another country?" she wants to know.

I'm embarrassed that we share a language.

On my way back to the hotel I stop at a restaurant advertising a terrace with views.

"Do you open at seven or seven thirty?" I ask.

"We are open now and until eleven," says the waiter.

"Now?" Shock must be written all over my face.

"Yes – for you Americans. We know you like to eat early."

"I'm not American. I'm Canadian. But yes – we do tend to eat earlier than Europeans. How about a reservation for …" I count to six on my fingers seeking the right Italian number. "… *Sei*? I'd like to watch the sunset from the terrace."

My wish is granted with a smile.

When I arrive, a table is set on the terrace, and a blanket provided. "If you get cold, you may please come inside," the waiter says.

The sun sets in a glorious display of oranges to deep purple while I sip chardonnay and enjoy a delicious *cinghiale in dolceforte* – Tuscan boar stew – by candlelight. As I reflect on the past couple of days, I realize the route signs have appeared in logical places, there's been no roadside garbage, people are consistently friendly, and my previous unease has given way to a simple enjoyment of the journey. After the usual complimentary limoncello, when I pay my bill, I notice the waiter has forgotten to charge me for the wine.

"Because you are not American," he says with a grave bow.

Day sixty-five. 27 October. To Colle di Val d'Elsa.

The early morning streets are empty save for a Zamboni-type street sweeper. My lone footsteps ring against the damp clean cobbles as I walk through the town, then leave through an imposing 13th-century gate.

As the sun lifts from behind the eastern hills, silver light fingers streak across the vineyards and orchards. I descend into the valley and immediately labour up another hill. Turning back, I see the towers shining golden. Valley mist begins shifting and climbing, blurring, then blotting the cypress and olive trees on the lower slopes. Soon San Gimignano becomes a mist-bound island. The magic catches my breath.

The mist working its magic.

"*Venire. Vieni qui.*" A harvester beckons me to come into a nearby olive orchard.

I join him and several others. A man offers me a cup of coffee from a thermos. We all sit on the dew-damp olive nets spread beneath the trees and watch the mist rise up the walls, embrace the towers and obliterate the town. No one speaks. When the harvesters get to their feet, so do I. Handing back the mug, I thank them for much more than a cup of coffee.

I walk on, the recipient of another Gift of the Way, my sense of peace absolute.

While descending the far side of a hill I've just climbed, I pause to take another picture of a landscape that continues to entrance. Hearing voices, I turn to see two other walkers catching up. Greeting each other and continuing together – as is the way – I learn that Katheryn, a GP, and Josh, in IT, from Michigan, are on their honeymoon. They're walking three days of the route, their luggage, which includes wedding attire, being transported by an agency that has booked them into luxury accommodation. They tell me a story about going on a canoe trip on Lake Michigan, being caught in a storm, getting washed ashore in Canada and kind Canadian border agents giving them a ride home in their boat.

Still later, the two Germans I'd met in San Miniato catch us up. I perform introductions, and we continue together, all with different reasons for being where we are, but united in our enjoyment of this moment in our journeys. At a large trail map we part ways. I'm taking the shorter – and more urban – route into Colle di Val d'Elsa. They're taking the longer trail to Abbadia a Isola. Stuart is right, I am a twenty-five-kilometre friend.

I don't feel lonely until I enter some woods and gunshots shatter the day's peace. Birds take flight from nearby shrubs. Wearing a light blue and white blouse and faded blue skirt, my pack an even more faded teal, I'm sure – I hope – I present a bright spot in the surrounding countryside. Even so, I stop and scan the ridge above – where I think the shots came from. Seeing no one, I hurry on.

More shots. More fluttering birds. Heart pounding, I keep walking while scanning the surrounding woods and ridge above me. I'm on a track that climbs the slope of a steep-sided valley. I understand just enough about shooting and hunting to know that I'm between the hunters above and their intended targets in the open fields of the valley bottom.

More shots. So close. Afraid, I start jogging – the best jog my sore-footed, pack-laden, sixty-eight-year-old body can manage. Soon I'm huffing. I keep jogging as I pass two vehicles. The hunter's vehicles, I expect. I keep jogging until gasping, I reach the top of the ridge and stumble out onto a paved road.

Dumping off my pack, I sink onto the grass verge at the edge of the road. With shaking hands, I pull out my water bottle and take a few sips. Sweat drips from my hairline and down my back. Five minutes later, I pull myself back to my feet and continue, glad once again to be out of the woods, but aware of increased pain in my foot and struggling to keep a limp from my stride.

Once settled into a room at my hotel in Colle di Val d'Elsa, I phone Stuart. He and David are in Monteriggioni. I've checked buses and let them know I can catch one scheduled to arrive in Monteriggioni at 8:39 AM. They say they will wait. Even as I eat my solitary dinner in a crowded restaurant, I feel the joy of knowing tomorrow will bring more camaraderie.

Day sixty-six. 28 October. To Siena.
Waking much too early to a din outside the window, I open the external wooden shutters and look down to see yesterday's quiet street transforming into a market. My bird's-eye view offers an interesting perspective as truck sides open and awnings sprout. Racks and tables emerge to be hung and stacked with clothing, leather goods, shoes, kitchen items and farm produce.

Three hours later, picking my way through shoppers crowding the stalls, I walk across the square to the bus stand. Showing my ticket for the 8:25 AM bus to Monteriggioni – on the Siena route – I ask other waiting passengers where my bus will stop. A team of women unites to provide instructions each time a bus swings into the stand. Several buses have Siena marked as the final destination, but none bear number – 130 – the only bus that stops in Monteriggimoni.

At eight forty, I call Stuart. "My bus still isn't here. I think you should start walking."

"Don't worry. We're not in a rush," says Stuart.

I go back to anxious waiting. The women continue assuring me as bus after bus rolls into the stand, then leaves. I gather that my helpers are also waiting for a bus that hasn't shown up at the expected time. Another bus arrives and some of the women tell me to get on while others say it's not the right one. Undecided, I hop on and motion to the driver to read my ticket before pulling out into traffic. He pulls my ticket into his cubical and shakes his head, but as I turn to get back off – against the stream of folks getting on – he changes his mind and points to a front seat. A young woman vacates it with a smile and moves back with the crowd. Outside the women argue and shout but the driver calls out to them, and they settle down, waving goodbye as the bus pulls away.

Glad to be going somewhere, I call Stuart. "I'm on a bus. Not sure to where."

He tells me that he and David are enjoying another cup of coffee in the morning sun and are prepared to wait.

Curious, I pull out my iPad and bring up Pocket Earth. I see Monteriggioni not very far away, but the bus turns off towards another town. A man sitting beside me taps my shoulder, points to the driver and says, "Monteriggioni." So, I sit back and enjoy the views as we wander around the countryside.

After a few more turns, the bus comes to a halt on the highway, and the driver indicates I should hop off. He points up a narrow side road heading towards Monteriggioni, now less than two kilometres away. It is then that I realize, I'm not on the official bus to Monteriggioni. I'm on the bus of a kind driver who is, at the very least, making an unscheduled stop and who may have driven out of his way.

With no time to show enough gratitude, I shout a heartfelt "*Grazie*" as I jump down.

Faces smile and hands rise in the windows to wave me on my way. The bus has dropped me by the highway in a valley. Being a mediaeval town, Monteriggioni perches atop a very steep hill. Good defensive position, but a brutal start to my walking day. I huff and puff up that hill, stopping a couple of times to catch my breath, but hurrying to meet up with David and Stuart who have now waited well over an hour.

Through the town gate I pant, ducking between a large contingent of Asian tourists flinging their selfie sticks around like weapons. I can't tell which way photos are being taken – towards the scene in front or at the lip-pursing face behind, so give up on trying not to photo bomb and hope my hot red face doesn't ruin too many photos.

David and Stuart leap from their square-side seats. We greet, then set off into what becomes a blistering day under the Tuscan sun. Despite the unseasonal summer heat, we relish the glory of the sweeping vistas that may not be much changed since the early 1300s when Dante Alighieri penned his *Divine Comedy*.

After being banished from his home in nearby Firenze, he wrote the epic while wandering from town to town reflecting on social injustice and political turmoil. I find myself considering that the social and political situation in Italy remains unsettled. However, on this day in Tuscany as the boots of three happy pilgrims stir dust and bees gather pollen from drought-stressed blooms, a sense of contentment prevails.

Towards day's end, we catch up with the American honeymooners, Josh and Katheryn, and once again I make introductions. These cocktail-party niceties performed on ridge-top trails have an element of the bizarre. Being a habitual forgetter of names, I'm never at ease with this sort of interaction at home, but here I am, host-apparent, feeling the joy of being in the company of others and somehow remembering the names of people I've just met.

> *But something gleamed on me, whence so intent*
> *To gaze thereon my baffled vision grew,*
> *That my confession out of memory went. ...*
> *Such faces, fain for speaking, came to sight; ...*
> *To see of whom they were, I turned mine eye; ...*

Dante Alighieri, The Divine Comedy, Paradiso, Canto III, *circa 1320, first printed 1472 Melville Best Anderson, translator, 1922*

Upon arrival in Siena, we enjoy beer together, then Josh and Katheryn continue to their fancy hotel while we three walk quite a bit further to a campground where we stay in small cabins. David and Stuart return to town to meet their Austrian friend Theresa whom they'd met on the Camino Francés a few years ago. They invite me to go with them, but I've done enough walking for the day. I eat at the campsite restaurant where I'm chastised for not having a reservation and given a draughty table by the door.

Day sixty-seven. 29 October. To Ponte d'Arbia.

We set off into Siena where we meet up with Theresa and buy takeout breakfasts to eat on the main square. From a recycling pile, Theresa scoops a large piece of cardboard to sit on. We've no sooner made ourselves comfortable and started sipping coffees when along comes a too-plump-for-the-job police officer who informs us that eating on the square is not allowed. We look at all the people eating at the surrounding restaurants and move on – the message is clear.

When Theresa suggests we visit the duomo, David and I go with her while Stuart, claiming fatigue, sits with our packs. During our moment of tourism, the duomo's bells ring and disturb the roosting pigeons. Avoiding pigeon bombs, we rejoin Stuart and march out of town. Again, the day's temperature climbs and again we swelter along the shadeless Tuscan ridges.

As the day progresses Stuart becomes more and more tired. Feeling unable to continue for the remaining distance, he catches a train to a station just past, but closer to our destination, and walks back. My foot is sore enough that I'm tempted to join him, but the landscape compels me to keep walking. David, Theresa and I arrive in Ponte d'Arbia at the same time as Stuart. Theresa has booked at a B&B, the rest of us go to the hostel where the manager has us sit outside while he admits people one at a time for a lengthy check-in procedure.

One of the young men we met in the shop back in Gambassi Terme comes out to wash his clothes. His friend has returned to Frankfurt, but Atul has decided to continue to Rome. We chat while the sun sets and a damp chill sets in, but still we wait our turn to be invited inside. Impatient and cold, we go to the door and when someone exits, slip in before it swings shut. We occupy the space in front of the manager's desk where we're informed there is no Internet, but we're assigned a room. One chilly room. Three beds. No bedding. No heat. I haul out my sleeping bag. Stuart and David don't have sleeping bags so will sleep in their clothes.

We join Theresa at the restaurant across the road where we receive the too common refrain – no reservation, no dinner. An Italian couple, also staying at the hostel, enter behind us. They have no reservation either. They engage in animated, cross-sounding conversation with the restaurant's gate keeper. After fifteen minutes we're told that if we sit as a group of six, we can eat. Once we have occupation of a table, the service is good and the company entertaining. The restaurant fills. Even if we weren't tired, we'd have not been permitted to stay longer than necessary to devour our delicious meal and drink smooth Tuscan wine.

We exit to a parking lot full of cars.

"What's here to attract so many people?" I wonder to the others.

"Maybe it's just a normal Saturday night," suggests Stuart.

"This is a holiday time," says the Italian woman who sat with us at dinner.

We look at her. Blank faced.

"November 1st is *Ognissanti* – All Saints' Day and the 2nd is *Il Giorno dei Morti* – All Souls' Day. Many people – like us – are enjoying a long holiday by not working on Monday either."

Now I understand why I've not been able to find accommodation in San-Quirico d'Orcia – my next stop on the route.

Day sixty-eight. 30 October. To Gallina.

Theresa is catching an early train back home from the station down the road, so we meet outside in the cold, foggy dark at five thirty. Our route takes us up into the hills where we walk by the light of our headlamps into the glorious enchantment of a Tuscan dawn.

"I think I may be getting a cold," says Stuart.

"Maybe that's why you felt so tired yesterday," I suggest.

"I guess so. I still feel really tired."

"What do you expect with no coffee," I joke, not thinking about what Stuart's scratchy throat and dripping nose might really mean.

Once at the station in Buonconvento, I say goodbye to Theresa and also to David and Stuart as they're catching a later train to begin their journey home to England. I've not walked with them for long but have enjoyed the generosity of their company. We promise to stay in touch.

I'm now confronted with a challenge. The closest accommodation I've been able to secure is in Gallina – still forty kilometres away. I decide to hitchhike a few kilometres down the road, reasoning that I can manage thirty-five. David, Stuart and Theresa stand on the other side of the road offering encouragement as vehicles rush past. A couple stop, but no one is going more than a kilometre or two.

Then Atul comes striding along. "Why are you hitchhiking?" he wants to know.

I tell him. He hasn't been able to find accommodation either but is going to see what happens when he gets to San Quirico d'Orcia.

"May I walk with you?" I ask. I'm shivering and my hitchhiking hasn't been successful.

"Of course."

Waving to my cheerleaders and wishing them safe journeys home, I turn and march down the road with Atul. The idea of no place to sleep at the end of the day no longer seems so daunting. We stop for a dismal breakfast and the very worst cups of coffee either of us have ever tasted, then carry on.

Atul is in IT as a contracted program developer. I don't know what that means, but it gives him flexibility to choose his own work schedule. His English is so perfect I hear only the faintest German accent and don't embarrass myself by trying to speak German.

During our lunch stop, I phone the hostel in San Quirico d'Orcia again. No one has picked up previous calls, and because of no Internet last night, I don't know if anyone has replied to my e-mail. This time a woman answers.

"*Buongiorno. Due letti del Pellegrino, per favore*," I ask, my pronunciation deplorable.

"No beds tonight," she tells me. "I speak English," she adds in a kind tone.

I ask if she knows of a bus that would take us from San Quirico d'Orcia to Gallina where I do have a bed. There are no buses, but she gives me a phone number of a taxi driver who often drives pilgrims. I thank her, then call the taxi. The driver tells me he can pick us up at three o'clock.

"I think that's too early," I say. "We still have too far to walk. How about four?"

He agrees and I breathe easy.

Atul isn't keen on the taxi and says he'll walk to Gallina. So, my next call is to my hosts in Gallina to ask about a bed for Atul. They are fully booked but will put an extra bed in my room. I confirm with Atul, he agrees, and I hang up the third call, satisfied that the Way has provided.

As we walk through Torrenieri, we notice an empty sidewalk table at a busy restaurant. After our abysmal breakfast, we're hungry and neither of us has much food because there was no place to shop in Ponte d'Arbia. Fortified, we continue through a stifling day and walk up another hill and through the gate into San Quirico d'Orcia just before three thirty. The town is packed. We try to find a place to sit for a beer but to no avail.

Walking past the hostel we see it opens in a few minutes. Atul helps me find the pharmacy where the taxi will pick me up, then runs back to check one more time if he can get a bed. I'm still waiting – it's not yet four o'clock – when he reappears with a happy smile.

"I have a bed," he says.

He goes on to tell me that people are arriving from their cars with wheeled suitcases. He suggested to the host that walking pilgrims should not be displaced from a pilgrim hostel by car-driving, suitcase-wheeling tourists. The tactic worked and he was assigned a bed. He'll see me tomorrow at the hostel in Radicofani. I take a photo of his passport and promise to register him if he's late.

The taxi arrives, and we drive out of town past an oncoming traffic jam that stretches over six kilometres.

"So many people coming to San Quirico for the holiday," says the driver. "This is where I drop the pilgrims," he says a short time later as we arrive in quiet Gallina.

"Do many pilgrims get a ride with you?" I ask as he helps me settle my pack on my shoulders.

"Maybe up to ten every day in the summer," he tells me. Then he smiles. "Don't worry, you are still a pilgrim even when you get a ride sometimes."

I cross the road and knock on the door of the hostel. No answer. Seeing a woman entering her house next door, I call out. She points into an olive orchard behind the houses and mimes harvesting, so I leave my pack and enter the orchard.

Nets lie spread under the trees. As I walk further into the orchard, I hear the sound of a generator-powered olive harvester. These devices, some looking like giant bottle brushes and others looking more like long-pronged rakes, are held up into the branches to vibrate the olives loose. Some olive operations use large vibrators supported by specially adapted tractor arms, but in this orchard, I find one of my hosts scooping fallen olives into a basket while the other reaches a hand-held pole with spinning prongs up into a gnarled olive tree.

They stop work, give me a warm welcome, and we discuss the poor crop. The heat and drought have been devastating. The olives are fewer and smaller than usual. The couple presses for oil and won't have much to sell this year.

When I'm shown to my room, I see they've added a bed. Explaining that Atul was able to find accommodation in San Quirico, I apologize for adding unnecessary work to their busy day. They don't seem upset. Now they have an extra space for another time, they say.

I ask about Internet. There is none for the hostel, but they welcome me to use their private Internet and provide the password and a lawn chair outside.

The village restaurant is closed, but my hosts have arranged for me to have a take-out meal. I'm to walk to the restaurant at seven and it will be ready. When I arrive, I'm presented with a large bowl of pasta and another of salad. Do I want red wine or white? I choose white and am given a 500 ml jug. This all costs €10.00. I walk back to the hostel carrying a teetering tray. There's a good reason I've never been a waiter. I'm not a competent tray carrier. By the time I arrive back at the hostel, I have, at best, 400 mls of wine. Plenty.

Day sixty-nine. 31 October. To Radicofani.
The fatigue of yesterday's twenty-six kilometres is still with me as I trudge along. I only have twenty kilometres to walk today, but in the heat, I just don't get into a good stride. Perhaps I miss the camaraderie. I feel a need to hurry because tonight's hostel provides beds on a first-come-first-served priority, but my legs are heavy and incapable of sustained effort. I take a break every couple of kilometres, my foot screaming in pain. Shoes off, I poke at my forefoot seeking the crepitus of broken bones. Of course, there is none, but something is wrong and besides taking lots of ibuprofen and smearing my foot with liberal amounts of Voltaren – far more than recommended – I don't know what to do about it. Well, I could stop walking – but somehow that no longer feels like an option. Rome is calling.

Radicofani – another mediaeval town – clings to the top of another steep hill. Despite having felt the slowness of every step, I arrive in the main square by noon. After lunch and beer have eased my pain, I call the hostel number. Receiving a lot of instruction in Italian, I'm only able to figure out that there is a door by the church. There are many doors by the church, but after inspecting several, I discover one that indicates "*Ostello*." I ring the bell and hear a buzzing inside. No one comes. I phone again and receive an aggravated earful that I don't understand.

"I am at the door," I say. "*Je suis à la porte*," I try. Maybe the yelling man speaks French.

Apparently not because the yelling gets louder.

"*Un letto. Pellegrino, per favore*," I insist. I have no idea if there are any beds. Maybe this man is telling me the place is already fully booked.

Then another voice comes on the phone. "Someone come," a woman says.

"*Grazie.*" I sit on my pack and wait.

Soon a stomping man, about my age, arrives with a key. He starts yelling the moment he sees me. Yells while he opens the door. Yells the whole way up a flight of steps and continues yelling while he points out a room with two bunk beds. He slams a registration form on a table and demands my passport. I pull it out along with my pilgrim's credential. He flips open the pages with such violence I think he might tear them.

Reaching across the table, I take my passport out of his hands. "That's enough," I say. "This is a hostel. I am a pilgrim."

He understands the tone. This is his mother speaking.

Blinking, he says, "*Mi scusi.*"

"I should think so." I don't bother smiling.

Again, there is no Internet, which is inconvenient because I want to book tomorrow's room, but sun streaming in an open window offers a perfect place to dry clothes. I've showered, washed clothes, and hung them in the sun by the time more pilgrims arrive. Two Italians. Mr Grumpy doesn't yell at them.

I notice he's left some blank registration forms on the table, so sneak an extra, fill in Atul's information and add the completed form to the pile. I then spread my stuff onto two beds. More pilgrims arrive. Mr Grumpy counts forms and looks puzzled. He counts occupied beds. I make no comment. A group of German cyclists arrive. Mr Grumpy grumbles about their bikes, grumbles about their shoes, grumbles while they register. Except for the two top bunks in my room, the hostel now appears full.

A shop in town sells hefty lunches to pilgrims, so I limp out to get a ham and cheese extravaganza as tomorrow nothing will be open. Then Atul arrives. Having walked over forty kilometres, he's exhausted. He goes to the shop and buys his lunch. After securing both lunches to the ledge outside our window – not wanting to chance marauding from the fridge – we go out for dinner together.

"Atul, there are lots of young people here. Wouldn't you rather go out with them?" I ask.

He says not. He's a thoughtful young man, Fly's age. We share concerns about the wellbeing of refugees. He's well-travelled, and his dual ethnic background – Indian/German – provides him with a perspective not available to me as a white-skinned woman.

We get back to the hostel to find a young Italian woman has arrived and taken one of the top bunks. Atul had met her earlier in the day. Antonella, a teacher living in Rome, is only walking for two days. She's on her way out for dinner as we're falling into our beds.

Day seventy. 1 November. To Acquapendente, Lazio.
Headlamps on so we don't disturb Antonella, Atul and I are awake and packing with minimal rustling at five thirty. However, Antonella wakes and decides to join us. We slip out into the dark streets, tramp down the hill and away across a wide valley. Now in the southern reaches of Tuscany, the landscape is becoming flatter.

We stop for a picnic breakfast in the shade of a tree, sip water and wish for coffee. I notice a sign. We're outside a B&B. I point this out to Atul and Antonella. They regard me with a "so what" kind of look, but I hop up and walk through the gate into a large garden.

Seeing a man, I call out. "Do you have guests this morning?"
He nods. "*Si.*"
"Are you making coffee?"
Another affirmative.
"May we buy three cups?"
He smiles but shrugs. "I'll check with my wife." He disappears into the house and a moment later re-emerges. "Take a seat in the garden. Coffee will be right out."

I go back to the gate. "Coffee," I say to my two companions. "We're to sit in the garden."

We make ourselves comfortable on a terrace with a view back to Radicofani and across heat-shimmering hills in the direction of our walk.

The coffee arrives with delicious cakes and breads – special for today's *Ognissanti* festivities. Our surprise breakfast consumed, when we try to pay, we're given a tobacco tin and asked to donate what we like.

We walk and walk. Atul could walk faster but he doesn't. I could walk faster than Antonella, but like Atul, I know going ahead is the wrong thing to do. We started as a threesome. We will finish as a threesome. Our route is longer than anticipated due to a detour to avoid the dangers of rushing traffic on the busy Via Cassia to Rome. We will walk thirty-three tough kilometres before the day is done.

During that long day, I consider my Italian Quandaries. Most Italians I've met have been warm and kind, but in some, the open hostility towards foreigners – or maybe pilgrims in particular – has been fierce and undisguised. Maybe this is the time of year when people in the hospitality industry are exhausted and look forward to their own vacations and adventures. I suspect, however, that something more insidious is at play.

On 22 October, Italians elected a radical-right prime minister – Giorgia Meloni. Her Brothers of Italy party, with neo-fascist roots, is ultra-conservative and holds an anti-immigration, anti-globalization stance. Her ideologies are apparent in the *sporchi stranieri* sentiment I've encountered enough times to put me on guard. While with other pilgrims, I've felt sheltered from the implied threat and have relaxed into enjoying all the beauty this area has to offer, but the unease of walking alone again through potentially hostile territory lurks.

In the heat of the afternoon, we climb our last Tuscan hill and step through an archway into the Lazio region. The last regional border I'll cross before reaching Rome. With only eight more days, I treat myself to a moment of imagining the final steps to the Vatican. My foot is so painful, I'm not convinced I will make it, but with each kilometre my chances improve.

Despite having left the hostel in Radicofani before dawn, night falls before we reach Acquapendente. As is often the case near towns, the route brings us onto a busy road. This one is narrow with frequent bends. I don my headlamp, Atul and Antonella hold their phone flashlights. Rapidly approaching and passing vehicles alternately blind us or illuminate the road ahead. Atul and I keep anxious watch for a trail that will lead us away from the dangers of the road, avoid a long hairpin bend, and take us up into the walled town.

A break in the guardrail alerts us to a rough path descending into a ravine. Casting our lights around, we glimpse the trail marker, so pick our way down a steep slope, then along a forested trail. I sense the mediaeval town walls looming somewhere above, but our vision is restricted to tight circles of bobbing inadequate light. Dense forest crowds the trail obscuring any potential glimmer of starlight and cloaking us in near-palpable darkness.

With a sudden crashing and squealing, an enormous boar erupts from the brush. Short tusks gleaming, snout high, mane bristled, the beast dashes across the trail just ahead of Atul and me. Gasping, we stop, each stepping closer to the other. Antonella, who has dropped behind, screams in terror. Rustles and grunts from the bush on both sides of the trail indicate the monster isn't alone.

"Come on," I yell to Antonella. "We have to stay together."

Antonella remains alone and vulnerable in the dark. "They are dangerous," she sobs. "We need to go back."

"No! We're over halfway. We must stay together. If we make big noises, we'll scare them."

I have no idea what the correct protocol might be when encountering boars in the dark, but have read enough to know they are unpredictable and ferocious creatures. I understand her fear. I share it. So does Atul. But we don't have the privilege of indulging in terror. We yell at Antonella again, and she scurries towards us. Once together, we continue, hearts pounding, senses scanning the bush.

In English, German and Italian we shout, "Don't come out." "*Komm nicht raus.*" "*Non uscire.*" to an unknown number of potentially multi-lingual boars that continue to grunt and rustle nearby.

Even though we're weary from the long, hard day, when we reach a flight of stone steps leading up to a gate in the town wall, we stumble up into the light as fast as our legs will carry us. Feet firmly planted on the cobbled street, I turn and look back down into the dark where hunched shadows emerge from the forest. Now that we are gone, the boars will spend the night digging up the path as they forage for roots, grubs and fallen acorns.

Later in a bright-lit restaurant, noticing boar meat on the menu, that is what I order for dinner, savouring every succulent morsel.

Day seventy-one. 2 November. To Bolsena.
Antonella has caught an early bus home to Rome. Atul and I meet in the still-dark square. After coffee and pastry at a café, we walk out of town as the sun rises.

We trudge along a busy road for a short distance before the route leads us onto a quiet farm track, fields spreading out on either side. We've both relaxed into the pleasure of walking through tranquil farmland when I hear small pops about six metres behind us, then similar sounds the same distance in front accompanied by small puffs of road dust. My immediate thought is too disturbing to contemplate. The pops and puffs happen again.

I glance at the road behind me. "What is that?" I ask.

Atul will have a more logical explanation than the one my brain is considering.

"Those two hunters over there by that shed. They are shooting," he says.

"But there's no animals or birds," I protest, my mind still refusing to believe.

"I guess they are trying to intimidate us then," says Atul.

"Well, it's working," I respond. "Let's hope they are very good shots. And sober."

There is nothing we can do except keep our pace even. We don't look in their direction. I add being terrorized by hunters to my list of Italian Quandaries. When the farm track ejects us onto a path along a short stretch of the Via Cassia, we endure the roar of rushing vehicles with a sense of relief. Here there are no hunters firing shots in our direction.

Later, we climb a rough trail through forest, the scenery

much wilder than in Tuscany. When we emerge, we see Lake Bolsena below. Occupying the crater of an extinct volcano, the lake shimmers silver in the day's heat. We ply rural trails winding through orchards and forests above the lake until descending into the attractive town of Bolsena.

After a beer in the square, Atul goes to find a bed in a church hostel, and I head to a lakeside hotel. The receptionist notices me rubbing my foot while she's checking me in and asks if I'm injured. When I tell her my foot is sore, she says to wait, then disappears beyond a door, moments later returning with a bowl of Epsom salts.

"Use the bidet to soak your feet," she suggests.

Following her advice, I put the lid down on the toilet and sit with my feet in the bidet while checking and sending e-mails and making tomorrow's accommodation booking. A peculiar but restorative habit I will repeat for the rest of the walk.

Atul and I meet for a pleasant dinner. He has slowed his pace for me, and I've increased mine for him but tomorrow we'll walk separately – each at our own speed – and meet up again at our destination.

Back at the hotel, I remember my promise to phone Stuart to let him know that I made it safely to Gallina.

He answers with a breathless, "Are you OK? Are you ill?"

"No. So sorry," I say. "I'm just beat at the end of the day. I forgot to call."

"Kim. I have COVID. I must have had it the day I was so tired. The night we shared the room."

"Ah. ... Well, I'm not sick." I count back the days. "That was five days ago. If I'm going to get COVID ... I guess it could happen any time. But no symptoms yet."

We chat a bit more and after hanging up, I sit for a moment. The Way will provide, I decide. And the Way better not provide me with COVID.

Day seventy-two. 3 November. To Montefiascone.

I start the day by digging out my rapid test kit and sticking the swab up my nose. I'm negative.

The route climbs out of town back into the hills, along forest paths, then farm tracks past olive orchards. The drone of generator-driven olive shakers attests to a harvest well underway. Atul catches up with me while I take a rest. We chat for a few minutes – he'd taken a wrong turn. He carries on, and later I catch up with him while he eats lunch. It's a good lunch spot so I stop too. As has become our habit, we share fruit. Half my orange for him. Half his pear for me, then he leaves me to rest a bit longer. As the day progresses, clouds gather and the temperature drops.

The entry into Montefiascone is through a rundown industrial area. But as the route climbs a steep slope into the old town, the urban landscape becomes more gentrified. I sit by a fountain to catch my breath and see my charming little hotel across the road.

The receptionist makes me a seven thirty dinner reservation for the hotel dining room, explaining that that is the earliest possible time. Happy not to have to go anywhere further today, I go up to my top floor room where I find a massive terrace with a fabulous view. After hanging my washing out, I settle with a beer but within minutes rain begins. I rush inside with laundry and beer as rain, driven by powerful wind gusts, lashes against the windows and door, and a vicious storm obscures the view.

Atul calls. He's staying further up the hill in a chilly convent run by surly nuns. I suggest he join me for dinner at the hotel and he agrees. Hobbling downstairs, I let the receptionist know there will be two of us but am told that dinner is only served to hotel guests. When I explain that I'd really like to eat with my friend who is staying with the nuns, the receptionist tells me to wait a moment and returns with the manager. They agree to make an exception.

"You must eat at seven, not seven thirty. The nuns will lock your friend out if he isn't inside by nine o'clock," the manager explains.

"Not a problem," I say.

I call Atul. The convent is miserable, the weather inclement, so he comes down to the hotel and we discuss troublesome social issues, the global spread of right-wing politics and the climate crisis while sipping fine Italian wine – on the house – until our early dinner. Atul will catch a bus to Rome in the morning, then return home to Frankfurt. We make no promises to stay in touch but exchange contact information and assure each other that should I ever be in Frankfurt, or he in the Comox Valley, there will be a welcome. We hug, and he sets off into the rainy dark before the nuns lock him out.

I will miss the company of my wise young friend.

Day seventy-three. 4 November. To Viterbo.

The hotel provides a hearty breakfast including a lunch panini to take with me. The storm has been replaced by dense fog, so as I climb further up into the old part of town, I can't see more than three metres and have to navigate across the town's hilltop park with Pocket Earth.

Down the far side of the hill I walk, and near the bottom I emerge from the fog onto flat terrain. Before long, I see Viterbo stretched at the base of a low hill in the distance. When the clouds dissipate and sun shines, I pull off extra layers and tuck my rain gear into my pack.

Five minutes later, an enormous splash of water hits the side of my face. Then another. Looking up, I see an ominous black cloud bank racing towards me, sheets of rain, a grey swath beneath it. The wind hits with such force that I bend at the waist to avoid being blown over. I struggle back under my poncho as it's whipped this way and that, my legs soon covered with red welts from it thrashing against them.

The rain turns the track into a slippery quagmire. I walk in the grassy centre as water runs with increasing force down either side. When the water level rises to cover the centre, I hop over to the raised verge. The surface is uneven, and the grass long. My wet legs gather seeds and bits of grass, and my shoes fill with water. Cold water runs down my back and even into my armpits.

I have one of those bladders that demands release at least once during a morning's walk. Even when walking with others, I've always managed to find a shrub or tree behind which I can make a discreet stop. I carry a Kula Cloth – an antimicrobial pee cloth designed for use by all of us who squat to pee – so leave no trace. Every evening I wash the Kula Cloth with my smalls. It's a game-changing piece of gear for female adventurers. Today, as the urge becomes more pressing, there is never a sheltered spot to squat. Several times I stop and scan the surroundings, and every time I'm in view of traffic or houses.

A bright orange shape approaches. It turns into a young cape-clad Swiss man who has been working in Rome for two years. He's walking home. We wish each other well, each of us buoyed with the knowledge that there is at least one other person foolish enough to be walking in this weather.

Later, a muddy cyclist splashes past, then a bedraggled dog with his gum-booted owner. A spandex-clad jogger sloshes by. We all greet each other with determined smiles while my bladder protests the lack of privacy.

There is a Via Francigena monument near the town's entry, but it is inaccessible on the far side of a busy road with no crosswalk. Another Italian Quandary. I continue through the ugly modern outskirts, then through a gate in the 12th-century wall into the convoluted cobbled streets of the ancient town.

I find my B&B up a metre-wide alley off a narrow, cobbled pedestrian street. The door is locked, but I had made a phone call – as instructed by the owner – thirty minutes prior to arrival. That was twenty-seven minutes ago. Surrounded by the bulging, crooked walls of 500-year-old buildings, I wait with toe-tapping urgency and am grateful that with the advent of indoor plumbing, no one will open a window above to hurl down nightsoil. A display of tarot cards and occult items outside a small shop with ancient, latticed windows invites investigation, but my need to pee now occupies all my attention. A man wheels a handcart laden with fresh vegetables to a restaurant just around the corner. I debate following and begging to use the toilet but don't want to miss the arrival of the B&B host.

After a fifteen-minute wait, I make another call. Fifteen minutes after that a woman arrives, explains she's the host's friend, that the host speaks no English and that she will be along soon. I shiver and ask Friend about a dinner reservation. She calls the restaurant to which the delivery was made and makes one for me. The torrential rain has let up, but a drizzle persists. We stand, she dry under her umbrella, me soaked, teeth chattering and bladder cramping.

Ten minutes later, Host arrives with a swirl of conversation directed at Friend. She ignores me, unlocks the door and we go inside to a vaulted dungeon-like reception area. I pull out my passport and credential and hand her both.

She uses her phone to take a picture of my passport and shoves away my credential.

"No stamp." The first words she's said to the person who's paying €60.00 for the night.

No one else has refused to stamp the credential. I'm disappointed but the need to pee is more intense. Host then pulls out a tourist map and starts pointing.

"She will show you the important sights," says Friend.

"Please tell her, that's OK. I have a map. Right now, I would like to go to the room."

There's a quick translation.

"She says she will show you the map first."

"Please say I don't need to see the map. I do need to use the toilet."

Another translation. Much more is said than I said, both women talking and gesturing, then Host shrugs and leads the way upstairs, through one door, then up more stairs to another. I pull off my mud-caked shoes and carry them. She pauses in the doorway and begins speaking again. I hurry past, dump my wet pack and shoes on the floor, run to the bathroom and shut the door. While my distressed bladder empties, I pull off sodden socks, dump them into the sink – where muddy water oozes onto the white porcelain

– and listen to the women arguing. I emerge and Host indicates I'm to come downstairs so she can show me the map.

"Please tell her thank you. I have a map. I promise to visit the sights. But now I must get dry and warm." I point at my wrinkled white feet to emphasize the point.

After another translation and argument, Friend smiles at me. "There is no heat because of the war in Ukraine. But the water is hot. There is an extra blanket in the closet."

With a hand on Host's shoulder, she ushes her out of the room. Listening to raised voices trailing down the stairs I begin peeling off wet clothing. There's not one hook in the entire unheated room. I rig up a drying rack with my clothesline and trekking poles, sit with my feet in the bidet filled with hot water, then use the hairdryer on my shoes that have leaked a large puddle onto the floor.

Day seventy-four. 5 November. To Vetralla.

Although I'm staying at a B&B, which implies an included breakfast, Host has left me instructions to walk a few blocks to a café where I will be given coffee and a croissant. The tiny café has no seating, but the lady behind the counter has a stamp for my credential. I'm given a miniscule paper cup of espresso and told I can choose one of several bakery items. I buy another for lunch, step out into a grey chilly morning and lean against the wall where I eat while vehicles splash by.

I break my promise to visit historic sites and tramp out of town, stopping at a fruit market to buy a pear. Over the past couple of weeks, I've enjoyed the juicy, flavourful Italian pears and mention this to the salesman.

"Oh, we grow the best pears in the world," he tells me, kissing the tips of his fingers and flinging out his hand. "*Deliziosa*," he says as he pops a second huge pear into the top of my pack, then adds a few grapes.

"*Grazie*," I say as I try to pay him more.

He waves my hand away. "No. No. *Un regalo* . A gift," he says.

I walk away, my pack heavier but my heart lighter. It takes so little to change the course of an interaction. A smile or a frown. The desire to extend kindness or the need to be mean. My determination to journey well is inextricably tied to the nature of these daily encounters, and I'm thankful that for every difficult interaction there have been more that have lent joy to the moment.

Yesterday's rain and windstorm have abated, but as I walk, I see numerous branches – some quite large – scattered on the track. Soon the route enters a forest where I step around a few more branches. Then more. As I pick my way through storm debris, a man catches up. We greet each other. He is Marco from Venice. He's walking to Rome.

"This route is closed today due to fallen trees," he says. "So how about we walk together."

"It's closed? How do you know?"

"There was a small paper note tucked under a branch," he says. "In Italian. Not obvious."

"But you came anyway."

He shrugs. "It's this way or walk back and along the road. This isn't as dangerous as walking along an Italian road."

Soon we are climbing over and under a tangle of fallen trees. They've come down in all directions and block the path. We clamber, crouch and crawl. Marco breaks trail and reaches out to give me a hand over some of the biggest trunks. It takes us over an hour to cover less than a kilometre, and once on the far side of the windfall, we meet several men carrying chainsaws. They say something to Marco but don't seem annoyed that we defied the sign.

Once we are out of hearing Marco grins at me. "I told them we saw no sign."

Now partners in crime, we walk together until I stop for my picnic lunch, and he continues, his young legs hurrying him on his journey. As I arrive in Vetralla, the wind rises again. When I hang my laundry on the line on a rooftop terrace at my accommodation, it dries within a few minutes.

That evening, I have dinner at a pizza restaurant recommended by my host. The pizza is delicious, and as tomorrow is Sunday, I order another to take for my lunch, asking that it be wrapped in foil so I can stuff it in my pack. When I go to pay, I've only been charged for one pizza and a glass of wine. I point out that I owe more, but the cook and the waiter join in their insistence that the second pizza is a gift for the road.

Day seventy-five. 6 November. To Sutri.
Now nine days post-exposure, I again begin my day with a COVID test. Again negative. I know testing when non-symptomatic can provide a false negative, but I feel confident now that I've dodged the COVID bullet.

Leaving the guesthouse, I anticipate turning left but see the Via Francigena sign pointing right. Signage has been accurate for the past several days, so I trust I'm being led in the right direction. Four kilometres later, when the signs disappear at an intersection with a highway, I realize my trust has again been betrayed. Careful study of the route marked on Pocket Earth assures me that my best option is to return to town and start again.

Back in Vetralla, I meet another walker standing on the sidewalk reading his phone. He, too, is puzzled by the sign. He has the same route information as I, so we set off together and after a couple of blocks come to a Via Francigena marker pointing in the right direction. The man pops into a café for breakfast. I continue. My foot already throbbing, I trudge along feeling a deep weariness seeping into my entire being.

At every intersection, I consult Pocket Earth because the route markers have been sabotaged. Each time I select a track, the markers reappear after several metres, their small red and white flashes providing assurance. After wandering through extensive hazel nut orchards, the route descends into a forested ravine and across a rotting bridge. One of the two support beams has broken so the bridge hangs across the river on a precarious slant. The railings are rotted and useless. I cross, hoping I'm not the pilgrim for whom the bridge breaks.

The day remains chilly, and after I huff up to mediaeval hilltop Sutri, my B&B host offers to turn on the heat.

"Are you allowed?" I ask.

"No. Not really. But just for two hours. The room will be much more comfortable."

When the radiators rumble to life, I hang my laundry next to them and soon the room is cozy. Upon my return from a delicious steak dinner at a restaurant in the atmospheric town square, the heat is off, but my laundry is dry, and the room remains warm.

Day seventy-six. 7 November. To Campagnano-di-Roma.

I buy breakfast to go from a small shop, then with renewed energy and confidence march down and out of the town that has occupied this volcanic hilltop since Etruscan times. After the Romans ousted the Etruscans and occupied Sutri – they called it Sutrium – they carved an amphitheatre out of the surrounding tufa – a soft, porous rock formed when volcanic ash is compressed to a cement-like consistency. Although the amphitheatre is closed at this time of day, I pause and peer through the gate to marvel at the still-beautiful oval, surrounded by tiers of seats that once accommodated up to 9000 spectators. A damp bench offers a breakfast spot. While eating, I imagine horses pulling chariots along the nearby Via Cassia and gladiators entering the amphitheatre to the roar of fans.

Much later, as I walk along a farm track, dogs begin barking from behind a solid fence as I approach their gate. From frequent experience with barking dogs, I know they'll chase up and down and leap against the gate bars, noisy in their greeting but of no threat. This gate, however, is open and two large white dogs – Maremma sheep dogs – dash out onto the road. Their tails don't wag, and their barking is fierce. This breed has a gentle-giant reputation, but these dogs are telling me to get the hell away from their property.

"Go home." I use a firm low tone and angle towards the far side of the road.

The dogs bark and snarl.

I walk and talk. "Nice beasts."

"Scary brutes," my inner voice squeaks.

"I'm just walking by," I tell the growling dogs.

"Please don't kill me," my mind implores.

In a nearby field, a farmer stops his labours with a shovel and looks in our direction. These must be his dogs. I'm torn between my fear of being mauled, my anger with him for leaving his damn gate open, and an overpowering desire that he come to my rescue. He does nothing. Perhaps he's burying the last pilgrim who walked past his gate. Or maybe he knows the dogs won't tear me to bits. I walk on, now past the gate and gaining confidence that the beasts won't pursue. Behind me, they stop their din and re-enter the gate. In the field, the farmer goes back to his work. On the road, I revel in joy that I'm still in one unbloodied piece.

Desiring to leave some trace of where I am, I stop at the church in Monterosi to sign the guest book. The last person to sign before me was a man named David from Vancouver. He passed here two days ago and has walked from Canterbury. He will have arrived in Rome today, I realize. That thought propels me through the rest of the day.

Not many kilometres later, I notice a large flock of sheep grazing in a nearby field. A breeze dries the sweat from my body, bees hum in the hedgerow. My foot isn't bothering me, I don't feel hungry or thirsty, I am content in this moment of tranquility.

From the vicinity of the sheep – happening too fast to comprehend – three more Maremma sheep dogs erupt, then surge beneath a sagging strand of barbed wire to surround me, ears back, lips curled, teeth bared, snarling. I have no choice but to stop walking. My heart leaps and my sense of humour fails.

"Twice in one day?" I mutter. Then fury overrides fear. "Sit the fuck down and shut the fuck up," I bellow at the advancing menaces.

Two of the dogs drop to their haunches and relax their ears. The other crouches and bares more fangs.

"You too," I snarl back.

The dog drops to his belly.

"Good dog."

I pass within two metres of his watchful eyes, but he remains still, pressed against the road, ready to spring up and tear out my throat at any provocation to his flock. I continue, my pace slow, so I don't trigger their instinct to chase fleeing prey. Looking back over my shoulder, I see the threesome rise and follow, but they don't close the distance. As I continue past the limit of the field, the dogs stop, then turn and trot back to their sheep.

By the time I arrive at my hotel in Campagnano-di-Roma, I'm limping. A detour to avoid the Via Cassia has turned an anticipated twenty-four-kilometre day into thirty-kilometres. There is no Internet in my room and dinner is not available until seven thirty, so I sit in the empty dining room, looking up accommodation for tomorrow while my stomach rumbles and foot throbs.

Day seventy-seven. 8 November. To La Giustiniana.

My foot protests as soon as I step out of bed. Yesterday's limp and my worn-out insoles have produced a hot spot under my heel. Not a blister yet, but the potential is there. Painful forefoot and heel – this is going to be a tough day. Before leaving, I want to check my e-mails, but the dining room is locked. Grumbling, I head to a nearby café for a coffee and croissant and buy a substantial sausage roll – I think that's what it is – for lunch.

Today's egress from town is well and properly marked, and I'm soon enjoying a hilly walk along a quiet lane. A church perched atop a hill offers a bench in the sun with a glorious view, so I pause there for a break and to inspect my foot. A blister has developed. Needle sanitized, I pierce it, sticky plasma squirts out and relieves some of the discomfort when I stand on it.

I'm sitting – bare feet up and drying in the sun – when Marco strides into the churchyard, greets me and suggests we continue together for a short time.

"I walk too fast on my own," he says when I worry that I will be too slow for him.

As we walk, he tells me about his father's vineyard near Venice. Marco is a university-educated grape vine pruner, working in his father's and other vineyards. While he talks about grape vines with the passion of someone dedicated to the art of their care, the kilometres slide by.

When I take another break to inspect and re-dress a horrible mess of torn skin and raw flesh, that was once my well-calloused heel, Marco carries on. The insides of my shoes have been disintegrating over the past couple of weeks – the result of months of sweat and stomping through puddles and walking in the rain. I replaced insoles once and need to do so again but have been unable to find any. My bandage supply is now getting dangerously low. I sit on the grass doctoring both foot and shoes and take another ibuprofen. I'm low on those too. Having done the best I can, I struggle to my feet and take a painful step.

"A bloody blister is not going to stop me getting to Rome," I scream at the universe.

A disturbed crow caws back at me and flaps away from its perch in a nearby tree. I take a breath and take another step. Then another. I've meditated for years. This is time to put that practice to good use. More kilometres pass under my shoes. Breath by breath, step by step I close the gap between where I am and where I want to be.

At a trail intersection, a sign with a photo of the Maremma dogs appears to warn people to avoid walking in one direction, so I take the other. Both trails bear Via Francigena markings. Both will lead to Rome.

The route I take offers a scenic tour past numerous archeologically significant Etruscan sites. An advanced Bronze Age culture, that reached its zenith in the 6th century BCE, the Etruscans were probably the first to cultivate grapes for making wine. They invented the chariot and entertained themselves with gladiatorial competitions. Many aspects of their culture were absorbed by their successors – the Romans – including the wearing of togas.

As I near La Storta, Marco comes running back down the road towards me. Having taken a short cut, he realized he'd missed the

Etruscan sites, so he's hurrying back before returning to catch a train into Rome.

Once in La Storta, the route joins the Via Cassia. There is a sidewalk, but the din of constant bumper-to-bumper traffic is more than I want to contend with. I stop for a beer, then go in search of a bus to take me five kilometres along the Via Cassia to La Giustiniana. Finding a bus stop, I ask a young man waiting there if he knows which bus I should catch. He does. He's catching the same one. It will be along in five minutes, and I need a ticket before boarding.

"Where do I buy the ticket?" I ask.

He points back down the road – the way I've come – tells me I can buy a ticket at the tobacco shop and offers to run back for me. Although tempted to accept his help, I say I'll be right back and jog – yes, my motivation is strong enough that I do jog – down the road and into the shop. The man doesn't understand my dreadful pronunciation of La Giustiniana so I give up and ask for a ticket to Roma. It costs me €1.50.

Dashing back to the stop, I arrive before the bus and in time to see Marco coming towards us. He stops for a wonderful Italian hug and double cheek kiss before jogging away to the train station. The bus arrives and my bus helper – a chef who has returned to Italy after four years working in Manchester, England – says he'll let me know when I should get off. The traffic is so congested I begin to think I could have walked in less time but now that I've stopped walking, the pain in my foot rages.

Alighting from the bus, I see the grounds of Casa per Ferie JPII Dom Polski – my accommodation for the night – across the street. As soon as I enter the gate, the street noises fade. Trees, statuary, garden beds with shrubs and flowers border the drive up to a large square building. Inside all is hushed. A group of nuns with hands folded walk through the lobby and smile at me. At the reception desk, a lay woman checks me in and takes my dinner reservation. I climb the wide steps and find my little room at one end of a long hallway. The bathroom is at the other end.

I sit on the bed and pull off my shoes. No bidet here to soak my feet, but in the bathroom, I find a plastic basin – that will do.

There is no menu, but the set four-course dinner, served by the smiling but silent nuns, is one of my favourite meals of the journey. Each guest – there are four of us – is provided with a carafe of either red or white wine. The place wraps me in a healing sense of calm, and even before falling asleep, I feel the renewal that will see me through to the gates of the Vatican.

Day seventy-eight. 9 November. La Giustiniana to Rome.

As I eat breakfast, one of the nuns places a paper bag on the table. Inside is a generous picnic lunch. When I check out, I ask about paying for it and the receptionist tells me it is a gift from the sisters who wish me well on the last leg of my pilgrimage to Rome.

"How do they know I'm a pilgrim?"

Her enigmatic, "They can tell," doesn't really solve the mystery. Maybe it's my worn-out shoes and faded blue skirt.

Leaving the tranquility of the convent, I'm assaulted by the roar of the Via Cassia but along it I must walk for just over one kilometre until I reach the Riserva Naturale dell'Insugherata. With relief, I turn away from the traffic, but as I enter the reserve, I notice evidence of a recent fire that has scorched several trees.

Further into the park, the trail – which has been dug up by boars – is overgrown with nettles and brambles. At the intersection where I anticipate a way marker to point right, there is none. I check Pocket Earth. Yes, this is where the route turns. I look around for the trail marker and find a damaged post lying in the woods. Vandalism. Further on, at another intersection the route turns left, but again the markers have been destroyed. Several information signs about the reserve, the vegetation and animals have also been covered in graffiti. I sit for a few minutes at a broken picnic table and wonder about the reasons for the gratuitous damage. In some other places in Italy, signs have been knocked over by farm machinery. Accidental or deliberate, I don't know. But this sabotage is deliberate. A chill of discomfort that has nothing to do with the reserve's roaming boars brings me to my feet. Upon emerging onto a busy street choked with morning rush hour traffic, I feel relief.

Stepping around some overfilled dumpsters, I walk past a man sitting on a bench. He's surrounded by a rumpled blanket and bags; his hat lies on the pavement at his feet. I'm a couple of paces past as my hand reaches into my pouch and connects with my wallet. My fingers fumble for change. I have none – well, not enough, so I settle on a €5.00 note and turn back.

"Will this help?" I ask, leaning forward and tucking the note into his rough hand.

He nods and smiles, "Thank you."

I now notice another bench next to his. Time for my mid-morning breakfast. I've dumped my pack and sat before my brain considers the morality of enjoying breakfast beside a homeless man who may not have eaten for some time.

"Would you like to share my sandwich?" I ask, unwrapping the nun's gifted ham-stuffed bun from its napkin. "Ham," I add. Maybe he's vegetarian.

He nods so I remove the ham, tear the bun in two, redistribute the ham and hand him his half with the napkin.

"Water?"

He nods again and hands over a stained cup. I pour, then we sit back and eat.

"Where are you from?" he asks.

"Canada."

"What are you doing here?"

"Well, I've walked from Canterbury. Today I hope to get to the Vatican."

He nods. "A pilgrim?"

"Yes."

"Where did you come from just now – today?"

I pull out my iPad and show him. "I walked from here," I point. "Then down through the Riserva Naturale. Then along this road – to here."

He studies the screen with the ease of someone familiar with maps and taps the pink area marking the reserve. "*Mamma mia.* That place is dangerous."

"The boars? There are signs of digging. But they sleep during the day."

"Boars! The least of your worries. Desperate – angry – people go there."

"I noticed vandalism – graffiti and garbage," I say without admitting to the unease I'd felt.

"I bet you did." He pauses and points at the dumpsters. "This has become a filthy city. I've had garbage thrown on me while I sleep." He pauses and looks at me. "Roma is in trouble. Italia. It's worse since COVID. You need to pay attention to stay safe here. Understand?"

I nod. "I do. I'll be careful. Thank you." I close my pack and swing it to my shoulders.

His smile returns. "Next time I will sing for you," he says, tapping his guitar.

"Next time," I say before slipping into a crowd of pedestrians to cross the busy street. On the other side, I turn and look back. He raises his hand in a sharp salute.

I return the gesture and feel a flicker of recognition pass between us.

Walking on – marching – I notice my mood has lifted, our conversation resonating and drowning out the incessant roar of traffic. A homeless man – a veteran, I'm sure – whose name I never asked, has provided me with a shred of insight into a national crisis of which I've witnessed so many symptoms.

I enter a city park and climb through trees to the top of a hill. The trees thin and I walk to the edge of a bluff. Below, the Tiber threads a silver ribbon, and the dome of St Peter's rises from dense clustered buildings that spread to a hazy horizon. I sit on a bench. It wobbles on a broken base and has a loose board. Garbage litters the ground around empty waste bins. Bells toll. It's noon. I await a visceral response to my first sighting of St Peter's. There is none.

Both my feet throb today, burning and cramping with a vicious intensity I find hard to ignore.

"You're not there yet," says the mean voice in my head.

"Don't get your knickers in a twist," I argue back. "I can handle the pain for a couple more hours."

I pull myself to my feet. Always the first few steps after a rest are the worst. I hobble, then push through the misery and find a bearable stride. Down the hill the path continues through the forest until I'm ejected through a pile of spilled, stinking garbage and out onto the road.

Traffic. Hard pavement. Dodging other pedestrians.

Don't vehicles stop at cross walks? Apparently not.

Is that dog shit? Yes, and I just stepped in it. Scuff my feet through this bit of dirt.

Sidewalk vendor approaches.

"No, I don't want a watch."

Beggar lifts his hands.

"No, I have no change."

Deep breath. Two more kilometres. Can't lose my mind now.

There's a bar right outside my destination – B&B Leonardo Suites. I collapse into a chair and order a beer while I call the B&B for the door code. I can see the high wall of the Vatican from where I sit. One more kilometre. Less.

I receive a text from Fly. His flight is delayed, but he'll arrive this evening. I should zip over to the Vatican now and get my certificate. First, I check into our room and drop my pack because packs aren't allowed in St Peter's. I lie down just for a moment. My eyes close. The sun has set when they open. Too late to go to the Vatican now. I go downstairs to the bar, sit at "my" table, order a bottle of wine and watch the sidewalk.

Fly texts, "My flight has landed."

I text, "Take the train to Termini Station."

He texts, "I'm on a train. Think it's the right one."

I text a smile emoji, "Take Metro line A towards Battistini and get off at Cipro."

He texts, "I'm on the Metro."

A few minutes later, he walks down the sidewalk towards me. We hug.

"Did you go to the Vatican yet?" he asks as he takes a sip of wine.

"No. I fell asleep."

"Good," he says. "I'd like to go with you." He takes another sip. "Mmmm. This is good wine."

I smile. "This is Italy."

I'm glad Fly wants to come with me when I get my certificate. It's a moment I'd like to share. After dinner, when we go upstairs to our room, he notices my limp.

"Why are you walking like an old lady?"

"I am an old lady. It's a long story."

Fly laughs and so do I.

Before we sleep, I show him a couple of pictures of my journey through Italy.

"This is where a friendly woman taught me the word *pomodoro*. At this tiny café in Filetto the beer was cold and barkeep kind. And Tuscany ... Tuscany just needs to be experienced." Looking at my photos, I know the positive experiences outweigh the challenges.

Day Seventy-nine. 10 November.
To the Vatican and St Peter's.

Pilgrims don't need to queue to go through security to enter St Peter's, but so early in the day, the lineup is short and I'm not sure if Fly would be allowed to skip the line without a credential. So, we wait our turn with fellow tourists. Once inside, we're directed to a small security wicket where I show my credential. It has one remaining square for one last stamp. The guard looks it over and provides that stamp.

"You started in Canterbury?"

"*Si.*"

He pulls out a certificate and a form. I complete the form. Name? Nationality? Where did you start? When did you start? How did you travel? Why did you make this pilgrimage? Signature.

After I complete the form, doing a better job responding to the reasons for making the pilgrimage than I did in Santiago – to improve cultural awareness, to gain broader perspectives, to connect with local people and other pilgrims, with no mention of having fun – he fills in my name and hands the certificte to me with a smile.

"*Grazie,*" I say.

"*Prego.*"

As we enter the basilica, my tears come. Tears of relief, of joy, of exhaustion, of disbelief, of remembrance. The last time I was here was with Dad in 2015. He died in March 2022, and I still miss him. The time before was with Mike, and I still morn him. The first time was just after my ninth birthday when I visited with Mum and Dad. Now at the other end of my life, memories pour with my tears.

"Why are you crying?" Fly looks around, hoping no one sees his mother sobbing.

Dabbing at my eyes, I smile. "It's complicated."

Like Dad, Fly is uncomfortable with displays of emotion. I see Mum's blue eyes and her wide smile in his concerned face. But, most powerful, is the presence of Mike in this son we raised together.

Standing beside Fly, surrounded by memories, I gaze up into the dome. Like Sigeric's, my journey has taken seventy-nine days. Like Sigeric, I didn't walk every step of the way. I have, however, walked over 1500 kilometres of ancient roads to Rome. Bruised, blistered and tired, I am at peace.

We wander through the vast basilica, our footsteps echoing on marble floors created from pilfered Colosseum marble. We pass pillars purloined from Rome's pagan temples. We admire Michelangelo's La Pietà, inspired by his admiration for Dante's *Divine Comedy*.

> *Daughter of thine own Son, thou Virgin Mother, ...*
> *Lowlier and loftier than any other, ...*

Dante Alighieri, The Divine Comedy, Paradiso, Canto XXXIII, *circa 1320, first printed 1472 Melville Best Anderson, translator, 1922*

On our way out, Fly notices a sign. "Look, for €8.00 we can climb to the top of the dome. It's just 551 steps."

We buy our tickets and start up. I feel unfettered joy and understand that it was the wonders and hardships of the pilgrimage that mattered. I am renewed. Wings beneath my feet, we race each other up and up.

Acknowlegements

Writing this book has been a collaborative effort from start to finish. It would not exist without the help of many.

Thank you, Mum. I wish – how I wish – you were still here to celebrate the long journey to publishing *Canterbury and Other Tales*. From the beginning, you ignited and fanned the flame of my curiosity and my love of both walking and writing. You remain a guiding light.

Kay, Barb, Sandra and Mary, your kindness in accepting me into your vibrant circle of hikers took me far on my healing journey. Joan and Sandy, I wish you were still here. You remain in my memories. Thank you.

Sally, half the fun of the Pilgrims' Way was walking with you and enjoying Tim and Gail's warm and generous hospitality.

Marianne, you were generous in accepting the single rooms, coping with hostel accommodation and learning how to research and book on-line. Thank you for being such an accomodating travel mate.

Pat, quite simply – most of these adventures would not have been had you not shared your walking passion. I know you suffered more from disappointment in not completing our Via Francigena pilgrimage than I did in continuing alone. I had the adventure, my physical journey complete while you continued a solitary road to recovery. As I write these words in the spring of 2023, you've recovered, while from time to time, my feet still hurt. Even so, we're planning our next long walk, hopefully along the Appian Way south from Rome to Brindisi. I look forward to kicking off our shoes, leaning back on our packs and watching fair-weather clouds float by. We won't need to rush. This walk is just 930 kilometres.

Gabby, Iris and Dave, David and Stuart, Raoul and Andrea, Theresa, Katheryn and Josh, Atul, Antonella, and Marco – your camaraderie on the road to Rome made all the difference. Thank you for sharing your pilgrim journeys with me.

David, Andrea, me, Stuart. Me and Atul. Fellow pilgrims and friends.

Paul Chinn. www.pilgrimagepublications.com Your Lightfoot guidebooks along with your thoughtful e-mails with suggestions and encouragement guided me from Canterbury to Rome. Thank you also for the time you borrowed from important environmental activism to spend with these stories and to share your expertise.

Trevor McMonagle. My editor and friend. Your patience always astounds me. Your care of my manuscript – dissecting, rearranging and suggesting – you do much to mold the stories into publishable material. Again – I thank you for your encouragement, faith and wise counsel.

Melanie Davy. A sharp-eyed proofreader, your British perspective has been insightful and your attention to detail essential. Where do those peculiar typos come from? And so many spelling disparities between the UK and Canada. Thank you from the other side of the world.

Brenda Sawatzky. Proofreader extraordinaire, you remain the comma queen but so much more. A kind friend who helps massage sentences with proper punctuation, and with whom I share wine – after adding the commas, of course. Thank you.

Michel Pelletier. Reading aloud is one of the best ways for an author to hear the syntax and lyrics of a piece and to confirm clarity of the story. Thank you for the hours you spent listening to me reading this book to you on Messenger.

To dedicated friends who helped me proof the proof copy – Anne Denninger, Pat Gould and Brenda Sawatzky – thank you for finding those pesky details that had somehow kept escaping our notice.

Jeanette Taylor, Margo McLoughlin and Danny Ramadan. My mentors and workshop instructors – you provide the guidance and feedback that encourages the solitary task of turning adventures into well-written stories. Thank you for your faith and encouragement.

Jane and Rob Weiss of www.rwnetworks.com. Jane, I love my website design and all your support as publicist. Rob, you keep me from tossing my laptop out the window when it gets its knickers in a twist. Thank you both for putting up with my complete lack of tech knowledge.

Christine Dickinson, Helen Fox, Martha Gerow, Eugene Hrushowy, Paul Kendrick, Kay Kennedy, Glenn Lawson, Ian McIntyre, Janet Miller, Jan Pearce, John Peters and Dave Young. Fellow authors and writers, your valuable commentary and critique over the years helps me improve my craft. Thank you.

The Comox Valley Writers' Society cvwriterssociety.ca, The Federation of BC Writers www.bcwriters.ca and The Writers' Union of Canada www.writersunion.ca – membership provides vital assistance and advice for an author's creative pursuits. Thank you for your support of our writing community.

Other books by Kim Letson

Pomegranates at 4800 Metres – Journeying at Home and Away (2018) weaves a vibrant tapestry with themes of love, courage and generosity. Letson invites the reader to share her experiences: working on Mount Washington, kayaking in the waters around Vancouver Island, losing her husband to brain cancer, then travelling to Tanzania, Nepal and Morocco.

Praise for *Pomegranates at 4800 Metres*:

Bruce Kirkby – adventurer, author
... At times gut-wrenching, at times spellbinding, this heartfelt memoir is a powerful reminder of the heights to which curiosity, kindness and bravery can carry us. Bravo Kim!

David Esson Young – ship's master, author
... descriptions of the lands Letson journeys to and the people she encounters are vivid and evocative. ... she's tough enough to defy risk, endure pain and most importantly, to grow in self-awareness and confidence.

Soul of a Nomad – The Journey Continues (2020) traces the author's life traversing Canada, rounding Cape Horn, riding the Patagonian Pampas and Mongolian wilds. From Greek islands to North Cape, through Thailand or along the Silk Road, Letson's journey reflects her curiosity and adventurous spirit. Readers meet characters imagined and real: ancestral ghosts, the author's intrepid parents, lighthouse keepers, an Auschwitz survivor, gauchos, Roma and nomads. Set within historic and literary contexts, *Soul of a Nomad* shares sixty-five years of journeys and revelations. Evocative descriptions nestle amongst hair-raising anecdotes, every page encouraging the reader to explore further.

Praise for *Soul of a Nomad*:

Dr James Deutsch – George Washington University lecturer, folklorist, author
... *a lifelong journey that never fails to delight the reader.*

Chris Harker – safari guide, fellow adventurer, author
... *with boisterous good spirits and self-deprecating humour, Letson brings us with her to many of the world's "roads less travelled"* ...

Christine Dickinson – historian, author
.. *A highly recommended read for all observers of humanity and those with an interest in travel.*

Margo McLoughlin – storyteller, teacher, author
.. *Rich with sensory memories ... full of delight in the mystery and varied beauty of the world.*

In the Footsteps of a Roman Legion: Walking the Via Egnatia (2021) recounts how on a blistering September morning in 2016, intrepid friends in their sixties - Kim and Pat - set off on foot from Durrës, Albania towards Istanbul, Turkey. Tracing the route of a Roman road, the Via Egnatia, they dedicate their endeavour to raising funds for refugee relief. Owing to a guidebook that overstates amenities, the trek becomes more challenging than expected. As they negotiate hurdles, test their endurance, and encounter human smugglers and feral dogs, an indomitable sense of humour, a personified GPS, and an imagined Roman legionnaire see them through daily adventures.

Praise for *In the Footsteps of a Roman Legion*:

Evelyn Gillespie – owner Laughing Oyster Bookshop, Comox Valley
...*The Via Egnatia holds over two thousand years of stories ... And this is a gripping one - two travellers (sometimes three?) meet both*

generous hospitality and surprising hostility with resilience, cold beer and hot coffee. ... I was transported!

Joshua Levy – CBC/QWF Writer in Residence 2018, poet, winner of the CBC/QWF Fiction Prize, Prairie Fire Nonfiction Prize, CNFC/ Carte Blanche Nonfiction Prize, Grain Fiction Prize, and SLS Nonfiction Prize, author of *The Loudest Thing*
... Fun, funny, and endlessly thought-provoking, Kim Letson pulls no punches as she explores some of the bumpier corners of humanity, all while finding the time to celebrate life's small, simple pleasures. ... a page-turner.

Janet Miller – past-president CVWS, author of *Cross My Heart*
... in this compelling book, ... learn about Albania's concrete bunkers as the adventurers endure blisters, encounter poisonous vipers, vicious dogs, human traffickers and armed helicopters before finally relaxing in a steaming Istanbul hammam. ...

Wendy Wickwire – professor emeritus University of Victoria, author of *At the Bridge: James Teit and an Anthropology of Belonging*
... A gifted storyteller and seasoned backpacker, Kim Letson takes her readers on a hair-raising journey. ... In the Footsteps of a Roman Legion is a superb travelogue and travel guide, ... I loved this book.

About the Author

With a Canadian military father, Kim spent her childhood living in various parts of Canada and Europe. She and her husband, Mike Simpson, served twenty-year careers in the Canadian Forces. Retiring in the Comox Valley on Vancouver Island, they focussed on raising their two sons, Brian and Kyle, pursued second careers as professional ski patrollers on nearby Mount Washington and for a time owned a sea kayaking company based on the west coast of Vancouver Island.

Since Mike's death in 2007, seeking solace and following her nomadic spirit, Kim has indulged her passion for off-the-beaten-path international travel. When at home, she walks with friends, writes and enjoys her unconventional garden.

Canterbury and Other Tales: Treading Ancient Trails is Letson's fourth creative non-fiction book.

Follow this author on her website: www.kimletson.ca

Contact: kim@kimletson.ca

About the Author